Kohn Pedersen Fox
Architecture and Urbanism
1993-2002

Kohn Pedersen Fox
Architecture and Urbanism
1993-2002

Edited by
Ian Luna
Kenneth Powell

KPF

Introduction by
Joseph Giovannini

Essays by
Carol Herselle Krinsky
Kenneth Powell

Book Design by
Massimo Vignelli

RIZZOLI
NEW YORK

Preface

When William Pedersen, Sheldon Fox and I founded KPF in 1976, our intention was to make buildings that would engage and transform their environments. That was our vision.

This book presents recent efforts to fulfill and extend that vision. The projects represent a diverse range of building types, and vary in size and scope. They span the U.S.A. and are across the globe in thirty-eight other countries. The types of projects include academic buildings, museums, healthcare facilities, courthouses, airport terminals, hotels, corporate headquarters, mixed-use transportation centers, urban master plans, and a stadium.

Technology and the issues related to sustainability have been major focuses since the early 1990s, as demonstrated by our projects in Europe and more recently, a proposed stadium in Manhattan. These projects incorporate a strong environmental agenda that is redefining our firm's work.

There are many other projects that could not be included in this volume, but the total range of KPF's work is revealed here. We hope that the work speaks for itself.

We appreciate and thank all who made these projects successful. I have been fortunate these past twenty-six years to work with many talented people.

A. Eugene Kohn
President

Contents

KPF New York:
A Decade of Change

Joseph Giovannini

Kohn Pedersen Fox started business in 1976 when, in the middle of a deep national recession, the fledgling firm landed the commission for a prominently sited, six-story ABC news-broadcasting facility on West 67th Street in Manhattan. The size of its projects since has only increased. Within a decade of its founding, the firm had emerged as the pre-eminent author of large office buildings in the United States, a leader among a handful of American firms responsible for re-investing cities with the charisma that suburbs had drained in the decades after World War II. In its rapid rise, KPF arguably eclipsed Skidmore Owings & Merrill and Johnson Burgee in prominence in this specialized and coveted market, and it currently has some of the tallest buildings in the world on the boards.

Architects, of course, always welcome large jobs, but sometimes it pays to paint on a small canvas, in a more contemplative environment where the mathematics of efficiency and expense do not price out architectural innovation. By 1988, opportunities for retreating into small commissions were rare to non-existent at KPF, but a CEO for whom the architects had done a high-rise asked Bill Pedersen, who sets the design pace for the office, to design a weekend house in Vermont ski country, on a hillside facing the slopes of Mt. Stratton (Fig. 1). The resulting break-out plan for the four-bedroom house would deeply influence the direction of the firm, opening it to a way of thinking that helped drive its creative search for at least a decade.

The house commission came during a turbulent time for both KPF and American architecture, as the ongoing modern-versus-postmodern debates were themselves upset by the advent of deconstructivism, suddenly prominent because of a 1988 show at the New York Museum of Modern Art. The visions of such architects as Zaha Hadid, Coop Himmelb(l)au and Frank Gehry abruptly became, collectively, a force that challenged and altered practice, creating a deep malaise about the conceptual directions of design then prevalent. It was a moment to stop and think, and Pedersen did so at the drafting table, with a single-family house that released him from the normal constraints of large-scale work.

After an intense period of historicized buildings during the early- to mid-1980s, KPF had already been forging a new direction by revisiting a collagist approach that informed their earliest buildings. In the late 1970s, KPF designed towers with highly differentiated facades that responded to their respective exposures and contexts: adjacent facades might be designed with completely different curtain walls, and shared only their seam. A decade later, after the postmodernist interlude, the architects elaborated the approach and pushed their high-rise collages to extremes of integrated complexity. Always contextualists, KPF was now proposing different volumes for different interior programs

2. Kohn Pedersen Fox, 333
Wacker Drive (1979-1983),
Chicago, Illinois.

3. Kohn Pedersen Fox,
One Fountain Place (1985-
1988), Cincinnati, Ohio.

4. Kohn Pedersen Fox,
DG Bank, Mainzer
Landstrasse 58 (1986-1993),
Frankfurt am Main,
Germany.

2

3

4

within an overall composition of parts that echoed the diverse forms and multiple scales of buildings in the immediate city. The architects even broke open the skin to articulate skeletal members: the drive was for a rich complexity resonant with the surrounding urban contexts.

Pedersen developed the collagist idea at an heroic scale in the fifty-story One Fountain Place in Cincinnati (Fig. 3), with a cascade of volumes corresponding to different interior programs of the mixed-use building. An articulate structural hat composed of a tall, nearly solid facade shielding triangulated structural members crowned the composition. In a rendering, it was difficult to tell, whether the building (which was never built) was one, or several.

A tower that was built which consummated this line of thinking was the 1986 design for the DG Bank Headquarters in Frankfurt (Fig. 4), where Pedersen created a structure whose base, shaft and top were each complex within themselves. With its multiple towers and bases, all distinct but merged into the same floor plates, the building resembled a composite city. Concomitant with the emergence of this collagist sensibility was the architects' interest in Russian constructivism. Like their Russian counterparts, KPF created designs that broke the conceptual unity of the classical building into fragments that registered the internal and external complexities in and around a building. The architects articulated this architecture of fragmentation in the Marathon/IBM tower in Montreal (1988), with a layered, asymmetrical composition, and in an elegant design for the last parcel of Rockefeller Center.

From its first commission, KPF had intended to design buildings whose architectural order affirmed the order of the city, but what changed after fifteen years was the realization that the order of the city is complex; seldom does it correspond to the idealized vision and fiction of urban unity inherited from the Renaissance. In Frankfurt, Montreal, and in other projects, Pedersen and associated design partners William Louie, Peter Schubert and James von Klemperer broke the unitary tower into a constellation of parts, but one that still adhered to a notion of the difficult whole: the complex exteriors usually masked a tight plan and an underlying grid, and the parts gathered loosely around a stabilizing elevator core (known in the office as the stick in the popsicle). Whereas postmodernist skyscrapers built by KPF through the mid-1980s respected the classical ideal of breaking the whole into subordinate parts, each assigned to a place, Pedersen and his colleagues were giving the collagist and constructivist high-rise designs a syntactic freedom that dislocated volumes and architectural elements from what would have been their prescribed place within a unitary postmodernist whole. Still, the new buildings remained classical if not traditional in the sense that newly liberated parts retained a poised equilibrium. The new collagist and constructivist-inspired buildings might not be strictly axial and bilaterally symmetrical, but they were symmetrical in the original Greek sense of the word—balanced.

With the commission for the Carwill house in Vermont, Pedersen suddenly found himself surrounded by a natural rather than man-made context. Instead of dealing with a flat piece of land bounded by a street grid, Pedersen encountered a hillside facing a dramatic view of Mt. Stratton's slopes. The architect spent hours exploring the terrain, assessing views and light. The lure of the site was its rugged naturalism; even the recreational program of a family on vacation suggested informality. The architect who had broken the usual stiffness of the skyscraper into collagist compositions here decided to break apart the orthogonal geometry that, in Frankfurt and Montreal, still locked the proliferating parts into an overtly rational, right-angled order. In what must have been a difficult moment of release for an architect who was trained, like all other architects, to "master" the site, Pedersen allowed the main rooms of the program to find their own orientation. With 270 degree views and steep slopes, the panorama pulled the design in several directions, spinning the parts into a wheeling composition that Pedersen further animated, with chamfered corners and sharply angled roofs. (The free geometries and complex intersections presented the office with a new level of construction difficulty that necessitated a computer.) For all the fragmentation in the previous work, the whole remained static, but Pedersen here refused to domesticate the site, preferring to design the structure instead on the site's own terms, layering together craggy, thrusting forms that resembled a geological eruption.

There was, however, one vestigial impulse in the otherwise liberated design. Between the wedged shapes that housed principal rooms, Pedersen positioned Platonic solids—a drum and several point towers—that conceptually held the wings in place. In the first proposal, and in a second, less expensive, simplified scheme, which was built, Pedersen drove these static forms through the plan like stakes. The wings, then, did not drift off in Einsteinian relativity, but remained grounded in Platonic stability, as though tethered to immoveable posts. Only a single drum remains in the final version, but its central location as an entrance and staircase holds the whole composition. The small chamber negotiates the transition between outside and inside, directing visitors into the freewheeling wings. With one controlling, regular form, Pedersen pinned the building down, as he had done in Montreal, Rockefeller Center and Frankfurt, with the popsicle-stick elevator cores. Despite his recognition of the fragmentation of the city and in Vermont, and the fractal geometries of the mountainscape, Pedersen instinctively chose to stabilize rather than destabilize his buildings by emphasizing fixity. The asymmetrical designs were not fundamentally eccentric or, in the root sense of the word, ecstatic.

Since the founding of the firm, design for KPF's principals has been a record of progressive, incremental invention and discovery. In the early years of the firm, A. Eugene Kohn worked closely with Bill Pedersen responding to and reviewing his design ideas, and contributing to them as well. Gene Kohn supported an office culture whose collective temperament is inquisitive and even earnest: this "corporate" firm spends a disproportionate amount of time in the design phase, as compared to many other large firms.

In the cross-pollination of ideas on the design floor, Pedersen's schemes for the Carwill house were not dismissed as a dalliance or luxury. They were treated as research, and the results became integral to the investigations of the office. The house also built on KPF's established direction of unravelling the building into constituent parts rather than binding the building as a hierarchically ordinated whole: the break that Carwill represented was to take the idea further by loosening the underlying structuring geometries. KPF's design tendency, or at least one of its tendencies, was toward complexity, and Carwill simply compounded this tendency by radicalizing collage and fragmentation with a geometic play tinged with wildness.

The house was not only a mine of ideas for Pedersen; like a semaphore, it signaled the firm's willingness to support further exploration of territories difficult and unusual for a large, established firm. In the late 1980s and into the '90s, KPF was sometimes haunted by the afterimage of its popular historicized work: some clients expected the previous KPF and resisted change. But KPF would not be fossilized by its success in a trademark style. The firm, which had a history of mainstreaming ideas from the margins of the field, is predicated on design evolution, and after its dramatic success as one of the leading firms that brought postmodern historicism to corporate America, it had to reestablish its self-image and visual identity with new and solid content. The architecture that emerged with Carwill was about to change. KPF's modus operandi as an organization was itself predicated on self-assessment and self-correction. KPF was molting, poised to transform.

The adventurous single-family house is usually the province of boutique firms. Carwill had introduced KPF to uncertain and even difficult territory because it was unclear how edgy lessons about geometric freedom might be applied in large corporate or governmental commissions.

Shortly after Pedersen started working on the Carwill house, he and design associate Craig Nealy began the development of their scheme for the World Bank Headquarters in Washington, D. C., where KPF was commissioned to expand a complex of two office slabs to fill out the whole downtown block. KPF has a long aesthetic memory, and is able to call up from an accumulated repertoire the better aspects of past

5

6

approaches. Pedersen's newly revisited collagist approach suggested an appropriate strategy for adding to the existing structures. For the parti, the architects simply created a square doughnut, ringing the site in a suite of pinwheeling office blocks. In the center, the architects created a multistory atrium featuring a waterfall that cascades to a pool on the lowest floor. Especially during its postmodern phase, KPF developed an expertise in curtain walls, and the exteriors of the World Bank Headquarters benefit from years spent cultivating an illusion of depth in the shallowness of a facade.

In terms of their architectural search, however, what is especially revealing are the interior surfaces, which amount to an architectural diary. Though the massive office blocks are orthogonal, new architectural aspirations are written graphically on walls and carpet designs (Fig. 5), at times escaping the second dimension to occupy the third, as architectural projections. The architects inscribe freewheeling complexities on the surfaces, decorative abstractions that refer, in principle, to the Carwill house and related developments emerging in the field. Working within the Washington grid, for a banking client, within a tightly controlled governmental context, the architects push the envelop to the furthest extent possible. The graphics may be decorative but it also proved telling: the World Bank Headquarters was a transitional building aspiring to a new complexity. (Sometimes, as in Chopin's compositions, decorative grace notes can be extended until they become the structure itself.) The World Bank decorative themes anticipated further development.

In 1992, Pedersen both affirmed its collagist direction with the Mark O. Hatfield United States Courthouse in Portland, Oregon (Fig. 6), and went beyond the latent design tendencies of the World Bank to build strong, angular design pieces on the inside that functioned as exceptions to the overall orthogonal geometry. As in the Frankfurt skyscraper, Pedersen, working with senior designer Jerri Smith, broke out the constitutent programmatic elements—courtrooms and dependent agencies—into a tower and an attendant mid-rise structure, differentiating the facades with contrasting glass and stone treatments. The architects further differentiated particular elements like the air-foil roof and cylindrical entrance: in the dull context of surrounding mid-rise office buildings, the courthouse stands out as a highly ambitious piece of design. But inside, the lobby features an angular stairway, designed in forced perspective and rotated off the building's dominant orthogonal grid—Pedersen intimates multi-perspectivalism. The staircase itself takes the place of the Platonic forms in the Carwilll house that pinned the composition in place, but here reverses the intention, as though unpinning the otherwise orthogonal structure. As in many of Pedersen's designs, where he composes by a strategy of opposition—circle versus square, solid versus void, stone versus glass—he

positions the stairway to oppose static and dynamic, stable
and unstable. Materially, formally and philosophically, the
building is heterogeneous.

By the mid-1980s, KPF was already typecast as a firm
specializing in corporate and speculative high-rise structures,
but the firm decided to diversify its portfolio, and sought
institutional, governmental and transportation commissions.
In financial terms, overspecialization increased risk with
shifting market demand, and it restricted the development
of its architects. KPF pursued other kinds of work, and
landed commissions for the Revlon Campus Center at the
University of Pennsylvania (1990-1995), the Newport Harbor
Art Museum in Newport Beach, California (1990-1991), and
JFK Terminal One (1992). The influence of Carwill that had
been latent in the World Bank Headquarters and in the
Hatfield Courthouse surfaced in all the projects as complete
statements. Unfortunately, few were built.

But in 1995, KPF won the commission for the new, lean
IBM, headquartered in Armonk, New York, and the nature
of the commission for the computer giant proved the
occasion for a quantum leap forward. This large commission
proved an opportunity to elaborate the ideas in Vermont.

IBM, downsizing, was decamping from its big, bland,
geometrically rigid box; designed by SOM, the structure
represented the old, top-heavy, hierarchical IBM. The firm
was leaving behind the Bauhaus modernism of the
previous generation, and with it, a sclerotic organization.

The new site for IBM World Headquarters was at the top of a
heavily wooded hillside (Fig. 7). The rugged terrain offered
Pedersen the same logic that had motivated his design for
the Carwill house, and for the first time, he applied the
Carwill lessons at a large scale. Working with Greg Clement,
Jerri Smith and Douglas Hocking, Pedersen bent the long
building to conform to the site, like a jackknife with two
blades opening at either end. With the main body of the
building positioned near the edge of a hill, Pedersen angled
one blade toward the forest, and the other, in the opposite
direction, toward a landscaped parking forecourt. Instead of
an 'O' or 'U' surrounding a courtyard, Pedersen's 'S'
partially cupped the grounds so that neither the forest nor
the building dominates: each slips into and out of the grasp
of the other. Pedersen was dealing with open rather than
closed form. In the World Bank Headquarters, there may
have been a frustration between wish and possibility, but at
Armonk Pedersen brought the new architecture well beyond
the surface, into plan, elevation and section. Instead of
World Bank's boxy volumes, relieved by an aesthetic
apparatus of mullions and reveals outside and decorative
motifs inside, IBM presents tapering lines and angling forms
that always ease out of sight. The structure makes no
monumental claims on the landscape, but insinuates itself

7

8

9

10. Kohn Pedersen Fox,
First Hawaiian Center
(1991-1996), Honolulu,
Hawaii.

11. Kohn Pedersen Fox,
Buffalo Niagara International
Airport (1993-1997),
Cheektowaga, New York.

10

11

into its countours. The angled, tapering and rising forms, in movement and shape, are self-transformative, always becoming something else.

The one constant in KPF's continuous evolution was its attention to materiality (Figs. 8-9). KPF architects have developed an increasingly refined architectural palette, mastering stone, metal and the elusive beauty and variety of glass. At IBM, the palette is especially masterful: acid-etched mirrors and stainless steel, in their lack of depth, reinforce the spatial ambiguity set off by the forms. Pedersen balanced the wildness of the design's geometry and gesture with material elegance, so that potentially aggressive forms appear serene. The building is deeply civilized.

From a social point of view, the change in the IBM headquarters represents a paradigm shift from sputnik to ecology, from scientific domination over nature to cooperation with it. In terms of the firm's own evolution, KPF had not only translated the Carwill experiment to a large-scale building, but had also altered the principles conceptually: Pedersen finally unpinned the design; he removed the cylinders that had fixed the Carwill house to the site. No such basic geometries control the newly liberated IBM plan for a company itself interested in continuous change and adaptation. Removing the Platonic forms that had held the spinning shapes in place, Pedersen erased the vestigial yearning for architectural absolutes. He had stepped outside the space capsule into open relativity.

The most intractible building type is, probably, the high-rise, a product of multiplication tables. KPF tested its new design direction in a series of towers in Hawaii, including the First Hawaiian Center (Fig. 10). As in Vermont, Pedersen—designing with Peter Schubert—allowed the usually pure morphology of the point tower to be tugged in several directions, and the two principal facades were differentiated by orientation to sea and mountain views. Pedersen carved out the volume to expose glass elevators to the vistas. The tower, an irregular wedge notched to reveal the junction of the two facades, sits on a podium that is itself shaped to accommodate program and urban forces. On the trapezoidal site, Pedersen shaped the base as a parallelogram to allow space at grade for a mandated plaza and public colonnade. Half the podium is devoted to the three-story banking hall, and half to the Hawaii Museum of Contemporary Art.

The call of Hawaii's different blue and green natures, the ocean and the mountains, then, invaded the morphology of a building growing up from a conventional urban grid. The contradictory pulls distorted and diversified an extrusion that became prismatic. Deepening collage to the point of fragmention, differentiating the parts beyond the surface yielded complexity in a building type that is predicated on a process of extruding form straight up from plans.

12. Kohn Pedersen Fox,
*Rodin Museum (1995-1997),
Seoul, South Korea.*

13. Kohn Pedersen Fox,
*Rodin Museum (1995-1997),
Seoul, South Korea.*

KPF's new dynamic language, however, was especially well suited to airport architecture, a building category that has no set typology but that nonetheless encourages futuristic, technologically symbolic form-making. In 1993, KPF began design on the Greater Buffalo International Airport (Fig. 11). The parti for the entire complex was basically a simple H, but the architects lengthened and angled one stem of the H to accommodate the departure gates and fattened the link between the two stems for a concession area just beyond security check.

The poetry of the airport is not in its organization but its expression. Designed at the same time as the IBM headquarters in Westchester, Pedersen—in collaboration with Anthony Mosellie and Duncan Reid—lifted the building out of stasis with a series of formal moves that floated and dynamized the building. The architects start at the leading corners, which they explode into a type of anti-cornerstone of glass triangulated into a leaning pyramid. The tilted, transparent volume lifts the corner of the roof so that it appears to sail. Inside, the white ceilings, uninterrupted by grills and lights, are buoyed by light coming from clerestory windows ringing the edges. Piers are inclined, setting the structure in motion. As a metaphor of flight, the design is the direct descendent and heir to the brilliance of Saarinen's TWA terminal at JFK in New York, but as a building, it embodies an entire thesis about indeterminate space and form set in a flux of its own making. The constantly turning ceilings, leaning piers and angled floor plans set up relational conditions that turn the building into a field of change to be experienced on a path of discovery. The shifts of parts as they revolve in a relational constellation peak the curiosity of the eye, engaging the viewer in perceptual interactivity. The architects have designed experience as much as form.

Armed with a portfolio of impressive large-scale buildings, Gene Kohn and Paul Katz successfully exported KPF services abroad in anticipation of declining demand for office space in America. Open to progressive ideas, corporate Asia has proved a very receptive region for KPF. Hong Kong, China, Japan, Singapore, and Indonesia have all commissioned major projects scaled to their real or anticipated position in the globalizing economy. Some buildings are among the world's tallest. Asia has generally patronized modernist architecture firms since World War II, both as a defense against colonialist traditionalism and as a symbol of progressive thinking.

In some ways, Asia has proved even more receptive to KPF's approach than the United States, and, in fact, the firm's first museum was built in Korea. In 1996, KPF redesigned the streetscape at the foot of three high-rise headquarters structures for Samsung in Seoul, to humanize and link the ensemble of point towers (Fig. 12). The new interventions on Samsung Plaza culminate in the freestanding Rodin Museum, where two whorls of tilting glass walls, one 'C' nested in a

12

14. Kohn Pedersen Fox,
Shanghai World Financial
Center (1994-2005),
Shanghai, China. Elevation.

larger 'C', each with varying heights, encircle Rodin's Burghers of Calais and The Gates of Hell (Fig. 13).

Designed by Greg Clement and Kevin Kennon, the open, irregular forms and translucent surfaces of the acid-etched glass mystify the interiors, establishing a soft, atmospheric surround featuring the two monumental scuptures. The indeterminate edges of leaning, curving walls in a gestural plan turns visitors in an open space that revolves around the sculpture: unlike the modernist towers that hover above the museum, there are no axes or centers that place the visitor (and the works), controlling the promenade. Space, here, is conceived as a dynamic field, the forms reconfiguring themselves in unexpected, always changing relationships. Visitors determine their own path of visit, without prescribed points of view. The design translates into more fluid form the angular geometries of its immediate KPF precedents, but the principles of a relational architecture remain the same. Luminous inside by day and outside by night, the building forms an urban lantern and a civic landmark.

While its architectural progression has been evolutionary, the evolution has not been linear. After two decades of an intense and highly productive practice, KPF has a complex portfolio and repertoire, and KPF architects frequently revisit their past successes to develop them further through the advantage of hindsight. It is in Asia, in the 1990s, that Pedersen has proposed designs that return to the early Brancusi-esque forms that culminated in Chicago's 333 Wacker Drive, finished in 1983 (Fig. 2). Perhaps the forms are more sophisticated, with curving silhouettes that match the curving plans, but they are sculptural in the same minimalist way, and they are unitary. They also share a common strategy at the base, where fragmented structures negotiate all the internal and external forces pressing on the podium at the street. KPF has generated a family of related towers across Asia, which yoke complex podia to lithe, sculptural towers. KPF moves from collage to hybrids in the 95-story Shanghai World Financial Center (started in 1994), the 88-story Daewoo Marina City 21/Suyoung Bay Tower in Pusan, South Korea (1996), the Posteel Headquarters Tower in Seoul (1996), and the Roppongi Hills Tower in Tokyo (1991).

In volatile Asian economies, some of the projects have been canceled, and some are under construction. The 492-meter Shanghai World Financial Center, developed by Minoru Mori, will be the tallest building in the world when completed in 2005 (Fig. 14). The form, though monolithic, is elusive, a square prism intersected by two sweeping arcs: two of the four corners splay into a fifth and sixth facade that tapers toward the top in a 50-meter wide, symbolically Chinese circle. The base, however, might be a plan adapted from one of KPF's low-rise schemes, a composite of circles, squares and shards, all designed to gather the forces of the site—vehicular and pedestrian approaches, parking, plazas,

14

15. Kohn Pedersen Fox,
Plaza 66 (1994-2001),
Shanghai, China. Model.

16. Kohn Pedersen Fox,
Plaza 66 (1994-2001),
Shanghai, China. Lantern.

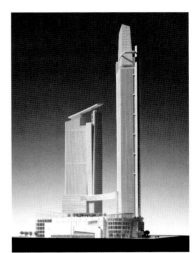

15

16

concourses and elevators—and translate them into vertical movement, up into the tower. Though a unitary form, the tower is self-transformative, with an always-changing plan, elevation and section, where no two floors are exactly alike. The form cannot be completely understood in a single glance. While the base connects to the city, the tower reads as an object against the sky.

The first skyscraper to be completed in this generation is the Plaza 66, in Shanghai (Fig. 15), a compex of two office towers, one sixty stories and the other forty stories, rising vertiginously from a retail mall situated in the old city (the total office space nearly equals that of the Empire State Building). In plan, the composite mall and the bases of the towers form a collage of curvilinear forms and lozenge shapes, all of which rise into the z-dimension, forming a three-dimensional collage. The architects—William Louie and James von Klemperer—striate the facades of the two towers with continuous vertical mullions, which make the towers soar visually up to sculpted tops. An inclined plane passing over the top caps the shorter tower, leaving a sculptural void. Belted by a free-flying frame, the top of the second tower transforms into a glass lantern (Fig. 16), which resembles the glass walls of the Rodin Museum. The design strategy may be collagist, and there may be self-referential memory in the composition, but the results are distinct within KPF's work, and unique in skyscraper history.

The formal beauty of KPF's designs often masks the architects' intention of designing public spaces that both connect to the surrounding city and cultivate an interior urban life. Pedersen has said that building is a social act of gathering people, and the subtext of all his buildings is urbanism, both exterior and interior. His recent design for Baruch College in Manhattan is a model of this urbanizing agenda (Fig. 17). Sited on nearly a full New York block, the base of brick, metal and glass supports a soaring corrugated metal roof whose gradual curve both recalls the arching roof of a nearby armory and forces perspective until the roof seems to vanish from sight. The building fits neatly into its urban context, while adding something strange and entirely unexpected.

But the building is most notable for the wisdom of its urbanism. Pedersen puts a bookstore on the street frontage along Lexington Avenue. On the side street along the north face, opposite the college library, he pulls the building line back about four meters to form a long, linear plaza that widens the street between the two buildings, creating a pedestrian plaza. One corner of the building leads inside to a corridor that, like a diagonal path across a college quad, forms one of the tributaries to what Pedersen calls a vertical campus. There are few buildings among Manhattan's high-rises with a section that pools people and breeds an interior public life, but Pedersen here has hollowed an eight-story

17

18

chimney of space (Fig. 18), with platforms and overlooks that foster a sense of community (the normal stack of pancake floors in New York towers usually divide and separate its resident population). At Baruch, a three-story, skip-stop elevator system guarantees a constant flow of students in the open stairwells sculpted around the elevators.

KPF's effort at creating a public life within and around a building perhaps achieves its most unexpected success in the notably anti-urban context of Tyson's Corner in Northern Virginia, where a famous (and infamous) mall gives the exurban center its only dependable venue of face-to-face encounter. Designing the headquarters for the Gannett Corporation (Fig. 19), Pedersen takes great care to socialize the urbanistically isolated building internally. With managing principal Robert Cioppa and designers Jerri Smith and David Lukes, Pedersen organizes the glass corridors on each floor of the 'U'-shaped complex so that they border the courtyard, all within sight of each other, and open directly onto the several levels of a stepped, landscaped roof that connects the two wings. Glass elevator towers placed in strategic apposition to the corridors also contribute to the pedestrian life of a car-dependent building type. The form of the 'U,' one wing longer than the other, extends into the surrounding landscape, interior pathways extend to the promenades and jogging trails around the adjacent pond.

Gannett, for KPF, is a virtuoso piece, conceptually, materially, socially, and formally. The crystalline glass volumes appear like an apparition when seen at a distance, a fragile, yet massive set of buildings unique in its mid-rise neighborhood. As at the IBM World Headquarters, the architects have shaped the volumes in angular geometries that glide subtly through the landscape, without any squaring frontality or anchoring moments that permanently fix the ensemble. To diminish the horizontal striping created by opaque spandrel glass, the architects applied vertical glass fins down each facade, that fog the surfaces with a green mist that softens the angular shapes, rendering the volumes indeterminate. Outside and inside, when struck by the sun, the fins play with the light, sparking such specular effects as stars and rainbows.

Gannett is a building of great scope, a full orchestration of a building's ability to establish a supportive work environment while shaping community and a relationship to nature. The form of the building is not an exercise in narcissistic beauty, but an instrument cultivating life in the building.

Gannett's glass veil endows the forms with the ability to transform themselves in different lights. The idea may be new to KPF's repertoire, but it represents the culmination of the theme of change and mutability that started with the Carwill house. Common to the buildings of the dozen years after the design of the Vermont house is a search for a

19 Kohn Pedersen Fox,
Gannett/USA Today
(1997-2001), McLean,
Virginia.

20. Kohn Pedersen Fox,
New York Jets Stadium
(2001), New York, New York.

poetics of change, the ability of a building to transform itself in shape and effect. Spaces and forms in KPF buildings merge into others in designs that are states of constant transition; entire walls bend out of sight, so that the mind can never fully understand a design and retire the building.

The nature of the change always changes, from building to building. Most recently a huge football stadium designed by KPF for Manhattan's side of the Hudson demonstrates yet another avenue of innovation. A professional stadium enjoys only a short season and a limited number of events, but KPF has designed a stadium that, at the push of a button, performs a ballet mecanique, transforming itself into an arena capable of accommodating smaller events (Fig. 20). The transformation is itself a performance.

The adaptability of the building, like the changeability of the skin at Gannett, the relational spaces and forms of the Buffalo airport, and the open, illusive blades of the IBM Headquarters all imply that the process of design in the KPF studios is open, changeable and relational: ideas rather than formulaic success drive the search. KPF grows and changes with each building.

19

20

KPF: Solving Problems in Three Dimensions

Carol Herselle Krinsky

The visitor to the offices of Kohn Pedersen Fox on West
Fifty-seventh Street in Manhattan may be slightly surprised.
The clean, white offices have no imposing reception area.
The plan and details do not reflect avant-garde design.
The partners occupy offices of compact size, and several are
far from a cluster of others at one end of the sixteenth floor.
None has a door, and A. Eugene Kohn, one of the firm's three
founders in 1976, and its president, occupies a desk at an
intersection of corridors, separated from the hallways only by
partial walls with large openings.

Just as entire buildings reveal important matters about their
sponsors, architects, and times, the open offices of KPF
suggest aspects of the firm's culture and of the partners'
personalities. An explicit aim of those in charge is to promote
collaboration within the firm in pursuit of the highest quality
result. While some comparably-sized architectural practices
have nearly separate studios within a larger structure, and
others are pyramids with one dominant person at the peak,
KPF partners and principals may participate in several
projects to varying degrees. Studios are temporary because
they are project-based, though people who work together well
or whose expertise is pertinent to a given job may collaborate
repeatedly, and some people develop specialized expertise that
is used more than once. Other than partners, no one has a
permanent desk; people move from one team to the next by
moving the computer and the telephone. Fluidity is seen as a
great virtue, and both James von Klemperer, a design partner,
and Gregory Clement, a management partner, independently
used the word "osmosis" to explain how the interchange of
ideas occurs. William Pedersen, another founding partner,
and others often put forward formal ideas that others adopt,
sometimes only later and in modified form for other projects;
the ideas "propagate." While the firm does not usually do
project reviews with pinups of current work submitted for
internal comment, projects are not spatially segregated, so
that it is almost inevitable that the participants in one will
explain the use of a new material, for instance, to participants
at adjacent tables. Mutual effort contributes to the leaders'
self-image and to their buildings. It helps in the continuous
stimulation of staff members, too. A young designer, Trent
Tesch, says architects "want to generate ideas, and if they are
allowed to have some range with these ideas, they generate
more good ideas. For the most part here, everyone feels he's
contributed in a meaningful way. This is unusual, especially
for a firm this size."

The partners take pride in nurturing home-grown talent,
promoting from within. Jerri Smith, a senior principal, has a
teacher's instincts and delights in working with student
interns and recent entrants into the profession. The partners
know that people whom KPF wants to attract will leave if
they are not challenged, if there are no clear architectural
objectives, or if they cannot achieve personal fulfillment
within a large organization—as of 2001, about four hundred

people in the New York and London offices. One lament is that the firm has so many talented designers that not everyone can be promoted rapidly; no corporation is composed only of executives. The people at the top appear sincerely to want interaction with those below. Here, as in other firms, the promotion of women to design partner in the New York office is an unresolved issue, but Jill Lerner is a management partner, and the matter is complicated by individual preference for work other than management, by the choice to follow a husband elsewhere, by the greater inclination among men to leave home and young children for three weeks abroad if business requires it, by the economic decline affecting architectural employment over a decade ago, which removed a now-partner-age cohort from the firm, and by an unconscious but perceptible tendency among men to be mentors to other men.

Another question arises often, but has as yet no answer, having to do with the firm's future. Kohn and Pedersen, who show no signs of exhaustion and continue to do innovative work, are thinking about the succession. Can a firm initiated by three men—Sheldon Fox has retired—become transformed successfully into a larger entity with more partners, multiple offices, and different practices for a different age? Pedersen says, "The new partners were created because they can bring a new level of creative energy to diverse new projects." One factor in a transition will be the maintenance of the firm's primary reputation for commercial buildings, which still dominate the list of jobs, while increasing its reputation for other types of work. "The modern city center," says Pedersen, "is largely composed of commercial buildings. If an architect professes to be concerned with urbansim, he has to be concerned about tall buildings and their ability to contribute positively to the city." Office building constitutes its most financially rewarding work (four hundred families depend on the financial rewards). Nevertheless, as more institutions and other clients understand KPF's successes in these areas, institutional practice has increased, introducing change along with opportunity. Fortunately for the architects, their ability to collaborate with other building professionals and to satisfy clients is likely to continue.

KPF's leaders welcome participation by the client. Partner William Louie hopes that clients realize that the building is as much their creation as that of the architects—because it is. What's more, he remembers with chagrin that as a very young man, he presented a design which he called "my" building to a client who had another idea about ownership! The partners and principals readily acknowledge the intelligence of clients who have worked themselves up to a position from which they are able to commit millions of dollars to building projects. The architects see serious collaboration as essential to a successful result, and repeat the truism that "great clients make great buildings." Some clients know what they want, whether or not their initial desires are

feasible or optimally desirable. Some trust the professionals to produce proposals, while others seek collaboration from the start. KPF's usual procedure is to devise several schemes that might fulfill the program, and then through a comparative analytical process, explain the strengths and weaknesses of each. The architects' initial preferred solution may be rejected or approved, but the decision will follow well-informed judgments in which the client participates fully. At the Gannett Corporation's new headquarters (page 314) in Tyson's Corner, Virginia, the client approved a certain spiral concept of form and circulation right away, but for Procter & Gamble's headquarters in Cincinnati, Pedersen remembers that John Smale, the client, felt that only after seeing four preliminary possibilities could he "better understand what he was hoping to achieve, which was to unite the old and new parts of the building in one entity. So we came up with a fifth idea, integrating [these parts]. By the time we had gone over all the possibilities, he could find valid reasons for his feelings, and then articulate them, and we could then respond to his aspirations." The procedure makes practical sense, because later in the enterprise, there will be fewer of the rude surprises that promote time-consuming acrimony and money-consuming lawsuits.

The general restraint of the white-painted offices suggests something about the personalities at the head of the firm. The partners and principals are strong individuals; they would not hold their positions otherwise. Nevertheless, Kohn and Pedersen are courteous and restrained in manner, commanding by example rather than by posing or by yelling at colleagues. Bill Louie speaks quietly and works in an uncommonly neat space. When Jamie von Klemperer reveals the expressive artistic reasoning behind a practical project, he does so in articulate plain English rather than the arcane language favored by certain fashionable architects. And for all the seriousness of KPF's work, there is room for humor; infant twins in T-shirts with a prospective client's logo form part of the firm's informal history. Not all the partners are equally reserved, to be sure, and no doubt, a choice of behaviors and approaches is appealing to clients who have to like—or at least trust fully—an architect whose building may risk the client's fortune. The most forcefully vocal of the younger partners, Paul Katz, expresses his opinions with wit and exceptional common sense. Clients can feel comfortable with architects who understand design (from which both Kohn and Katz moved into management), who agree that the client's financial health is essential to their own, and who understand that strangers who will work together for several years need to feel comfortable with each other. As Katz says, "Choosing an architect is something like choosing an airline. Some architects don't consider the safety of the sponsor's life," pointing out that a costly error can ruin a client financially. Anyone can recognize a taste for unpretentious, direct speech and level-headedness among all the partners, and surely this has helped KPF to secure commissions.

19

The fact that the offices have not been renovated conspicuously shows that the partners understand economy. Frequent renovation for the sake of temporary display is time-consuming and costly, and may even impress outsiders as wasteful. A client interested in efficiency and cost-control, even for a showpiece headquarters, understands the tradeoff between display and expense, and knows that the architects do, too. Nevertheless, Pedersen remembers that Sheldon Fox established a principle: "He never controlled the time [spent on a project] on the balance sheet. He understood that a manager was not there to track the hours spent on design."

The office detailing reminds visitors that the firm for at least a decade was prominent in designing postmodern or, as the architects might put it, overtly contextual buildings. Symmetrical layouts in parts of the office floors, rounded wall moldings, and other hints recall the firm's past direction as prominent designers of high-rise office towers with balanced forms, evocations of the 1920s, and details taken from Rome, the Crystal Palace, and the adjacent neighborhood. Whether it is because the architects have shaken themselves out of continuing mechanically along a successful course, or because tastes have changed throughout the architectural profession, KPF has included only small pictures of a few postmodern projects in a large book illustrating the firm's first twenty-two years of existence, even though internal planning may have been excellent and details carefully made. Pedersen regards those projects as representing a brief interlude, pointing out that other buildings, the ones prominently emphasized in that book, are his own designs, and that there was only a matter of two or three years between the completion of 333 Wacker Drive, the office building that made KPF famous, and the initiation of the DG Bank project in Frankfurt, the pivotal work that maintained contextual relations while refreshing a modernist approach.

This re-examination of modernism took place under new circumstances including foreign commissions, the use of computers, and developing techniques for enhancing environmental performance; the London office, under David Leventhal and Lee Polisano, often working in Europe where environmental controls are mandatory, has been especially attentive to ecological developments. Pedersen is immensely proud of KPF's technical strength and sound building practices. Younger partner Peter Schubert emphasized refined detailing as among the ways to promote a "more humanist" contemporary result, and considers it important for the firm's current reputation.

Along with IBM Quebec's headquarters in Montreal, the DG Bank (1986-93) shows the firm's fresh direction. It is still contextual in attempting to address several scales within the city, including five-and six-story apartment houses in Frankfurt's Westend and extensive vistas from upper floors toward the Main River. A passageway through the building accommodates pedestrians moving from a business district to a residential one, and shelters palm trees that give it the historically-evocative name, Winter Garden. Surface materials include traditionally suitable stone. Nevertheless, the building looks modernist because its conspicuously high tower's surface is clad in glass and painted aluminum, as is the face of a lower section that terminates a street vista. In later buildings, metal and glass dominate.

The architects see the DG Bank as an assembly of components—offices, apartments, the passage, shops, restaurants, and services. They hope to have created harmony from the many parts. No delirious or deconstructed jumble of forms, the bank appears from afar to be one tall tower joined by a central spine to a somewhat lower one. This building renews ideas behind 333 Wacker Drive in Chicago; there, one section curves to echo the form of the Chicago River, while the other is rectilinear, responding to geometric buildings and the city's grid on that side. In Frankfurt, the forms and materials have been calculated to provide spaces required by the program, of course, and to satisfy local environmental regulations, but they also break up a single shape in order to avoid overwhelming other buildings nearby. The architects see context as something that evolves by transformation, not by mimicry.

The idea of assembly informs several other recent buildings by KPF. Pedersen is especially taken with the idea of juxtaposition—of solid and void, high and low, spacious and confined. This is unlike the collage, for example, of the Educatorium, a multi-purpose building by the Dutch firm of OMA, at the University of Utrecht. There, within a discreet rectilinear glass and concrete enclosure, varied forms, spaces and textures appear in visually separate areas. In KPF's building, the variation appears outside as well as inside, so that the observer on the street can guess what happens within. Several floors with repeated square windows on the facade of the City University of New York's Baruch College (page 218) represent faculty offices; clerestory strips in solid sections of wall light lecture halls which are often darkened for multi-media presentations. The broader metal-framed glass plane of the Institute for International Economics (page 406) in Washington, D.C. conceals a lecture hall and most of the researchers' work spaces, while the narrow section contains the building's core. Newsrooms require broad, flat floor plates, so the Gannett Corporation's new headquarters reveals them by a protruding glazed block connected to adjacent spaces. More conventional offices for magazine publishing can be housed in a taller office tower. The various components are organized so as to evoke at close range the variety in a townscape—one with glass surfaces. (It is ironic that the architects, and perhaps the clients, apply an urban metaphor to a headquarters that abandoned the city.) While different in contour and surface material from an older wing to which it is connected, the horizontally emphatic, brick-clad annex for the Provincial Government offices (Provinciehuis) in The Hague (page 108) undulates gently from the older section as if it were always intended to be built. This project, directed by KPF's London office, demonstrates some commonalities of approach despite the second office's geographic distance from the first. The environmentally low-impact building fits into the low scale of the area without imitating anything nearby, or even following the contours of a park across the street. Here the distinctive parts—courtyard, annex with a planted berm at its base, and park form an open visual continuity, separable but fully coordinated. The result is easily appreciated from a glass-enclosed cafe on the ground floor.

KPF's flexibility in enhancing or smoothing heterogeneity—depending on the project—is especially important as the architects expand their work to Asia. In about 1985, Gene Kohn was impressed by an economist's prediction that Americans had to establish global businesses if they wanted to survive; earlier, the partners usually stayed home so as to provide constant service to their clients. By 1985, however, KPF had grown large and reputable enough to allow colleagues to visit clients. Asia and South America offered both puzzles and promise; in time, an office opened in London to handle many of the European projects. The traditional street patterns of Europe and North America are familiar to architects who remained awake in dark architectural history lecture rooms, so that they can form part of planning in western cities. These patterns are, however, rare in Asia. Some cities there have risen from farmland only recently, and in scattered increments. Few Asian cities emphasize continuous urban form; instead, the property owner expects to express his own desires, not to defer to nearby buildings.

Heterogeneity rules in individual buildings, too. Asian clients often ask KPF to design multi-purpose high-rises containing disparate facilities including department stores, hotels, apartments, offices, retail premises, and occasionally, cultural premises. Discontinuity and confusion need to be tempered for the psychological comfort of a city's inhabitants, and KPF's simpler modernist direction fits this need. Within the multiple urban forms of Shanghai, Pusan, Tokyo, Singapore, and elsewhere, the firm has recently designed several elegant towers that taper to distinctive, usually simple geometric forms. One, for the Dacom Corporation in Seoul (page 240), consists of two principal sections, one curved and the other with straight-lined walls. The entire structure is sheathed in glass to maintain a uniformly crystalline appearance. Even simpler is the tower section of the gigantic Shanghai World Financial Center (page 156), located in the new financial and trade center of Pudong, across the river from the older business district along the Bund. The new tower will make its mark with uninterrupted contours that taper in section, appearing to twist as they culminate in a plane pierced by a circle. This is not simply an artistic gesture or one that

creates a logo, although it is both. The cavity counters wind pressures, and it also creates a small measure of urban continuity by relating to the spheres of the television tower about a thousand feet away. As an added fillip, it can be said that the circle as a Chinese symbol of unity, created by North Americans in an international business quarter, stimulates thoughts of harmonious international relations.

Usually, KPF's designers spend little time on symbolic appliques, though experience has taught them about symbolism that some clients will not or cannot put into words—a CEO's drive for power, a need to express an institution's benevolence. They believe in architecture as an artistic pursuit that solves practical problems in three dimensions. Like many other good architects who have undertaken complicated commercial and institutional projects, they demand high standards of design; individuals say "Our firm is about design," or "design is why we're here." Tesch says that in working with Pedersen, the partner sets a goal, and "people work around him to put form to that idea...flesh[ing] it out with CAD and models." For an addition to the Philadelphia airport, built on a fast-paced schedule, they worked in this way "until every ounce was figured out and detailed. My job [and that of others working on the project] was helping him [Pedersen] see what his ideas were" in actuality. Design, then, is not ornament; it has to do with problem-solving, reason, and enhancement. In addition, KPF follows budgets and schedules rigorously, though delays sometimes occur since a building project is executed by many participating groups. To preserve their business beyond the working lifetimes of Kohn and Pedersen, they must respect and support the situation of their clients. None but fully-developed professionals could produce the range of buildings from the Shanghai World Financial Center to a wrap-around glazed pavilion for sculpture by Rodin in Seoul, IBM and Gannett Corporation headquarters buildings in the suburbs and the World Bank's offices in Washington, D. C., eight Bloomingdale's department stores, and the new building for Baruch College.

While most of the partners are disinclined to discuss abstract theoretical matters, they have conceptual ideas of their own, going beyond urban contextualism to a focus on interaction among the users of their buildings. (These aspects of humane modernism are pertinent especially to institutional buildings and department stores, since well-being in speculative offices depends principally upon tenant firms' own practices.) Pedersen points to examples such as the World Bank and Baruch College where "our buildings have transformed the culture of the institution" by changing the manner in which the people "function and interrelate" within their own corporate or institutional structure. When Baruch College's new building opened in September, 2001, it was hard to get evening students to leave at closing time, even before the coffee bar and cafeteria were in operation, and day students reported feeling proud to be in a building that made it clear that the city cared about their well-being. The World Bank commission (page 32) probably came to KPF in part because theirs was the only firm to propose keeping two existing buildings on the site. This idea promoted economy and enabled some workers to remain in place while construction was underway, minimizing disruption of operations. The initial plan envisaged an open-air internal court, allowing offices on two sides to have windows. The present glazed roof over the internal space keeps this idea, but also gives everyone the opportunity for all-weather socializing in and around the court. Supporting the goal of employee interaction and pleasure in the work environment are several kinds of spaces for conversation and coffee, from a basement cafeteria lit by light wells, skylights, and openings to balconies with tables and chairs. Staff members claim to work differently in this setting, and have gone so far as to schedule weddings in the central court—after work hours. The architects are also proud of having achieved a spectacular, luxurious-seeming result within a budget limited by the client's understanding that the World Bank must husband its resources to promote its work around the world.

At the Gannett headquarters, public tours are among the program's special features. The building includes editorial offices for periodicals and the newsrooms for the daily USA Today. Different functions receive different expression, but the separate activities connect at a large entrance atrium used for access to the reception desk and elevators, but also for large gatherings and dinners. Tourists walking in glass-enclosed corridors will see Gannett's employees in other corridors, and can look through windows to see the publishing operations. Moving people and a sense of busy activity are features provided for in the design. Staff can enjoy restful conversation and lunch at coffee kitchens adjacent to outdoor balconies, on terraces fronting the lower floors, and on low walls within the carefully-landscaped grounds. The garage, concealed by wire mesh that will carry planting, has on its roof tennis and basketball courts, while a hill on the site where a high-rise headquarters was originally to go, is now the location of a badminton court and softball field. These facilities are enticements to move to the suburbs—not everyone was happy to leave the city and its immediately-adjacent stimuli—and are useful break time amenities for those who work at odd hours on nights and weekends. The upper floors of the periodicals tower provide satisfaction for executives who from their heights can command a broad wedge of nature, landscaping, and impressive glass-covered architecture.

Corporate budgets make possible amenities that do not appear even at the World Bank. Public educational institutions normally face equal or greater limitations, but successful solutions are possible nevertheless. For the new Engineering Center building (page 354) at the University of Wisconsin-Madison, John Bollinger, the now-retired dean, wanted the building itself to be an educational tool, promoting "learning rather than teaching." This was to be done by emphasizing constant interaction among undergraduates, graduate students, and faculty, and by making the building components as visible as possible. As in Frankfurt, the World Bank, and Baruch College, all on constricted urban sites, the architects proposed an interior focus, which also suits Madison's harsh winter climate. In a tall, central multiple-use spine, students can assemble on several levels—in student club booths, on bridges and stair landings, in open areas near classrooms. The spine is also likely to become a major pedestrian passage from the engineering-and-science mall to a public street. All the internal building machinery is visible through transparent plastic panels, so that budding engineers can gradually come to understand construction. Guaranteed to promote conversation is a deep well along one side of the main floor passageway, from which people peering over a parapet can watch first-year students in the basement who are constructing their required floatable concrete canoes. The university officials requested an exterior that responds to the design of nearby buildings, so the architects (including local colleagues, Flad Associates) devised a metal and glass paneled wall with yellow brick facing that is clearly a veneer, showing students the difference between structural and ornamental elements.

For Baruch College, limitations were especially acute. Pedersen says that he was even warned away from working for the city, since officialdom and cost restrictions were said to crush initiative; in fact, the architect found the then-president of the college, Matthew Goldstein, to be one of KPF's best clients. The program included several departments of undergraduate instruction, separate facilities for executive education, faculty offices, lecture halls, student affairs offices, a large theater open at times to the public, and athletic facilities that are open to the public when intercollegiate games take place. The faculty offices had to have windows to the street, or windows into a central court. All this had to be inserted on three-quarters of a city block only about 200 feet wide, subject to zoning regulations. The compact, voluminous building addresses these matters. A tall but narrow tower would have been possible, but that would have meant time wasted in waiting for elevators; more elevators would have used spaces needed for other purposes. Instead, three-story zones with internal stairs for the individual instructional groups connect to a central skylit atrium that invites students to see each other all the time, reducing the separation between liberal arts and business students. Conversation can occur in spaces reserved near stairways and elevators, in student clubrooms, in the cafeteria, and on the north, opposite the college library, a widened sidewalk with benches that is intended for socializing. Sun will enter the skylight during at least half the year; no one need feel like Jonah trapped inside a whale. Window strips on the north and south faces light the ends of elevator halls, removing the sense of enclosure from elevator lobbies; on the exterior, the strips lead the eye rapidly upward, using the visual speed of a zipper to modify the other large exterior elements. The curving silhouette was intended to mitigate the building's bulk, although it may even emphasize it, and allow the building to fit snugly into the zoning envelope, making use of all permissible volume. Elsewhere on the outside, window patterns reveal the functions inside—classrooms, offices, mechanical services. Materials on the lower floors relate loosely to those of nearby buildings. Space-consuming athletic and theater facilities are underground, approached from separate entrances for convenient crowd-management. On the ground floor, a bookstore provides convenient service and income. Perhaps good architects produce their most ingenious work when they are asked to do the nearly impossible. In this case, the building is humane, lively, and inclusive, despite the constraints of site and budget.

Buildings that offer pleasure and arouse respect reveal the professional competence of the designers. Design must go beyond making exciting but unbuildable sketches and it is certainly not a matter of simply trimming boxes. It must address programmatic requirements and distribute spaces to suit them, then provide structure, surfaces, and details to enhance the user's experience. As Peter Schubert puts it, "We build beautiful buildings that solve the program." Paul Katz claims that although there may be other architectural firms here and there that do one thing or another in a superior way, no other firm offers equally consistent high quality in all aspects of design, management, and production. KPF's architects do not pretend to do all the work by themselves; they are quick to name associated architectural firms, engineers, landscape architects, contractors, local collaborating architects, and other participants. But insofar as they are the coordinators or originators, KPF earns its credits. Apparently disdaining large-scale commercial architecture, some theory-centered critics ignore the ingenuity of this work, or its humane imagination. Organizational capacity, well-rounded financial ability, and other real-life skills are essential to realize good design, no matter what its underlying approach may be. Observers may like or dislike the aesthetics—now varied ones—of KPF's buildings, but the totality of the work contributes substantively to making architecture a responsive and responsible art.

Carol Herselle Krinsky

KPF London: A Community of Innovation

Kenneth Powell

Kohn Pedersen Fox's London operation was launched in 1989—
it formally opened in April 1990—with high expectations and
a huge dose of optimism. Over the past twelve years, the
London office has become the base for a truly international
practice, working across Europe, into the Middle East—and
indeed beyond. Germany and the Netherlands have been
particularly fruitful points of growth, and southern Europe is
increasingly seen as an area for development. In short,
Europe, has warmed to the KPF approach.

In the beginning, however, the focus was on London itself.
Fuelled by Thatcherism, the development boom of the 1980s,
was rooted in the phenomenal growth of financial services.
The deregulation of the Stock Exchange in 1986—the so-
called "Big Bang"—had a huge impact on the capital.
London's established position as a world financial center,
alongside New York and Tokyo, became the springboard for
a revolution in investment banking and share trading.
Institutions that had previously had a token presence on the
London scene—including big American players like Merrill
Lynch, Salomon Brothers and Goldman Sachs—resolved to
develop major UK operations. The architectural consequences
of the "Big Bang" were no less radical. Trading floors and
deep-plan offices equipped to handle a hefty infusion of IT
were suddenly in huge demand. And American architects
were well-equipped to give London the new workspaces it
urgently needed. Given the downturn in the American office
market during the later 1980s (partly a consequence of
Ronald Reagan's 1985 tax reforms) the opportunities that
London offered seemed heaven sent. By the autumn of 1987,
the *Architects' Journal* reported that ten major American
practices were operating in Britain, though, significantly, only
three had opened offices.

For Lee Polisano, the KPF Principal who as senior partner-in-
charge founded the firm's London office (as Kohn Pedersen
Fox International), the events of the 1980s now look like the
archaeology of the European practice which has since been
created. Polisano and his colleague David M. Leventhal, who
came to London as partner-in-charge of design, recall a
gruelling period when they were making almost weekly
return trips between New York and London. London was not,
in fact, KPF's first point of contact with Europe. In 1984, the
firm had been commissioned to design a new United States
Embassy in Nicosia, Cyprus. More relevant to its subsequent
London operation was success in the 1986 competition for DG
Bank's headquarters in Frankfurt. (The building, the work of
partner William Pedersen, was completed in 1993.) Having
worked with developer G. Ware Travelstead in the U.S.A., KPF
was an obvious addition to the design team that Travelstead
assembled for his landmark development at Canary Wharf in
London Docklands. Travelstead's exit from the project and the
advent of the Reichmann Brothers (who finally got the
development off the ground in 1987) saw KPF's role change.
The firm was given two blocks as part of the master plan by

Skidmore, Owings & Merrill. They were designed from New York by a team led by Bill Pedersen and David Leventhal. With Canary Wharf underway, KPF scored a further success when it was selected to redevelop the former *Daily Telegraph* site on Fleet Street into the UK headquarters of Goldman Sachs (a commission largely secured through KPF President Eugene Kohn's contacts at the investment banking firm). Bill Pedersen's achievements as a designer and teacher is an inspiration which Polisano readily acknowledges, alongside the unwavering support of Gene Kohn. Indeed, it was Pedersen and Kohn who have done as much as anyone to transform the aspirations of American architects, with KPF seen by fellow practitioners as a benchmark for quality and innovation.

The Canary Wharf and Fleet Street projects prepared the way for KPF's European operation. The opening of the London office, with a staff largely recruited in London and embracing a wide national and ethnic mix, reinforced a growing realization that working in London involved not just importing technical expertise and design flair—commodities that a number of American practices offered—but equally coming to terms with the architectural culture of Europe.

KPF's arrival in London coincided with a period of intense debate about the role of architecture, extending beyond professional circles and generating intense media and public debate. The dominant theme in British architecture was high-tech (a term that its practitioners, led by Norman Foster and Richard Rogers, in fact, disliked). Foster's Hong Kong Bank and Rogers' Pompidou Center (done in collaboration with Renzo Piano) demonstrated the global appeal of this approach—both Foster and Rogers had, at this time, built relatively little in Britain. The anti-modern cause there had been given an enormous boost by the activities, from 1984 onwards, of the Prince of Wales, whose favored style was a rather literal Classicism.

There was a certain irony in the fact that it was the Prince who, as a distinguished visitor to Washington D.C. in 1990, spoke at a ceremony in which Eugene Kohn received the AIA's Firm of the Year Award on behalf of KPF. As critic Deyan Sudjic remarked, KPF's "dazzling" skill at infusing commercial architecture with inspirations from a wide range of sources, some of them distinctly leading-edge, was at odds with the Prince's conservative agenda. British critics warmed to KPF's magisterial 333 Wacker Drive, Chicago, and tended to forgive the firm for its excursions into postmodernism. "KPF has, more than anyone else, made postmodernism commercially acceptable in the 1980s," wrote Sudjic.

In Britain, and in Europe generally, postmodernism tended to be seen as an American import. By 1990, its influence in the design studios of KPF was rapidly waning—even the Canary Wharf blocks reflect a restrained approach to a style that

others used in a more full-blooded (and, it might be said, vulgar) manner. As a relatively young practice, KPF's approach to stylistic matters tended to be undogmatic and exploratory. It took naturally to the art of building in context —its skills in this direction were tested in the Peterborough Court, Fleet Street, project. In this light, the comments made in March 1990 by Lord St. John of Fawsley, chairman of the Royal Fine Art Commission, on the "American invasion" seemed less than temperate. It was an invasion, said Lord St. John, "more of Vandals than Goths." American practices, he continued, "are threatening London with a rash of quite unsuitable buildings. The revenge of the once rebellious colonies is to undermine our historic capital."

For Leventhal and Polisano, these sentiments, though not specifically targeted at KPF, must have been galling as they worked to build up the new office. The European operation was launched under the banner of KPF International—and the title was more than a token of intent. "We were determined to create a practice which would be truly international," says Leventhal, "rooted in Europe as much as in London." The very specific circumstances of London in the mid-and late-1980s would not be duplicated in Frankfurt, let alone in Hamburg, The Hague or Amsterdam. "In the USA, office floorplates of 43,000 square feet (4,000 square meters) were common," says Leventhal. "Working in European cities meant getting used to typical floorplates of around 9,000 square feet (800 to 900 square meters)—the sort of floor plans we'd done at Canary Wharf were ruled out." It was not just a matter of divergent technical briefs, but of cultural and political diversity—German regulations on access to natural light, for instance, and on energy use were far more stringent than those in Britain and a world away from American attitudes. Most European cities, for example, were predominantly low-rise in character. The office clearly faced a steep learning curve.

The London office started with a core of twelve people transferred from New York—Karen Cook, now a partner in the firm, was one of this contingent. The rest of the office was recruited in London. The timing of the move was unpropitious. After years of unallayed boom, the British economy was heading for recession and major commercial developments were the first victims. It made sense to diversify, both geographically and in terms of building types—no practice could survive simply on office commissions. Given the London office's expectations of European practice, there was a certain irony in KPF's victory in the 1992 competition for the De Centrale Tower, the tallest structure ever approved in The Hague. Lee Polisano, however, considers that it was the project at Bismarckstrasse (page 62) in Berlin which "set the tone for our work in Europe—it was so clearly not the sort of job you'd do from New York." The scheme was led by German planning and environmental regulations and became a testbed for exploring the context of Germany and particularly for KPF's growing interest in environmental issues. The corner site was on a main street, opposite the Deutsche Oper and amongst a mix of residential and commercial blocks. A truly urban, even civic response was needed—a detached object-building would have been utterly out of place in this location. One of the delights of working in Europe for Leventhal and Polisano was the pleasure of discovering at first hand an alternative modern tradition that they had known only from books and working with colleagues whose view of modernism was very different from their own. The orthogonal geometry of Mies van der Rohe was in tune with the American city grid but it was to Erich Mendelsohn—whose expressive architecture still resonated in Berlin, that KPF turned for inspiration at the Bismarckstrasse. The corner became the key to the design. The height of the development was restricted to just five storeys, with shops at street level. The detailed designs capitalized on the expressive and curvaceous aesthetic of the scheme—the lobby entrance became an elegant exercise in curved glass and slender framing.

The environmental program of the development was progressive. The in situ concrete frame provides a strong thermal mass to offset the impact of heat and cold. External shading is built into the floor-to-ceiling glazed façade panels. Opening windows are supplemented by an underfloor assisted ventilation system. The project was, in fact, far from extravagant—it was a matter of using standard components to best effect in line with a tight budget. The result is a streetwise building that has both real elegance and a sense of place. KPF's work on the interior fit-out added to a feeling of integrity, a sense that interior and exterior are integrated – the use of uplighters to illuminate office spaces is a typically inspired touch, elevating a spec office development into something special.

Bismarckstrasse came to KPF through a direct approach from the developer, but the early years of the London operation were characterized by intensive work on competitions, which were seen as a source of education and growth. A landmark event was victory in the 1994 competition for the Cyprus Parliament House (page 150) in Nicosia—sadly, it remained unbuilt in 2001. Out of the first thirty competitions which the office entered, it won a remarkable seventeen, a considerable proportion of them in Germany. For a time, KPF International operated an office in Berlin. The firm's European reputation grew steadily on the basis not only of its architectural but equally its master planning and urbanistic skills.

KPF's introduction to The Netherlands had been its work on the De Centrale tower—one of a number of high-rises that suddenly sprouted in the Dutch capital. The Provinciehuis project could not have been more different. The brief was an expansion and reconstruction of the headquarters of the Province (or region) of South Holland (page 108). KPF's 1994 competition-winning scheme addressed the specific functions and imagery of a public building (though the project was

actually a public/private collaboration). The existing 1960s Provinciehuis, a good building of its period, had to be integrated into the scheme, though an extension from the 1970s that functioned badly was demolished. As in Berlin, there was an exploration of modern roots. The work of the Amsterdam School and of Dudok offered a model for a highly practical, human-scaled, richly textured modern architecture that responded to the historic city. In contrast, perhaps to the aesthetic of the International Style, it seemed accessible and unintimidating—qualities that the end user wished to infuse into the project.

The key move in the scheme was the decision to create a great public space at the heart of the development, not an American office plaza but a partly tree-planted, partly open square in the urbane Dutch tradition. The new offices form two blocks, one a sinuous curve, the other a sharply pointed wedge attached to an existing block, that enclose the square. A very deliberate gap between the two offers views into the space. In plan, the buildings are highly cellular and employ central corridors. Exposed in situ slabs offer well-tried environmental benefits. The emphasis is on user comfort and a high degree of individual control over internal conditions. Opening windows are combined with double glazing. A heat exchange system offers substantial economies on heating and ventilation costs. The brick cladding on the street facades to Zuid Hollandlaan and Koningskade are not carried through to the courtyard facades, where sheer glazing is used.

KPF's Provinciehuis won critical praise in Holland, while the work of Richard Meier and Michael Graves—among others in the city—was seen in some quarters as alien and overly assertive. The Netherlands subsequently became an important sphere of operations for the firm. At the time of writing, six KPF projects are under construction in the country. The model of the Provinciehuis has clearly informed work on the ambitious masterplan for the Hoofddorp area, on the fringe of Amsterdam close to Schiphol Airport. The site is both constrained—surrounded by roads and rail tracks—and sensitive. The historic Genbiedijk, one of the most significant of Holland's monumental sea defenses, is designated as a World Heritage Site. Out of this difficult set of circumstances, the master plan seeks to create a highly individual commercial development that has a strong sense of place and offers real benefits in terms of public space. Two crescent-shaped towers flanking the rail tracks are seen as a new gateway to the area, but most of the accommodation is in lower rise buildings, set amongst green parkland and water.

On the southern edge of Amsterdam, close to a park and set on Berlage's great radial axis, the World Trade Center development (master planned by P. de Brujn) is conceived as a way of giving a new identity to an existing, somewhat uncompromising, group of four 1960s buildings (page 210). It is a matter of intensifying the use of the site, but equally of connecting them and making useable and enjoyable spaces around them. To create a benign, all-year-round environment a long-span 69-foot (21-meter), light-weight roof (designed in consultation with engineer Guy Battle) is being slung across a new piazza, where shops, restaurants and other facilities will inject new life into the complex. The roof is a sophisticated creature, incorporating lighting, fire control, and sound absorption provisions, acting as an environmental modifier for the space below. A fifth tower is being added to the development, featuring a climatic facade with a timber clad inner facade. This tower will eventually address a new public square, part of a series of civic spaces intended to animate what is virtually a self-contained urban quarter. The existing towers are to be reclad. The project is a classic instance of an issue that increasingly confronts cities, developers and architects: that of making intractable twentieth-century developments work for a new century.

The idea of a "big roof" has been developed with equally innovative effects in the very different context of KPF's ENDESA headquarters project (page 430) in Madrid. The client is a huge national utility and the building is large (970,00 square feet/90,000 square meters). The site is on the north side of the Spanish capital, a place noted for its extreme, desert-like climate—boiling in summer, icy in winter. With an area of 86,000 square feet (8,000 square meters) the roof is itself a tour de force, again engineered with the assistance of Guy Battle and incorporating a system of louvres, shading devices and photovoltaic cells to moderate and capitalize on the Spanish climate. The photovoltaic cells will be used to supply a significant portion of the building's energy requirements. A series of great thermal chimneys—dramatic architectural features in themselves—are a key element in the ventilation program for the central atrium, which is seen as a place for socializing and interaction, for breaking down the barriers between departments and hierarchies, a covered version of the typical plaza. The office spaces, generally five stories, are disposed in two blocks wrapped around this social space, with public areas at ground level and two levels of parking below ground.

ENDESA is clearly innovative, ground-breaking architecture, an example of KPF's ability to work within unfamiliar cultural contexts and fuse traditional and novel themes. In contrast, the ADIA hadquarters (page 296) in Abu Dhabi is recognizably part of a long line of towers which the partnership has built or projected around the world during the last quarter of a century. There were other tower projects, in fact, which emanated from London—several fell victim to the Far East recession of the late-1990s. The ADIA project was won in competition, but subsequently redesigned. In the redesign, the office revisited two unrealized projects, the Daelim HQ planned for Seoul and the curvaceous Coolsingel scheme designed for a site in Rotterdam. In both these projects, offices were disposed in two flanking towers, joined by a glazed atrium, so that internal spaces could benefit from optimum amounts of natural light. ADIA is a huge investment company, a key player in the economy of the Middle East. A high-prestige building with a strong sense of identity was required. The site was striking: close to the sea, amongst green spaces on the edge of the city. The building is designed to address the seafront and to draw in the green space that is extended as a new parkland zone around it. While the office floors are relatively conventional, the insertion of a series of "sky gardens" helps to create a memorable and enjoyable workplace.

KPF's British operation has so far focused almost exclusively on London and has been dominated by commercial commissions, so that the completion of the Rothermere American Institute in Oxford (page 138) is a real landmark for the practice. The Institute houses a library, teaching spaces and offices for American Studies at Oxford University. The competition for the scheme saw KPF pitted against a diverse group of practices, including Foster & Partners, Porphyrios Associates, and Evans & Shalev. At this stage, the project was far from assured—adequate funding had not been found. A major subvention from Lord Rothermere provided the shortfall and the Institute opened in 2001.

No site in Oxford is anything but sensitive. In this instance, the new building had to relate to a context provided by the Victorian premises of Mansfield College and Rhodes House (an institution which has itself provided a base for many American students and scholars over the last century). A green space at the heart of the site contained a defensive mound dating from the siege of Oxford during the English Civil War of the seventeenth century.

KPF's winning scheme took the form of a garden pavilion, a structure which sits elegantly within its green setting without dominating it. The garden square was, in fact, excavated so as to reduce the apparent height of the building and minimize its impact on the context. The parti is that of a traditional full height library, with classrooms below, overlooking the garden. To the rear, offices and support spaces are stacked. It is in the balance of materials and the fastidious attention to detail that the real quality of the building is to be found. The Institute is constructed on an exposed concrete frame. The plinth on which the library sits is clad in natural (Bath) stone, a close match to that used at nearby Mansfield. The facade of the library itself is an extremely lightweight mesh of steel and glass, incorporating shading devices (including fritted glass louvres) that draw on the experience of the practice's (so far) unbuilt Cyprus Parliament project. Natural ventilation is used throughout, using the mass of the concrete structure and the thermal chimney effect.

The Rothermere Institute is seen as a real breakthrough for KPF—rightly so, in view of the prestige of the project. Debate about the relationship between old and new architecture in Oxford has raged for many decades. Oxford's most distinguished modern complex of the 1960s, St Catherine's College, was built in an enclave well outside the historic core. More recently, new buildings have tended to reflect a considered mix of tradition and modernity—seen, for example, in Richard MacCormac's successful collegiate additions. The Rothermere Institute is, in this light, quite uncompromising—and all the more appropriate for being so.

The vocabulary of the Rothermere Institute—solidity counterpointed by the lightweight—was prefigured at Thames Court (page 166) in the City of London, a project initiated from New York but completed, in radically redesigned form, only in 1998 (The revised scheme provided a striking contrast to the recently completed Classical Revival office development just to the east). The site, at Queenhithe, close to Southwark Bridge, was problematic but also full of potential. To the north, it addressed Upper Thames Street, a thoroughfare that had developed into an urban motorway, with high levels of noise and pollution. The southern boundary of the site, however, was formed by the river Thames, with fine views to the South Bank. Developing anywhere in the City means dealing with the archaeologists—the site proved to be archaeologically rich and the remains of a Saxon dock were unearthed beneath it. Piling on the site had to be severely controlled, providing an engineering challenge. In addition, a derelict but listed warehouse survived, isolated from its original context, and a compelling case had to be made before consent to demolish it was eventually given. Finally, the development had to conform with the strict height guidelines laid down to protect views of Wren's St Paul's Cathedral.

Lee Polisano recalls realizing that this was a scheme that "had constraints on six sides—not only was it closely hemmed in by streets and buildings, but there were controls on what you could do in the ground below and the sky above!" Inevitably, the new 323,000 square-foot (30,000 square-meter) building evolved as a "groundscraper," with five stories of accommodation above ground—the fall of the site to the river allowed a further level of offices below street grade. In its urban form, Thames Court developed as a thoroughly European building, its groundplate closely hugging the line of the old streets. Its internal configuration, however, marked it as a hybrid of European and American descent. Featured were a mix of deep floors, on lower levels, suitable for trading spaces—that were still heavily in demand in London—and more conventional floors that, with the assistance of a stepped, daylit atrium, could be naturally illuminated from two sides. Externally, the sparing use of Ham Hill stone (in response to planning guidelines) gave the building an appropriately solid dignity and urbanity but was linked to a strategy for insulating the interior against street noise, with the massive stone portal on Upper Thames Street framing a glazed buffer zone that acts as a reception area. The edge of the office zone forms a secondary internal facade. From the lobby area, the route through the building is across a triple-height hall which contains escalators and lifts. The central atrium lies to the south and is the heart of the building, a serene space filled with light—a system of fabric paddles mounted below the double-glazed roof adjusts to track the course of the sun during a working day and can be manually opened or shut in response to external conditions. Motorized blinds and louvres counteract solar gain on the south (river) frontage, while windows along the western (Queenhithe) edge of the building are designed to open.

The controlled use of natural light is a key element in the scheme, with glass floors used extensively around the atrium, part of a strategy for channelling light into the center of the building. In keeping with this approach, the structural agenda is about lightness and economy of means, expressed in the virtuoso use of steelwork. (The use of a steel frame minimized the weight of the structure and thus reduced the need for new piling on the site—some of the basements from the existing 1960s building which had stood there were reused.) In the main atrium, the huge steel trusses supporting the upper floors contrast with the elegance of the castings specially developed for landings and stairs. Thames Court reflects a fertile collaboration between the KPF team and structural engineers Watermans—the building's echoes of the "functional tradition" are appropriate in the riverside context—but is equally a very carefully considered piece of urban architecture, which is both contextual and modern. Polisano recalls the great number of models made during the development of the designs, partly in response to the many planning and consultative meetings which the scheme generated—again, a far cry from the North American experience.

Mid City Place, a 377,000 square-foot (35,000 square-meter) office development on London's High Holborn, is another long-running KPF scheme (page 386), begun in the early days of the London office but started on site only in 2000, a decade after State House, a typically 1960s office slab which stood there, surrounded by a bleak open plaza, was demolished. High Holborn runs dead straight, a former Roman route connecting the West End and the City, and is dominated by a series of monumental commercial buildings, the earliest of them Alfred Waterhouse's Gothic Revival Prudential Assurance. The project enjoyed the advantage of a straightforward rectangular site. The urban scale, set by mundane post-war commercial buildings on High Holborn, became more domestic to the north.

The rationale of Mid City Place was linked to moves within the British property industry to secure high value, fast track floorspace using design-and-build procurement methods that depend on the involvement of contractors in the design process. (A spur to this process was provided by a report prepared by leading industrialist and manager Sir John Egan, which suggested that the construction revolution of the 1980s, which had drawn inspiration from the U.S.A. had lost its impetus). Mid City Place then was commercially driven from the start—the cladding system, for example, was developed in partnership with a cladding contractor. Internally, the deep-plan floors are consistent throughout, arranged around a glazed atrium and elevator and toilet cores, and the floors are adaptable to a variety of layouts—flexibility is the key to the diagram. While the scale of the facades relates to that of adjoining streets, the great curved roof which rears up above High Holborn gives the building a distinctive presence while providing a dramatic display of structural steelwork. On lower levels, masonry cladding helps to root the building to its setting. Designed and constructed within two years, the project fully addressed the demanding agenda set by the Egan Report.

The experience of Mid City Place was channelled into KPF's most prominent London project to date, the proposed landmark tower (the so-called "Heron Tower") at 110 Bishopsgate on the eastern edge of the City (page 394). The location at Houndsditch was close to one of the lost gates of medieval London. For the architects, the island site seemed to merit a marker more distinguished in quality than the drab 1970s blocks that stood there. A tall building was possible here, since the site was not within the area subject to the St. Paul's Heights Planning provisions. Indeed, it will form part of a clump of high buildings in the eastern quarter of the City, including Tower 42 (better known as the NatWest Tower, completed in 1979) and the forthcoming SwissRe Tower designed by Norman Foster.

At Bishopsgate KPF was able to draw on the practice's proven record at designing high buildings—this was the first such opportunity that had emerged in London. But Bishopsgate is not Chicago or Abu Dhabi—the proposed tower is shorter than the NatWest Tower and slender in profile, with a carefully studied form. The NatWest Tower, like its 1960s precursors, featured a huge central core, with relatively small office floors that today attract a limited range of tenants. At 110 Bishopsgate, floors are large and open, with cores concentrated along the south side of the building—a device which provides a helpful barrier against the sun. The northern elevation, in contrast, is transparent, revealing the stacked, generously planted atria that serve as the focal points of the vertical "villages" of office floors. A similar transparency is found in the east and west facades of the tower, with their low-energy ventilated skins.

A further contrast between this state-of-the-art twenty-first-century tower and those built in London during the last century is found in the approach to public space. 110 Bishopsgate is anchored to its site by a new public square, formed by closing the road to the north of the site—spaces of this order are precious in the Square Mile. From the square, the handsome facade of St Botolph's, Bishopsgate, can at last be properly seen and enjoyed.

The idea of an office "community" is central to this City project. It is assumed that a number of companies and organizations will share the building—the projected retail and catering facilities, including a rooftop restaurant, address the needs of these users as well as those of other City workers. The idea of an office lobby permeable by the public is novel to London (though standard fare in the U.S.A.). 110 Bishopsgate has been conceived as a commercial development which addresses the needs of the public domain, as well as a landmark of the quality that London's Mayor, Ken Livingstone, sees as vital to London's continued dominance of the European financial markets. In this light, the planning delays that have affected the scheme seem unintelligible. (At the time of writing, a government decision on the future of the project is awaited, following a protracted planning hearing in autumn, 2001.)

A little more than a decade after its arrival in London, KPF seems a thoroughly Europeanized operation. Of the four new London partners appointed in 2000, one (Fred Pilbrow) is British, another (Ron Bakker) is Dutch, balancing Americans Karen Cook and Jim Outen. The firm's current office base in Covent Garden, a stylish but far from extravagant conversion of a Victorian warehouse, is in tune with Lee Polisano and David Leventhal's aim to run a design studio not unlike the British practices which Polisano and Leventhal most admire (and increasingly find themselves in competition with) are those of Norman Foster and Richard Rogers. Little more than a quarter of a century old, KPF globally is a young practice. Its London arm seems determined to maintain its youthful, innovative, and radical approach. KPF does large projects, but it also seeks relatively small jobs, like the infill development being built in Long Acre, yards from the office, in the belief that the latter are often especially challenging. KPF has succeeded in challenging a range of British talents on their own ground, but in the process it has enriched London and the broader European scene.

Kenneth Powell

Selected Buildings and Projects
1993-2002

Arranged Chronologically

World Bank Headquarters

Washington, D.C.
1989-1998

The design for the World Bank headquarters complex was the winning entry in an international competition. Occupying a site on Pennsylvania Avenue, in an area dominated by buildings from the 1960s and 1970s, the scheme incorporates buildings by Skidmore Owings & Merrill and Vincent Kling into a unified entity.

The building consists of a thirteen-story block surrounding a large covered courtyard. The existing structures comprise two of the three masonry wings that frame the project's glazed north wing. Measuring 150 feet wide by 150 feet high (46 meters) and bathed in natural light, the courtyard represents the bank as a community, connecting and integrating the separate buildings and their diverse functions within one institution. The canted glass wall facing Pennsylvania Avenue rises from the ground to reveal the open-plan lobby, its adjacent public spaces, and the large central room. Establishing a dialogue between parts of great weight and great lightness, these elements create a strong urban presence, while symbolizing the institution's desire for transparency and accessibility for its constituents and the public at large.

Although Washington is a city of classical architecture, the design distances itself from that vocabulary because of its references to colonialism. Instead, the project is inspired by its context: it modifies and enhances the scale of Vincent Kling's modern building. The horizontally striated glass facade along Pennsylvania Avenue counters the vertical gestures that derive from and connect to the existing structures.

The individual architectural elements of pre-cast concrete and white-painted aluminum have been detailed to a high level of abstraction; their recombination and juxtaposition provides depth and variety of expression. Within the central court itself are linear watercourses, monumental flights of steps, and pyramidal glazed pieces. On the roof, conference room canopies, masts, and the bowed courtyard skylight give form to the building's programmatic elements and provide a distinctive profile.

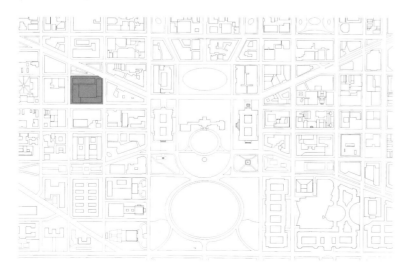

Typical lower floor plan

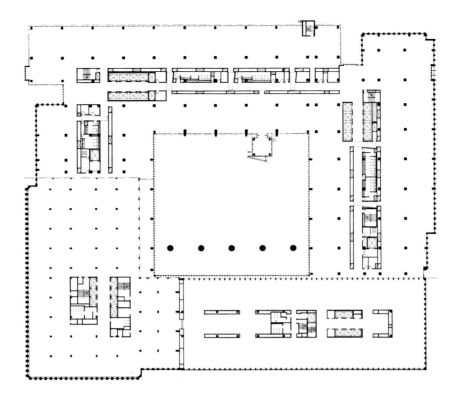

Ground floor plan

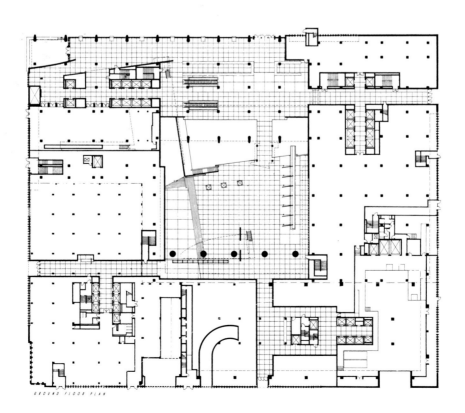

GROUND FLOOR PLAN

0   100 ft

Roof plan

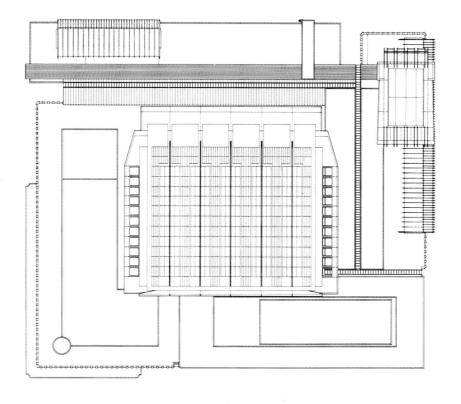

Typical upper floor plan

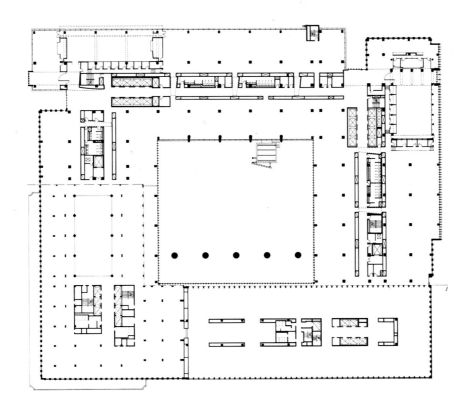

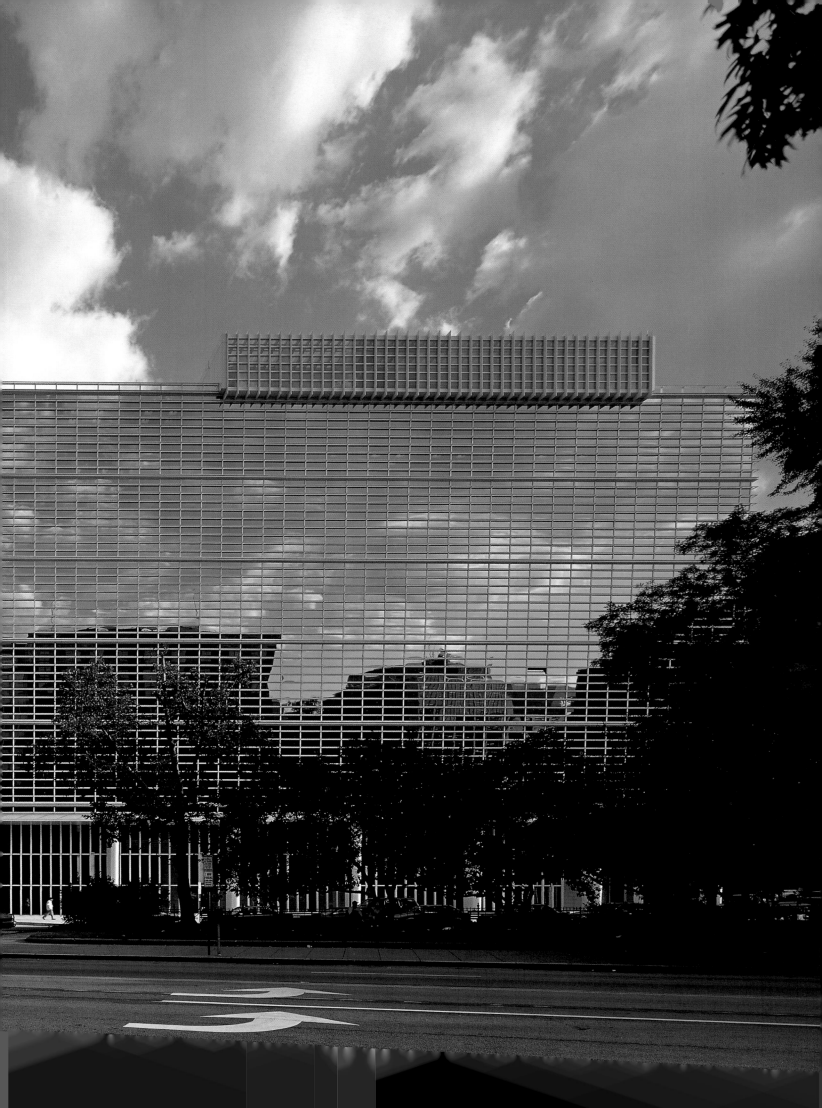

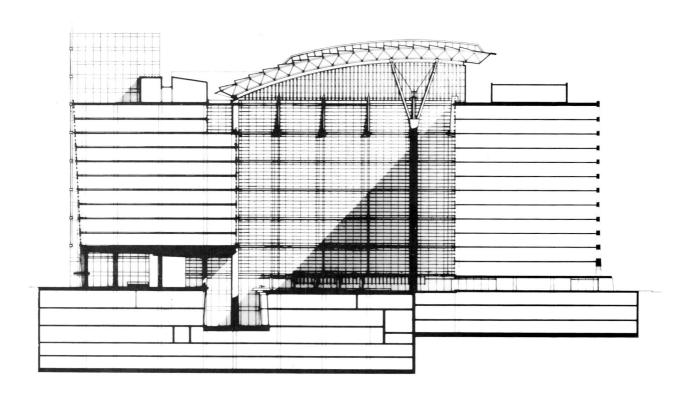

JR Central Towers and Station

Nagoya, Japan
1990-2000

The Japan Railways Central Towers is located in Nagoya, a growing city on the Noubi Plain halfway between Tokyo and Osaka. Adjacent to the tracks of the *Shinkansen*—the national high-speed trains that connect the city to the rest of the country—the complex houses the corporate headquarters of Japan Railways Tokai, as well as cultural, hotel, tenant office, retail and station facilities. The design solution addresses the structural problem of creating a complex, mixed-use building on top of an important transportation hub—linking rail, subway, and bus lines along a densely populated urban corridor. Organizing the large flow of people associated with a variety of use types, the solution defines distinct and separate circulation paths for pedestrians using different parts of the building.

The project is the largest commercial building in Japan. Its distinctive form is composed of two towers rising from a twenty-story podium. The base contains a multilevel department store, museum, health club, multipurpose hall, restaurants, and other retail functions. A two-story *sky-street* on the fifteenth floor—reached from the ground level through a bank of exterior shuttle elevators—connects public functions below to the towers above as it affords sweeping views of the city. The circular 59-story hotel tower provides a variety of room types and views; the 55-story office tower is formed by the juxtaposition of cylindrical and rectilinear forms.

The contrast between the towers and their shared base also reflects the desire to integrate the building into the urban context. Evoking parallel stretches of railway, the horizontal articulation of the podium provides a link to the low, surrounding structures. The uninterrupted vertical expression of the towers combined with the siting of the complex forms a monumental gateway into the city.

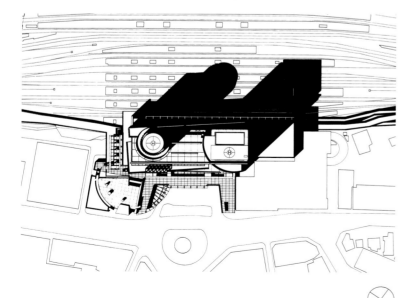

Typical high-rise floor

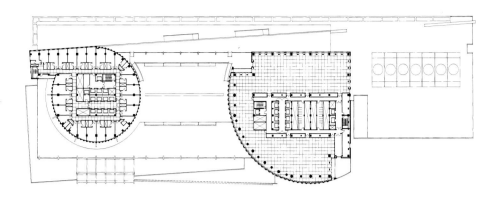

Sky-street floor

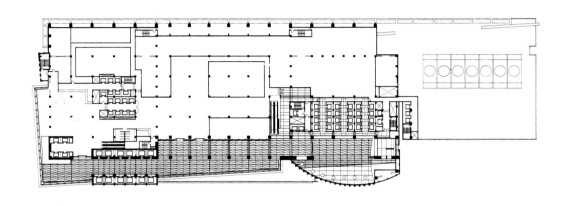

Ground floor plan

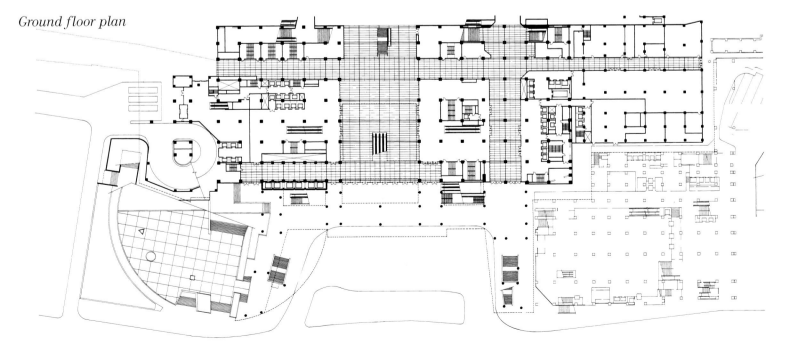

0   50 m

47

First Hawaiian Center

Honolulu, Hawaii
1991-1996

This 30-story bank headquarters and office building is on a full-block site in Honolulu at the intersection of Bishop and King streets next to Bishop Park, in the city's financial district. The building sets back from King Street, a major pedestrian artery, allowing for a public arcade and a zoning-mandated plaza at ground level.

The geography of Oahu inspired the skyscraper's formal language. A prism linked to the ground by a low podium, the tower volume serves as a compass marking four cardinal points on the island: the Koolau mountains to the north, the sea to the south, Diamond Head to the east and the city of Ewa to the west.

The parallelogram-shaped podium, housing the main entrance lobby, a three-story banking hall and an exhibition space for contemporary art, responds to the lower scale of nearby buildings and the angle of Merchant Street. It engages the office tower—composed of two nestled triangles that share an exposed elevator core—with the immediate urban context and shapes a series of gardens along the surrounding streets.

The facades are articulated with a limestone-and-glass curtain wall with vertical sun-shading to the east, and a metal-and-glass curtain wall with horizontal sun-shading to the west and south. The building's fenestration expresses each of its major parts: horizontally louvered windows frame views of the sea and the horizon; vertically proportioned fenestration faces the mountains; and the podium is dominated by a great wall of prismatic-glass louvers. These louvers fracture the light like a kaleidoscope, illuminating the interior of the lobby, museum and banking hall.

Typical high-rise floor plan

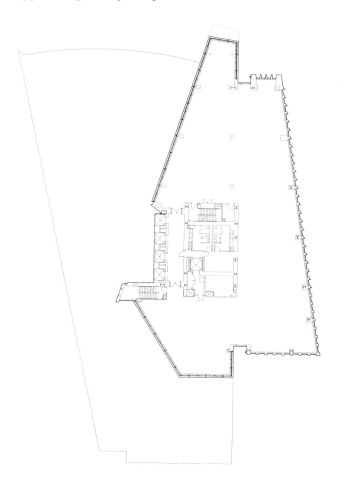

Ground floor plan

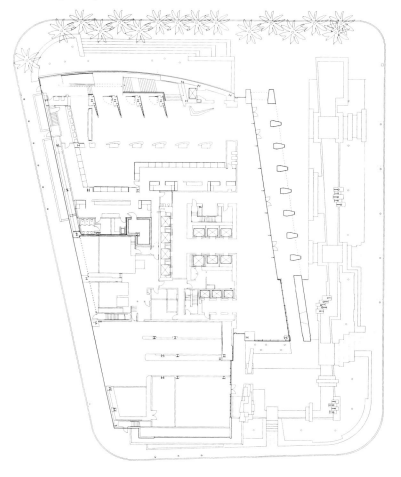

Typical low-rise floor plan

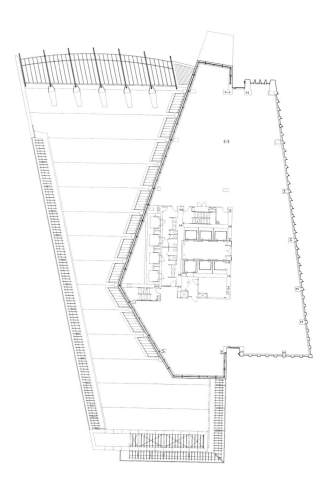

0   50 ft

Bismarckstraße 101

Berlin, Germany
1992-1994

The Bismarckstraße project was an important landmark in the development of KPF's European practice. Located on one of the main thoroughfares of the new capital, opposite the Deutsche Oper, the scheme represented a strong response both to the German philosophy of workplace design and to the cultural context.

The brief provided for largely cellular office space in the German tradition, spread over five floors, with shops at street level and basement parking. To the rear, the building faces a residential court and its stepped, landscaped terraces were designed to contribute to the overall amenity of the area as well as protecting rights of light. Its very strong form—reflecting a degree of homage, perhaps, to Erich Mendelsohn—accentuates the street corner and gives the building a definite landmark quality. The main office entrance is highlighted by the use of rear-illuminated glazing.

Though highly distinctive, the building combines quality with appropriate economy—a matter of using ordinary materials to best effect. The facade components are off-the-rack, but the use of full-height glazing ensures generously daylit working conditions. Exposed in situ concrete ceilings and opening windows are elements in a formula for low-energy running.

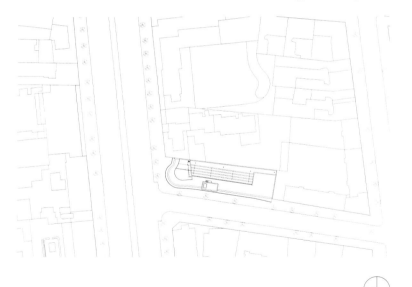

Typical floor plan

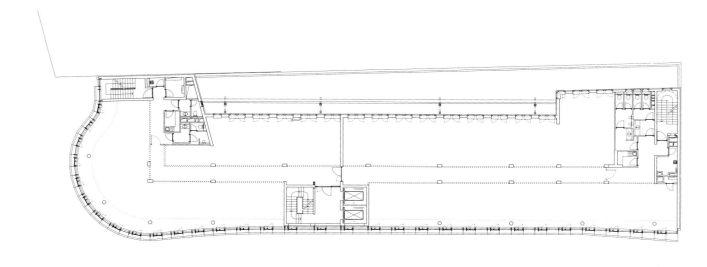

Ground floor plan

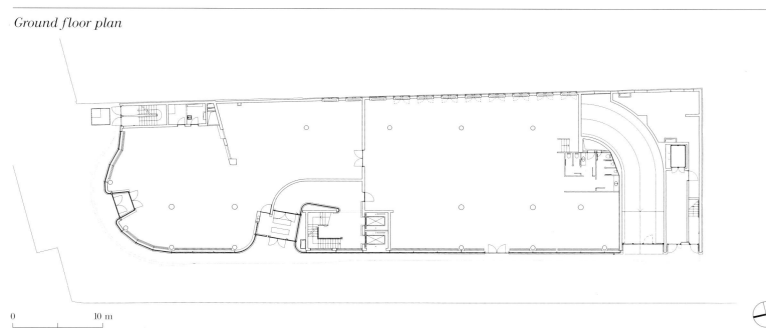

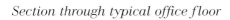
0   10 m

Section through typical office floor

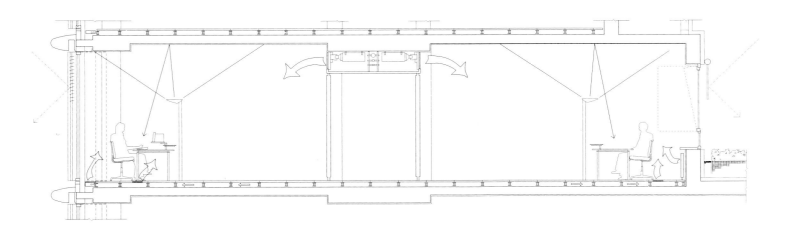

0   2 m

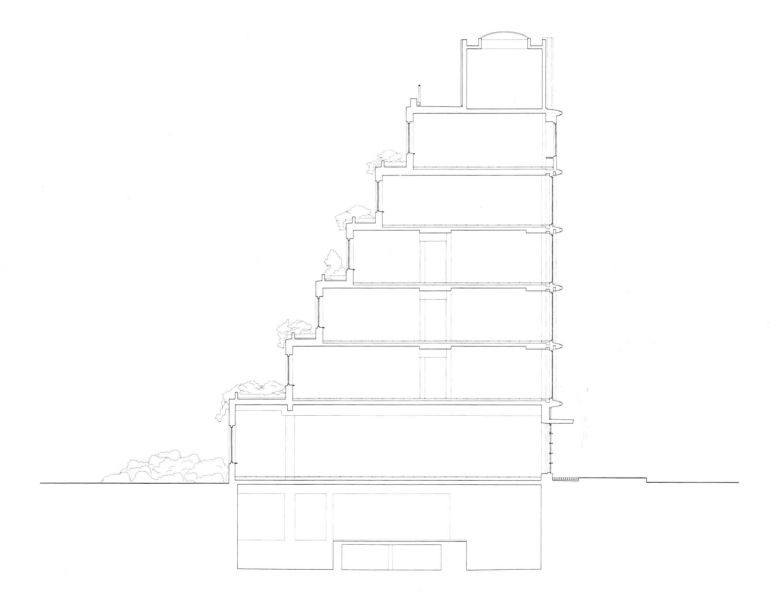

0   10 m

Mark O. Hatfield United States Courthouse

Portland, Oregon
1992-1997

The sixteen-story Mark O. Hatfield Federal Courthouse occupies an entire city block adjoining a public park. Fulfilling the diverse functional requirements prescribed by the General Services Administration's Federal Courts Program, the facility is composed of two dominant programmatic elements: the courts, and the agencies that serve the courts.

Within a 300-foot (91-meter) vertical height limit on the site, the architects created a single structure that efficiently serves both the judicial and bureaucratic functions. Each of the functional components is given a specific representation within the varying formal components of the overall design. The tower volume, for example, houses two courtrooms, judges' chambers, and a public gallery at each floor; the tower core contains secure elevators for prisoner circulation and restricted judges' elevators.

The dialogue between light and heavy forms dictates the expression of these functions on the building's exterior. The courtroom zone is given the appearance of weight, conveyed through a facade of Indiana limestone punctuated by narrow lateral openings. Small square windows above sponsor light scoops, trapezoidal volumes spanning across the upper zone of the restricted corridors to bring natural light into the courtrooms. In contrast, the judges' chambers and public circulation galleries are made light with a horizontally articulated curtain wall of reflective and transparent glass.

The lower portion houses administrative functions, and a nine-story limestone facade on the south and west mediates between the scale of the monumental tower shaft and the lower buildings facing the park blocks. The west façade with the public galleries opens toward the park. The curved elevator tower acts as a campanile to pin the northwest corner of the park, and the courts tower is capped by a curved metal roof on the other side that gestures to the Willamette River. On the east façade, functions are arranged to take advantage of the magnificent views of Mount Hood in the distance.

Typical floor plan

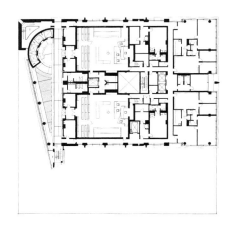

Ground floor plan

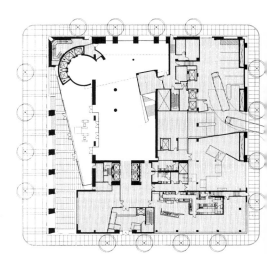

Section looking north

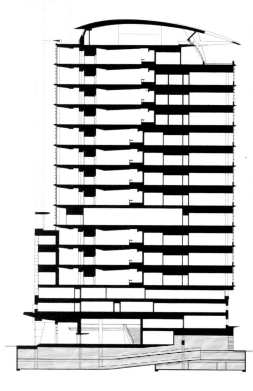

0   50 ft

Taichung Tower

Taichung, Taiwan
1992-2001

The design of this 47-story mixed-use building addresses a
demanding practical brief, as well as the physical and cultural
context to create a memorable landmark for the city of
Taichung, in central Taiwan.

The project developed out of an unbuilt hotel and office
scheme for a site at the end of a half-mile stretch of urban
parkland that allowed for uninterrupted views of the tower
from all directions. In the first scheme, the tower assumed a
strongly geometrical form, like the shaft of a great crystal
rising out of the geometry of the soil. As revised, the scheme
has taken on a far more organic and sculptural form. For the
client, the design resembled a great fish—a traditional symbol
of good fortune—and this concept was further developed in
the final designs.

The form of the building takes a theme familiar from other
Kohn Pedersen Fox projects—that of a larger whole cut down
the center and brought together to create an irregular and
dramatic profile. The tower tapers as it rises, accommodating
the larger public spaces at the base, and the smaller floor plates
needed for hotel rooms and office suites at the top. The 300-
room hotel occupies the middle levels of the tower.

The result is a gesture of great simplicity. The form is echoed
in consistent detailing: the variations caused by the use of
uniform rectangular facade panels is taken up in the panel
joints.

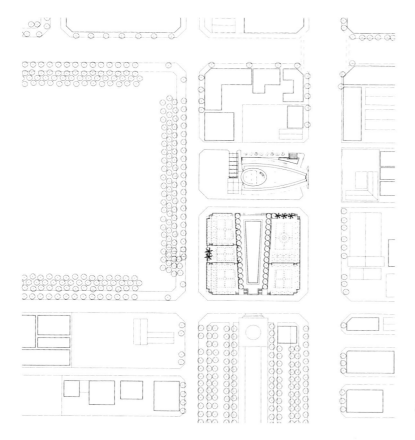

Typical office plan

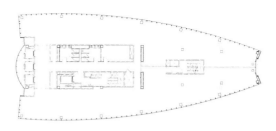

Typical hotel plan

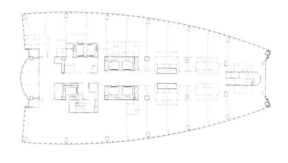

Restaurant floor plan

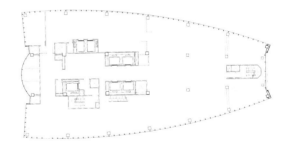

Ground floor plan

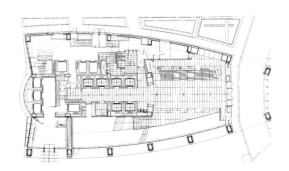

0   20 m

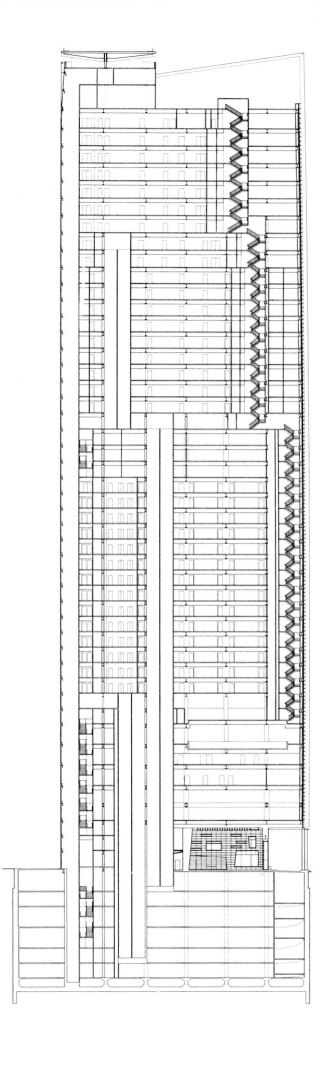

75

Dongbu Kangnam Tower

Seoul, South Korea
1993-2001

Rising to a height of a 35 stories, this headquarters tower for the Dongbu Corporation occupies one of the most visible sites in Seoul's southern commercial district of Kangnam-ku. Because the site is directly adjacent to the Posco building, which sets back from the main commercial boulevard of Teheran-Ro, its corner forms a significant boundary to one of Seoul's busiest intersections.

The design of the project evolved from the premise that the major forces internal to the program, as well as those external to the building, could be best articulated in a layered organization of the core, displaced to the south as an east-west line segment due to the small size of the floor plate. Views to the north, prized for their orientation to the Han River, Teheran-Ro, and a historically significant garden, are preserved

This layered order was developed and combined with influences from Korean traditional handicrafts, such as *shik-tak-bo*, in which cloth is patched together in random patterns. Above all, the intention was to compose the building within an organic rather than a geometrically reductive idiom. This method of composition was chosen so as to provide a counterpoint to the parade of rectangular box towers which make up the surrounding context. The diagonally folding expanses of curtain wall satisfy the client's wish to make a bold sculptural statement. The result is a north facing elevation characterized by a series of separate zones, each of which is canted to reflect a different part of the sky.

The eastern facade of the building is more graphically pronounced, as it displays the sloping edges where the curtain walls terminate in leading edges of stainless steel. Because the glass of the north and south facade is somewhat reflective, and that of the east and west facades is more transparent, the building invites entry from the corner. The main entry consists of a bridge which crosses over a sunken garden and penetrates the eastern curtain wall from the side. Flanking the bridge and the lobby to the north is a wall of textured glass whose patterns resemble *shik-tak-bo* cloths. This wall is a kind of light filter, which mediates between the experience of entry and the activity of the street.

Ground floor plan

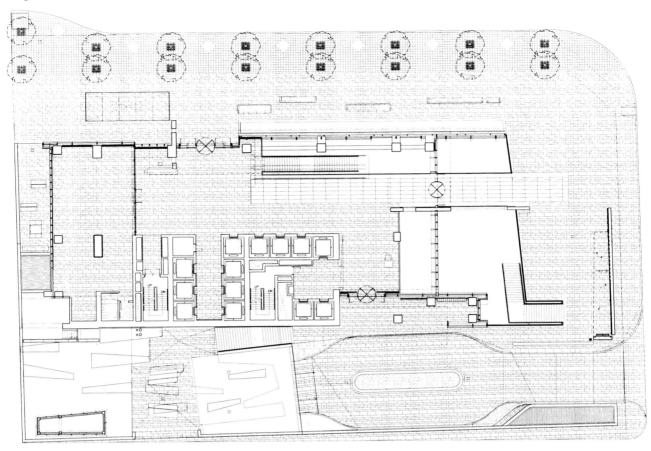

0   20 m

Floor transformation

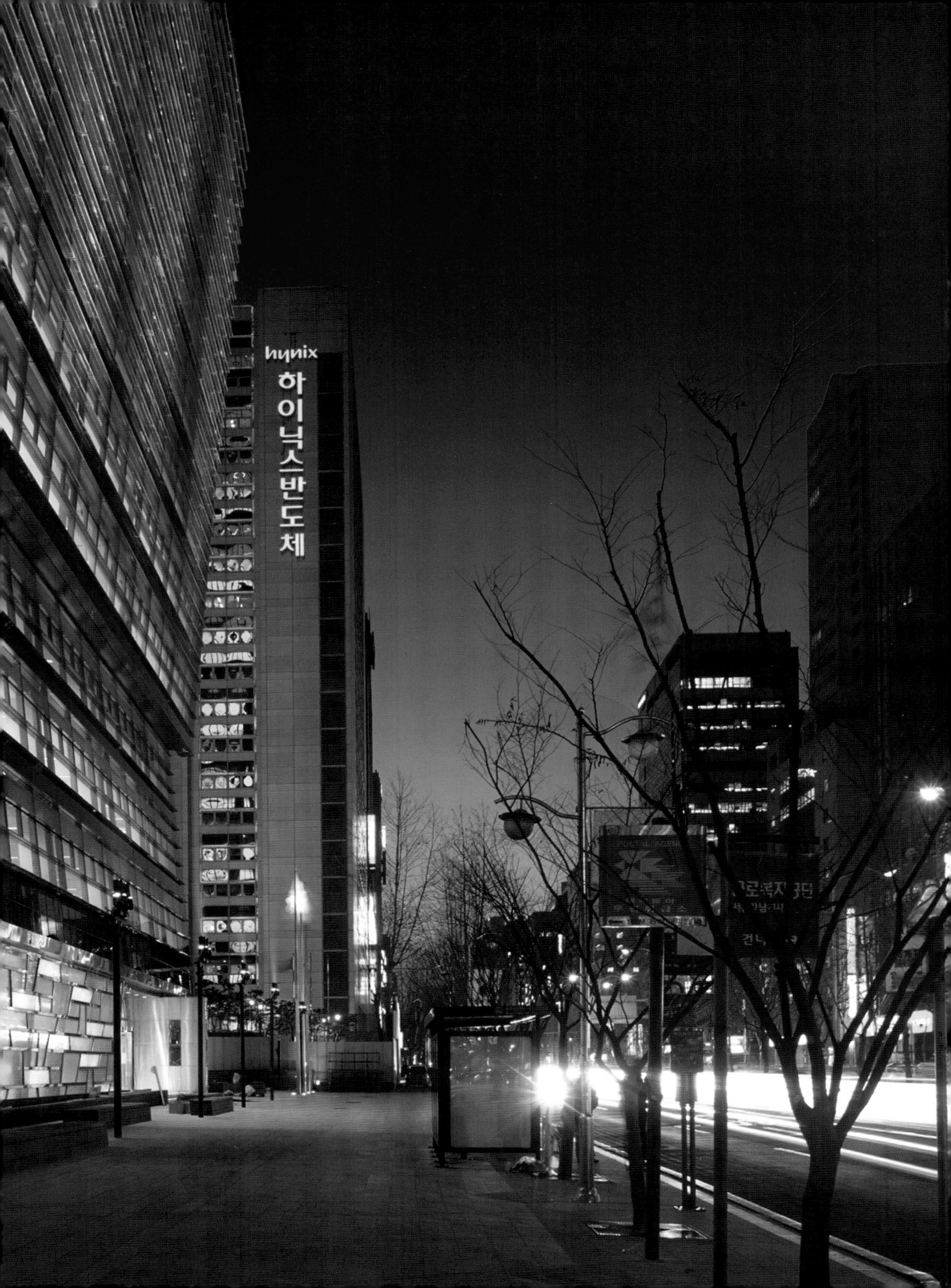
hynix
하이닉스반도체

Buffalo Niagara International Airport

Cheektowaga, New York
1993-1997

The main air transport gateway to the Niagara Falls region, the Buffalo Niagara International Airport serves the second-largest metropolitan area in New York State. Kohn Pedersen Fox, William Nicholas Bodouva & Associates, and Cannon Design Inc. formed a team to pursue and execute the project, and KPF led the design of the core and shell.

The new facility unites the represented airlines in one efficient structure, replacing two existing terminals. The scheme consists of three major components arranged around a tear-shaped road: an arrivals-departures hall, a concessions link, and a fifteen-gate concourse parallel with the east-west runway. The mass of the architectural volume is occupied by the arrivals-departures hall, that takes up two entire levels. On the departures level is the main ticketing hall and the security checkpoint, from which passengers gain access to the concessions link and the concourse beyond. On the arrivals level are all the airline operations, baggage handling and baggage claim areas. Outside the terminal is a corresponding landscape and parking program enclosed within the tear-shaped rotary.

Recalling familiar images of air travel and aviation technology, the airport design attempts to represent the ground-air relationship fundamental to the sensation of flight. Consistent with architectural themes first introduced in the design of modern airport structures in the 1960s, the aesthetic employed in the design of the three-part structure conveys this relationship in essential dualities of heavy versus light, static versus dynamic or solid versus void. The arrivals-departures hall establishes the architectural vocabulary for the entire facility as the fullest expression of the ground-air dialogue. Two parallel walls form the north-south boundaries of this room. The north wall is a massive, gently curving concrete arch that grounds the entire structure to the runway. In contrast, the south wall is primarily constructed of glass, its form not unlike an airborne wing. These two planes are connected by straight beam segments, generating spatial volume and bringing equilibrium to the two parts.

Building axonometry

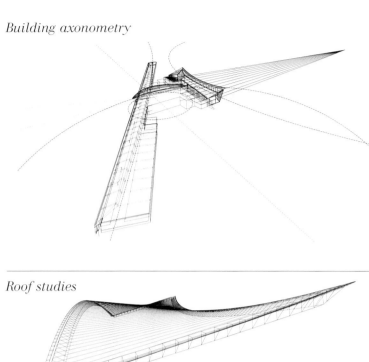

Roof studies

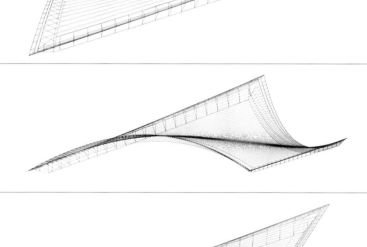

Site plan

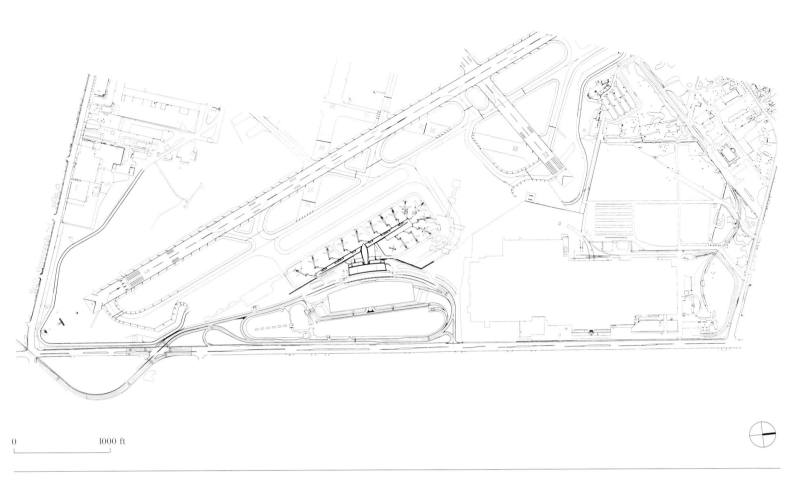

0   1000 ft

Departure level plan

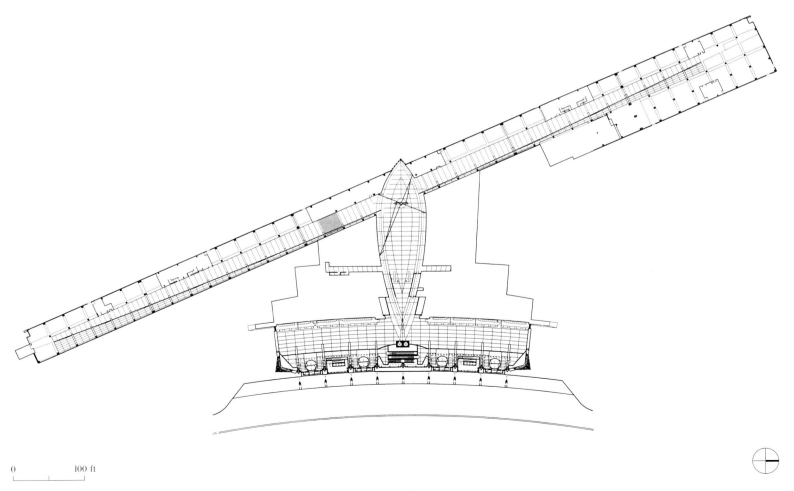

0   100 ft

William H. Gates Hall
University of Washington Law School

Seattle, Washington
1993-2002

Incorporating all the functions of the Law School at the University of Washington into one facility, the William H. Gates Hall is set on a gentle hillside bordered to the east by the tree-lined Memorial Way, a principal north-south axis within the campus. The new facility houses instruction and seminar rooms, a full research law library, a law clinic, a graduate program center, special conference rooms, student lounges, and faculty and administrative offices.

While many of the university's existing academic structures are arranged to form quadrangle spaces, the Law School stands alone at the northern edge of the university's core. The L-shaped building defines a courtyard and terrace that opens south towards the greater campus. Beneath the terrace the library occupies the lowest two levels, providing a plinth for the composition. The scheme responds to the geometry of the old quadrangle and the surrounding urban grid of Seattle, creating a distinct identity for the school while grounding it firmly to the university.

The project provides teaching spaces appropriate to the modern Law School curriculum, which emphasizes smaller classroom instruction, group discussion formats, practice skills training, and access to information technology. Classroom configurations were selected with pedagogical intent, from 25-seat seminar rooms with mock courtrooms to a 170-seat auditorium.

The concept of the school as community is vital to students and faculty. The spatial interpenetration between the two-story gallery, terrace and library invite interaction and reflection. The central focus of the library is the grand two-story reading room. It is flooded with light from four skylights at the terrace above and fritted glass at the south and east walls. Study rooms, computer consoles and lounge areas punctuate the reading room and stack areas. The generous use of glass—unusual for this building type—allows for the extension of the landscape into the interior; the conservatory-like quality of the space is reinforced and elaborated. Canopies and trellises protect benches at the gallery and perimeter from sun or rain and frame views in and out. The north and west facades act as a textured brick shell holding the layered, glassy volumes.

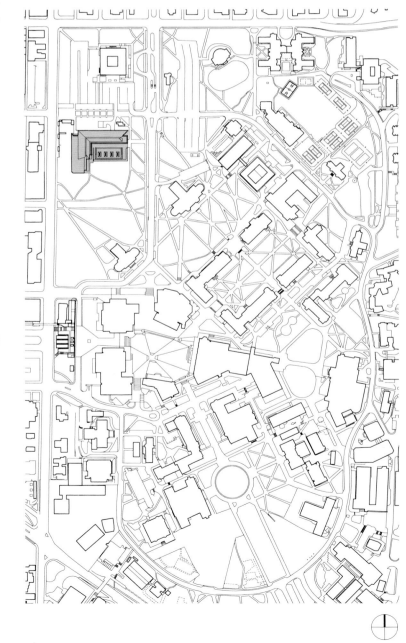

Ground floor plan

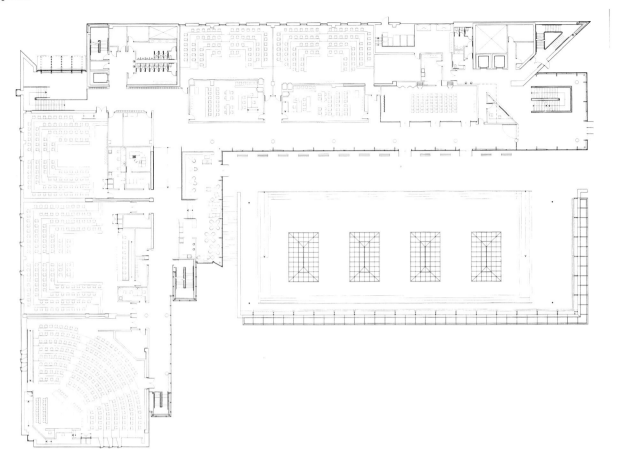

Library/basement level plan

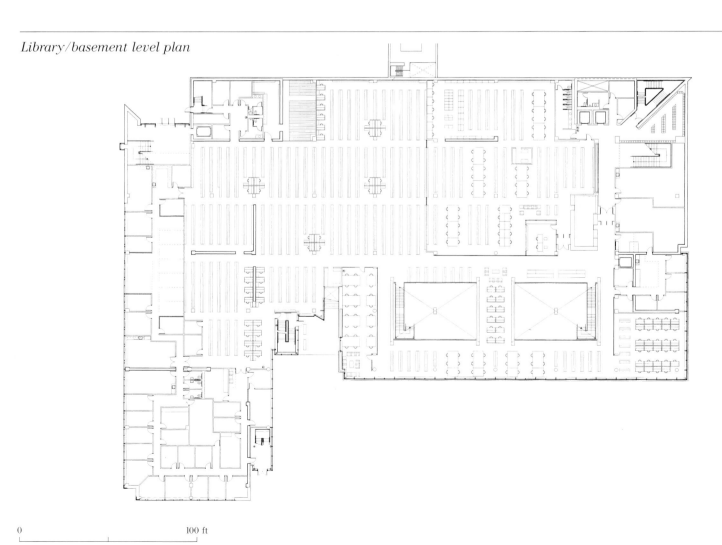

0   100 ft

Third floor plan

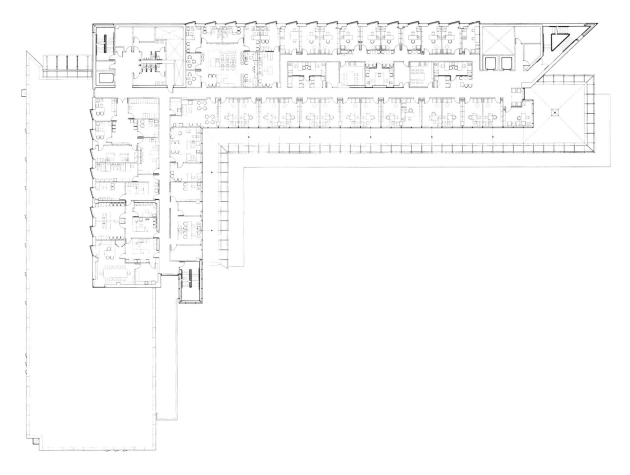

Second floor plan

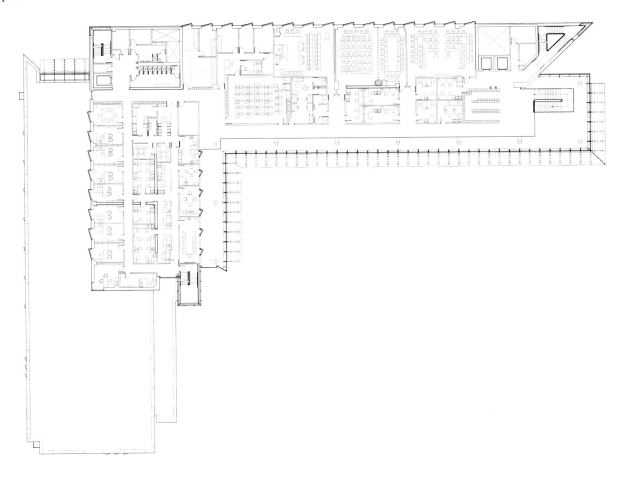

103

North elevation

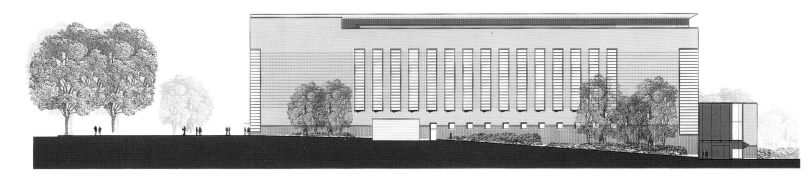

South elevation

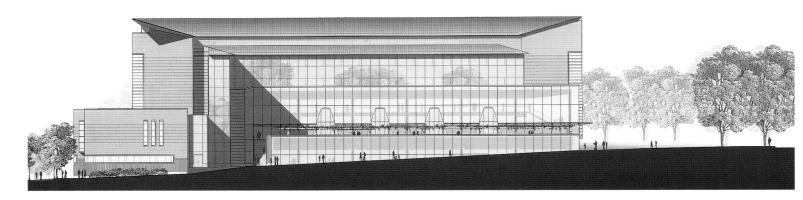

East elevation

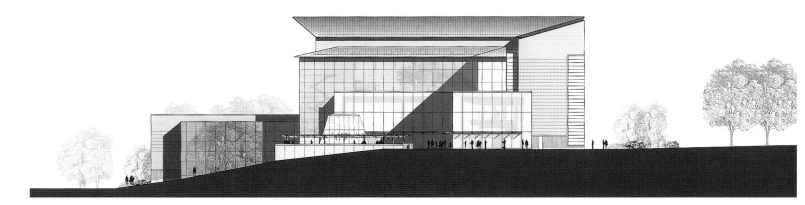

West elevation

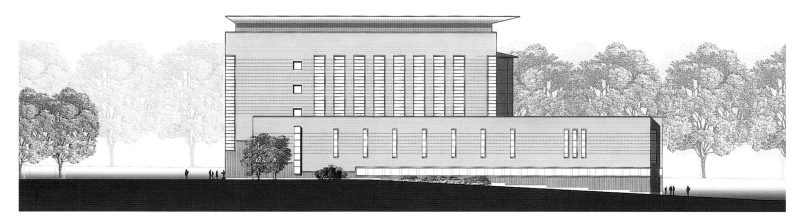

Section looking north

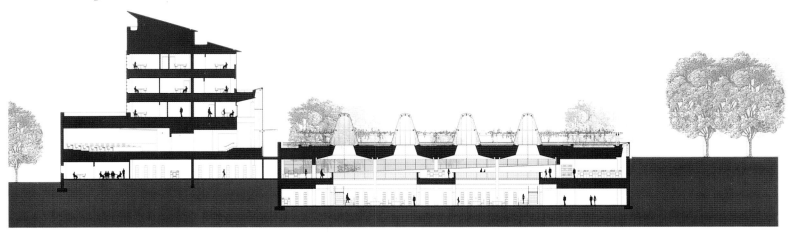

Section looking west

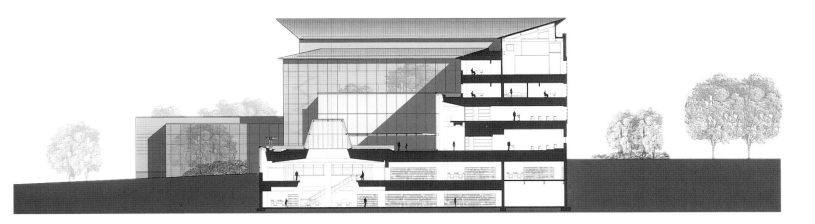

Provincehuis

The Hague, Netherlands
1994-1998

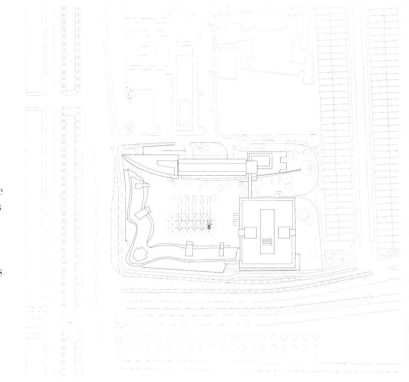

Provinciehuis, the headquarters of the Dutch provincial government of South Holland, is progressive in a number of respects—in its approach to workplace design, its environmental strategy and, finally, as a statement about the nature of government.

Won by KPF after an international competition, the project involved the complete refurbishment of existing 1960s buildings on the site (at the junction of the Zuid-Hollandlaan and Konigskade, close to the Malieveld park) and the construction of a 258,000-square foot (24,000-square meter) addition, together with the creation of a new public landscape linking the buildings. The decision to demolish a failed 1970's block increased the potential for a thoroughgoing redesign of the site.

The new building occupies the corner site to which it responds with a boldly curved form. On its street elevations, bands of brick facing evoke the romantic modern tradition of Willem Marinus Dudok and the Amsterdam School. Its slender floor plates—office spaces are generally cellular—make optimum use of natural light. To the rear, the building, constructed on an in situ concrete frame, faces a newly created square—the facades here (facing north-east) are predominantly glazed with infills of stainless steel. The design of the facades combines a high degree of insulation with opening windows—set in double glazed units—to give users control over their working conditions. The concrete slab is exposed internally and its thermal mass exploited as part of the heating and cooling strategy.

The new square is a welcoming place that can be entered at three points. Public spaces and the staff restaurant are located at ground level. Raised above the surrounding roads, the square contains both quiet and dynamic areas, a mix of hard and soft landscape. A water cascade along the northern edge provides a buffer against noise.

Provinciehuis transforms the image of the government building as a bureaucratic enclave into something public and genuinely democratic, while responding with vigor to pressing environmental concerns.

Typical floor plan

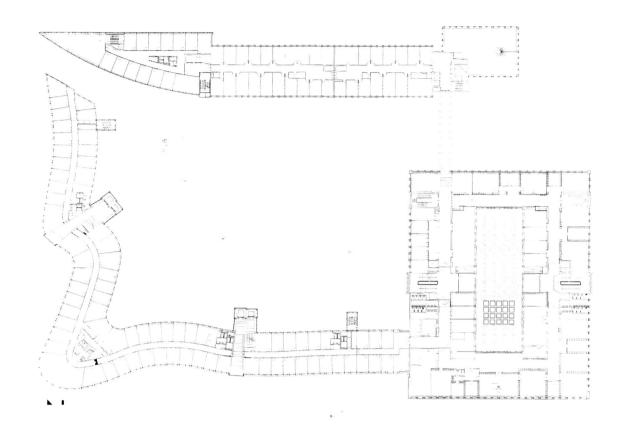

Ground floor plan

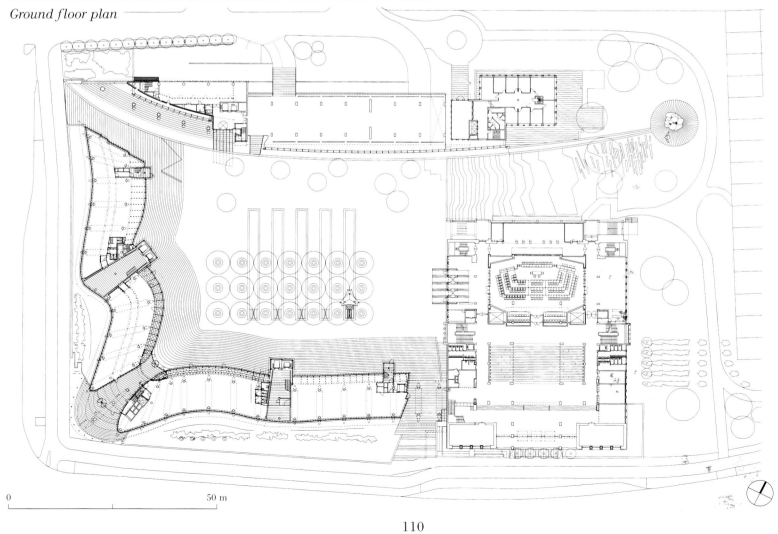

0   50 m

South elevation

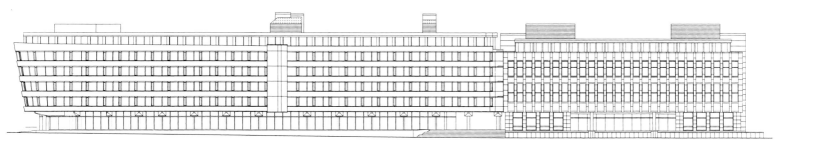

Courtyard section looking west

0　　　　　　20 m

Plaza 66

Shanghai, China
1994-2001

The assignment of combining a 60-story and a 40-story office tower with a major retail mall in the heart of Shanghai's old city posed several major challenges, the foremost being the need to mediate between Nanjing Xi Lu, a celebrated pedestrian thoroughfare, and the scale of such large structures. The program calls for a mix of retail, entertainment and extensive below-grade parking areas with over one million square feet (93,000 square meters) of office space in Tower I and 750,000 square feet (69,000 square meters) in a proposed Tower II.

The solution arranges a series of radially derived volumes—lozenge, cone, almond, and arc—in the manner of a collage. They are bound together in a five-story retail podium, but each of the component parts retains a formal independence. Each volume is distinguished by a canted sectional lean or cut, and establishes separate entry sequences as they come in contact with the street. The elements closest to the ground match the scale of historic structures, and reflect the busy street life of Nanjing Xi Lu.

The retail podium contains half a million square feet, and is punctuated by two major interior public spaces. Enclosed within curved volumes, these two atriums are cradled by the tower walls. The overall composition of the project is propelled skyward, as if influenced by the forces of a vortex. This spiral of building masses ascends some 922 feet (281 meters) to the top of Tower I, and is capped by a lantern formed of glass screens, illuminated at night and visible from all directions.

Ground floor plan

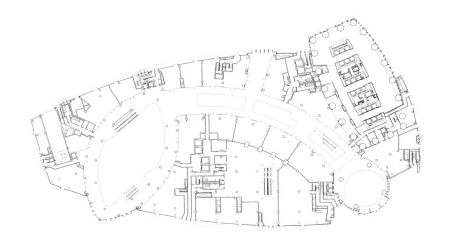

Roof plan

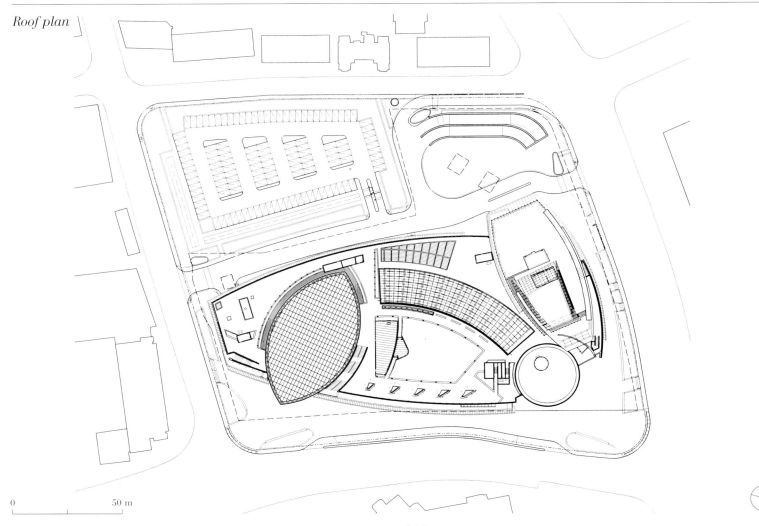

0   50 m

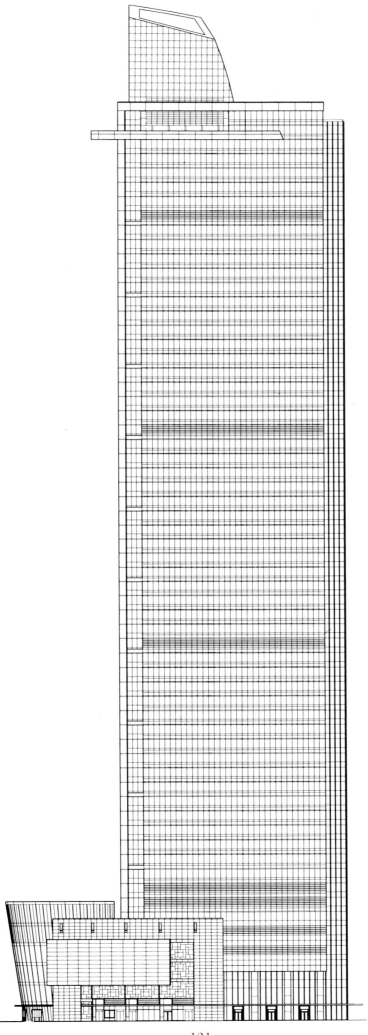

0   30 m

Singapore Exchange Centre

Singapore
1994-2000

As an urban development, the Singapore Exchange Centre
was conceived to fulfill both a practical organizing function
and an iconic role. The complex houses three important
financial institutions: the Stock Exchange, the Singapore
International Monetary Exchange (SIMEX) and a major
banking center for United Overseas Bank. It is located in an
existing business district, but also serves as the gateway to
Marina South, a major land reclamation project seen as
pivotal to the future growth of the city.

The site on Shenton Way is close to the established financial
district and the historic gathering place of Lau Pa Sat. The
five-story podium helps root the development in its setting
and contains a column-free, 88-meter long (289-foot) trading
room occupied by SIMEX at the first floor level, with retail
banking facilities at street level.

Sharing a common podium, the twin 29-story towers respond
to contextual circumstances—the proximity of other high
buildings, for example, and the desirability of securing views
out over the immediate neighborhood. As a result, the
facades facing Shenton Way are curved in plan. The roof is
strongly developed, composed of planes of masonry abutting
dramatically modeled roof canopies. The dynamic vocabulary
is intended to emphasize the vital mission of the Exchange
Centre in the economy of the city-state.

The scheme makes a positive contribution to the street by
providing a covered perimeter walkway at ground level,
thereby protecting pedestrians from the sun and frequent
heavy rain. In addition, the new square facing Lau Pa Sat
enhances an area of preserved colonial-era buildings and
provides the development with a prestigious "front door." As it
fulfills the requirements of modern financial institutions the
complex expands the public realm, and reinforces a well-
loved, historic district.

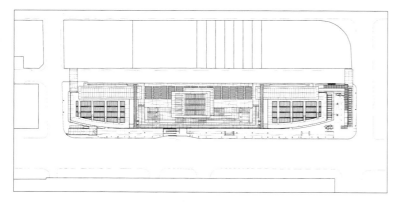

Roof plan

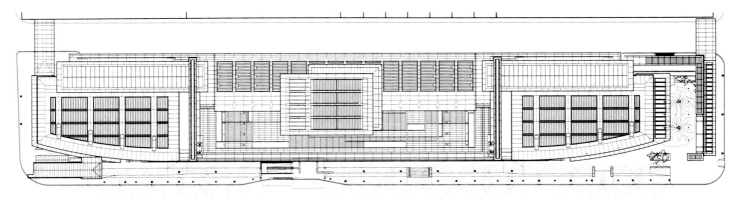

Typical office floor plan

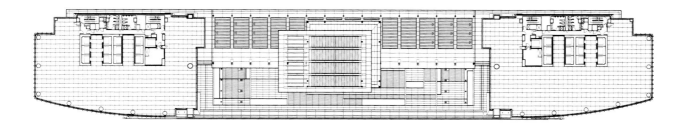

Typical trading floor plan

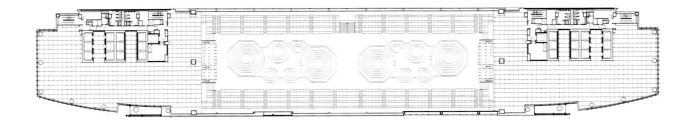

Ground floor plan

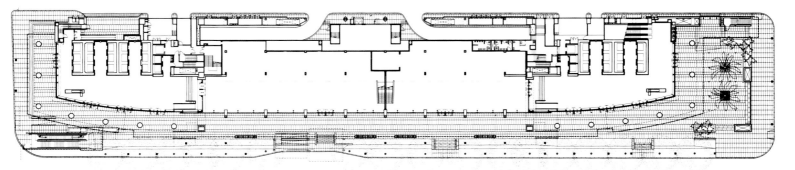

0   50 m

The Rothermere American Institute
Oxford University

Oxford, England
1994-2001

Dedicated by former President Bill Clinton in 2001, the Rothermere Institute has been described in the British press as one of the most beautifully built modern buildings in Oxford. It stands adjacent to Rhodes House, an institution with close American connections, and to the nineteenth-century complex of Mansfield College, in a leafy quarter north of the historic city center.

The Institute extends the University's teaching resources in American studies. Its centerpiece is the reading room— library stacks, academic offices and seminar rooms occupy the remainder of the building.

The Institute, as conceived in the competition-winning scheme, is a freestanding pavilion set within landscaped gardens, entirely modern in its expression but respectful of its context (which includes a defensive mound thrown up during the siege of Oxford in the English Civil War). The basic parti follows that of Basil Champney's library at Mansfield College: classrooms and ancillary spaces are located below the great volume of the reading room. The vocabulary consists of exposed concrete and natural Bath stone, balanced by finely detailed steel and glass.

The double-height reading room faces south over the garden—galleries containing study carrels look down into the main space. Classrooms are located below the main level, looking out to the garden. The principal, southern facade is strongly modeled, with fritted glass louvers to control solar gain and reduce the need for mechanical ventilation. Air conditioning is eschewed in favor of nighttime cooling, using the thermal mass of the structure, and an earth-connected heat exchange system set below the garden.

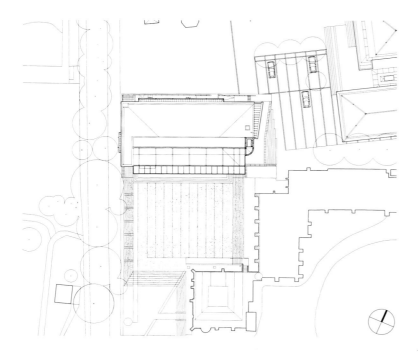

Reading room plan

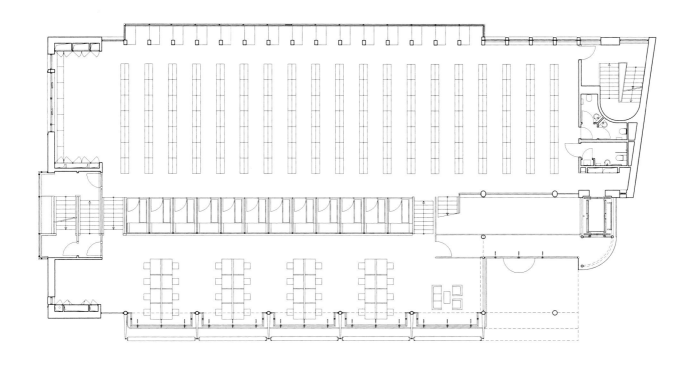

Garden level plan

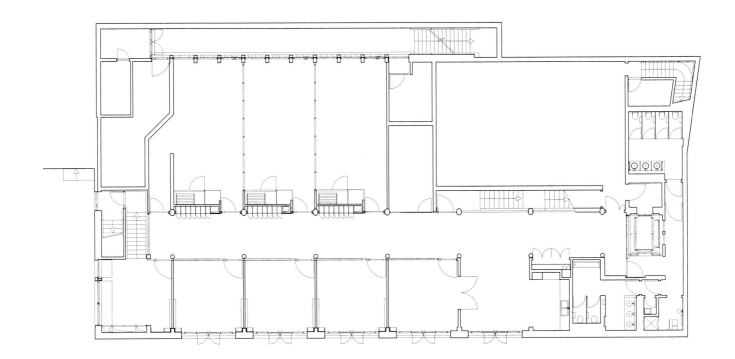

0   10 m

South elevation

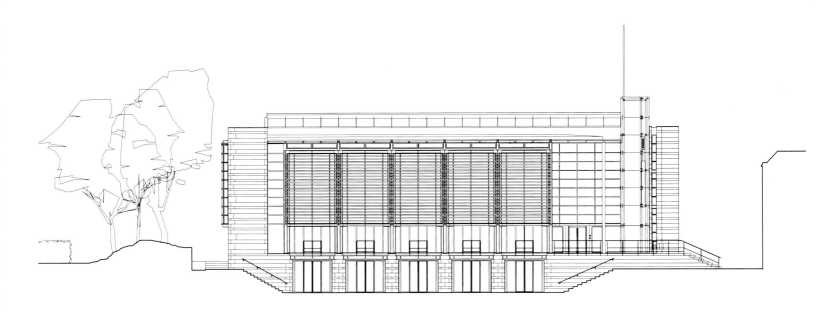

East elevation

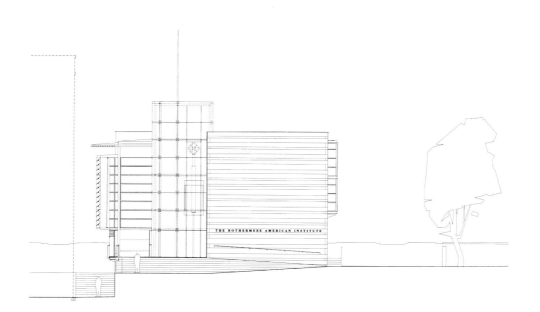

0   20 m

North elevation

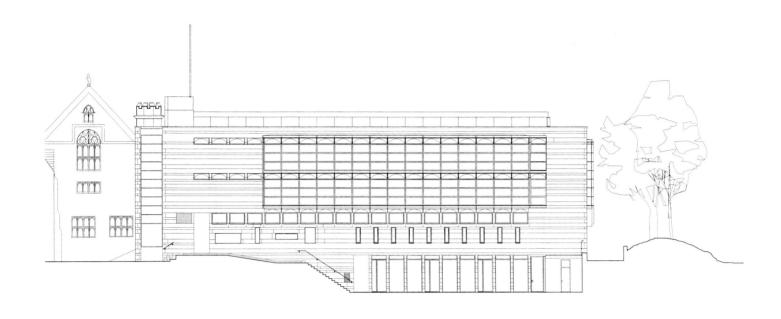

Section looking east

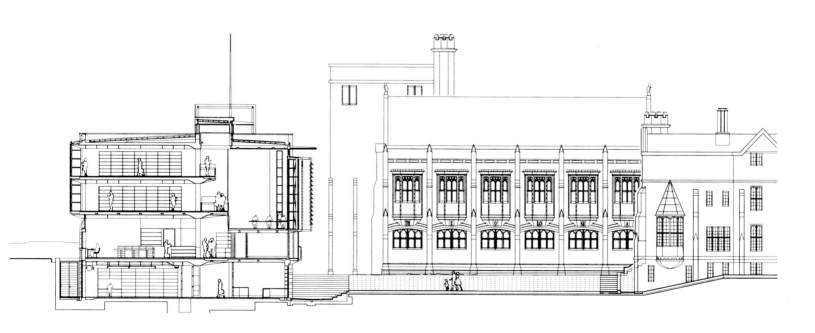

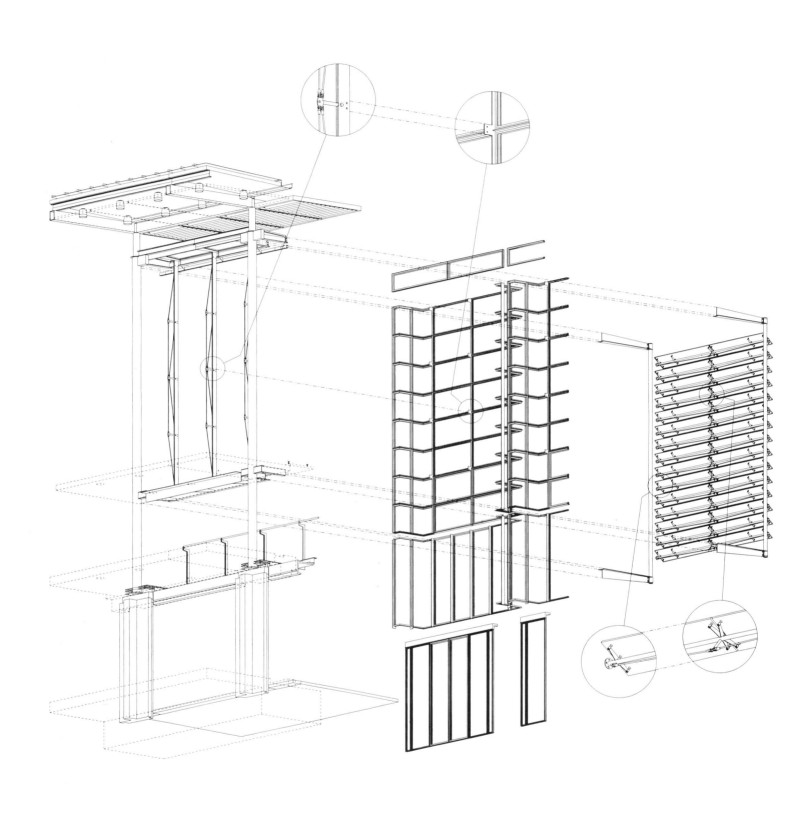

Cyprus House of Representatives

Nicosia, Cyprus
1994

The competition for a new house of representatives in Nicosia was won by KPF (with Cyprus-based D. Kythreotis & Associates) in 1995, though planning problems have since delayed the start of construction. The presence of notable archaeological remains close to the site is one significant constraint.

The site is in Monument Square, on the processional route from the presidential palace to the old city of Nicosia. Though relatively modest in scale, the parliament house accommodates the customary debating chamber with public gallery, plus committee and meeting rooms, library and other facilities for members, staff and public. The scheme is influenced by two factors: the contours of the site and the rigors of the Nicosia climate (where summer heat is extreme). The diagram of the building draws on the ancient Greek imagery of the *agora*, the place of public assembly, and the amphitheatre where the representatives of the people meet. The debating chamber is sunk into the slope of a low hill and contained within a great circular drum that is the heart of the building. The drum is clad in thin sheets of alabaster—a reference to Gordon Bunshaft's iconic Beinecke Library at Yale—protected by wooden louvers to exclude the hot sun. Extensive use of local stone cladding applied to the concrete frame is a further protection against the climate and a link with Cypriot building traditions. The main roof structure is of concrete cast in situ.

The adjacent public foyer, entered through a dignified portico which makes oblique reference to the language of Classicism, extends the outdoor public spaces around the site—it is a place for meeting and the interchange of views and ideas. The great roof is the element that unites interior and exterior, its deep overhangs offering shade and shelter. Meeting and committee rooms open off the foyer. At the rear of the building a private garden is created within the declivity of the hill, surrounded by the members' offices and library.

The building is environmentally efficient, with the thermal mass of the structure, extensive shading, and the stack effect produced by the double-skin wall of the chamber used to cool the interiors.

Entrance level plan

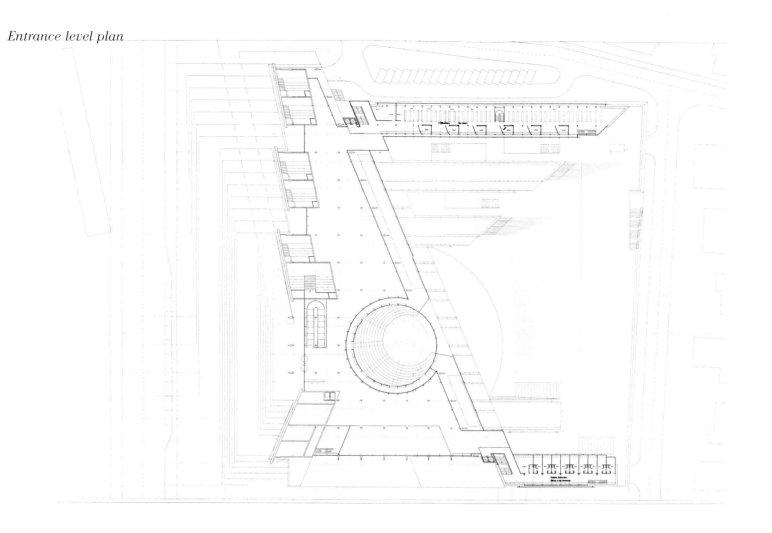

Basement/Chamber level plan

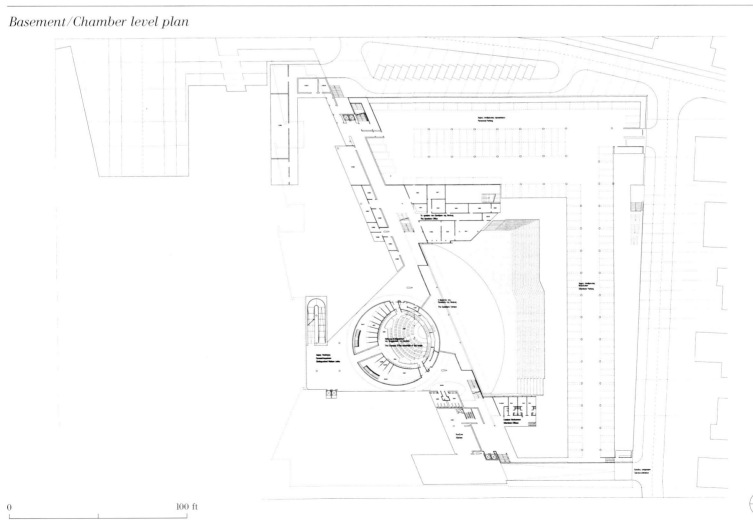

0   100 ft

151

Exploded axonometric diagram

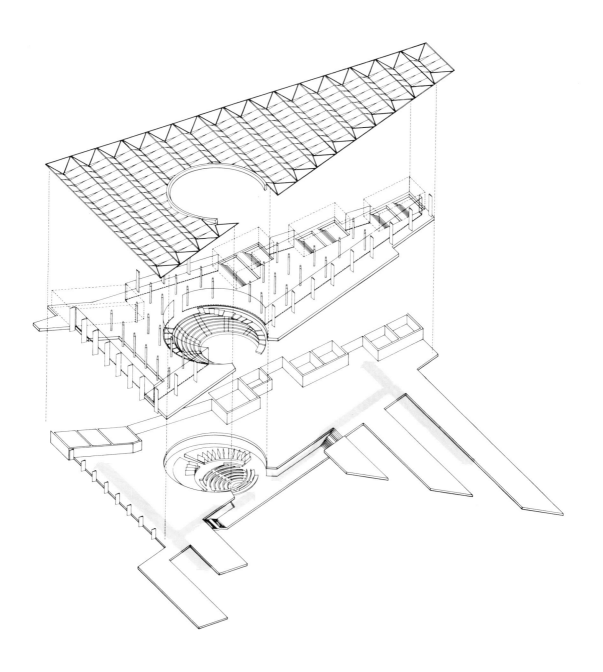

Section looking south

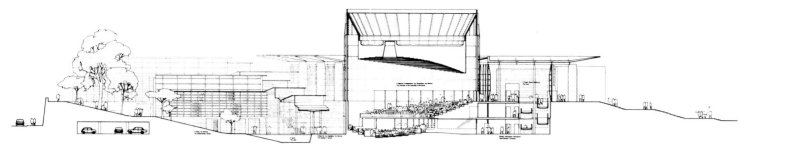

North elevation

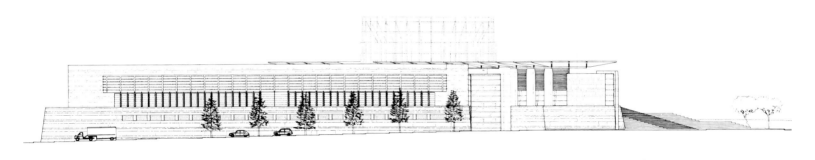

West elevation

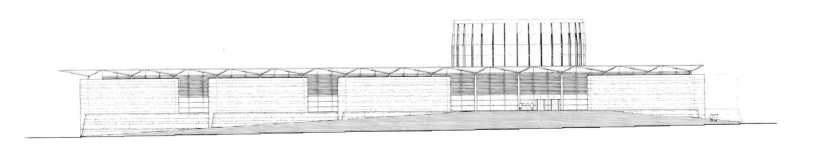

0   20 m

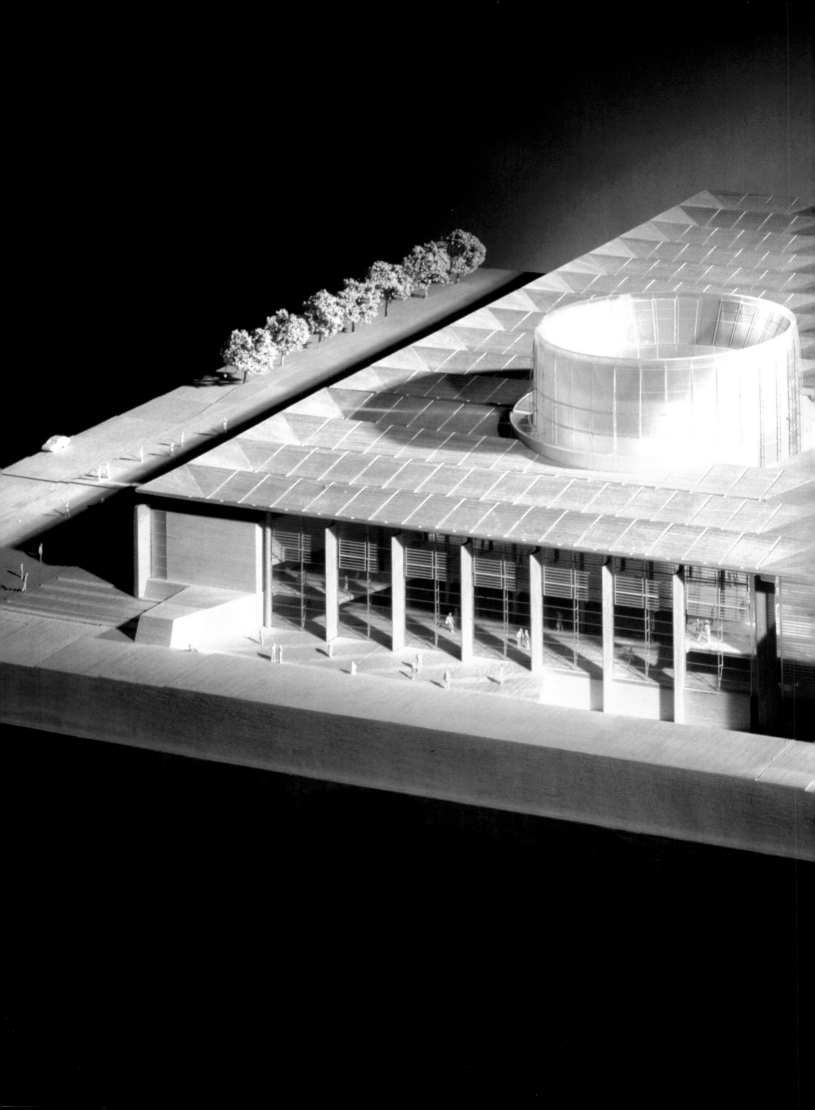

Shanghai World Financial Center

Shanghai, China
1994-2005

When it is completed, the Shanghai World Financial Center
will stand as the tallest building in the world.

The project is located on a key site in the Lujiazhui financial
and trade district in Pudong, which the Chinese government
has designated as an Asian center for international banking
and commercial interests. The rapid development of the zone
has resulted in a disjunctive urban fabric to which the design
of the tower reacts with monolithic simplicity.

The program of this 95-story project is contained within two
distinctly formal elements: a sculpted tower and a podium.
Corresponding to the Chinese concept of the earth as a square
and the sky as a circle, the interaction between these two
geometric forms gives shape to the tower. The project relates
to its context through an abstract language that attempts to
symbolically incorporate characteristics meaningful to the
traditions of Chinese architecture.

The primary form of the tower is a square prism intersected
by two sweeping arcs, tapering into a single line at the apex.
The gradual progression of floor plans generates
configurations that are ideal for offices on the lower floors
and hotel suites above. At the same time, the transformation
of the plan rotates the orientation of the upper portion of the
tower toward the Oriental Pearl TV tower, the area's
dominant landmark, a fifth of a mile away. To relieve wind
pressure, a 164-foot (50-meter) cylinder is carved out of the
top of the building. Equal in diameter to the sphere of the
television tower, this void connects the two structures across
the urban landscape. Wall, wing and conical forms penetrate
through the massive stone base of the tower. The varied
geometries of these smaller elements lend human scale, and
organize the complexities of pedestrian movement at the point
of entry, complementing the elemental form of the tower.

Second floor plan

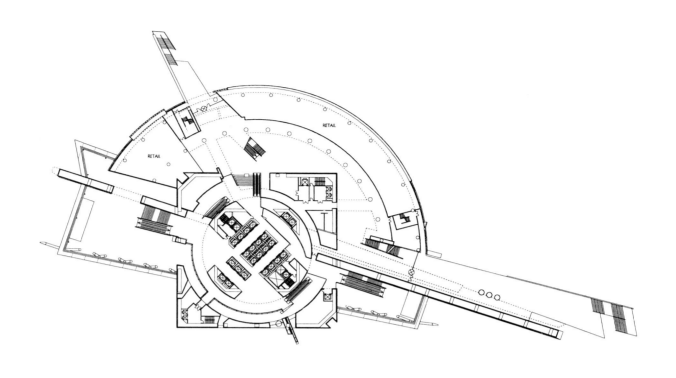

First floor plan

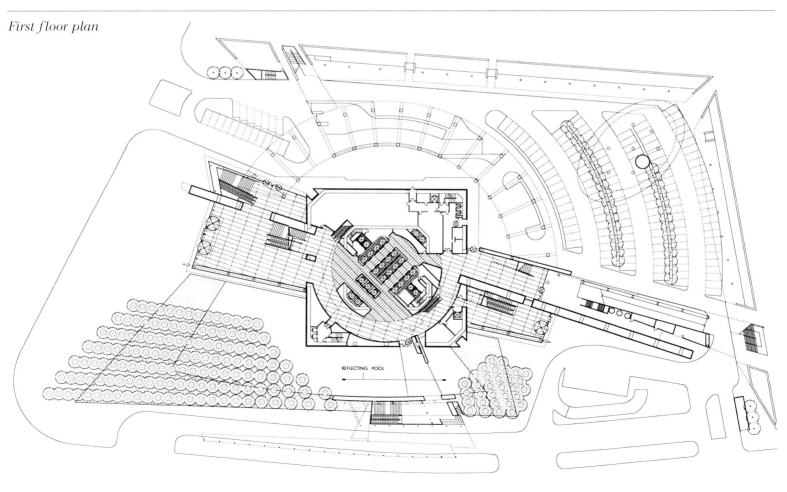

REFLECTING POOL

0   50 m

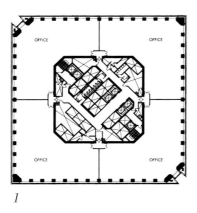

1

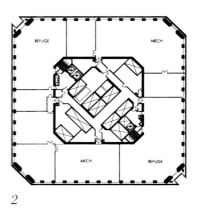

2

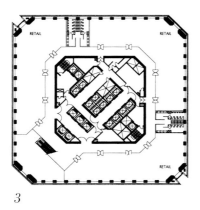

3

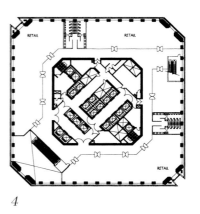

4

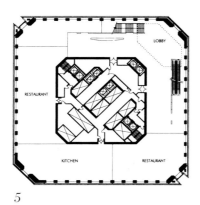

5

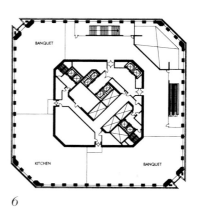

6

1   *Typical office floor*
2   *Refuge floor*
3   *Sky lobby 7th floor*
4   *Sky lobby 2th floor*
5   *Hotel lobby floor*
6   *Hotel banquet*

Floor transformation

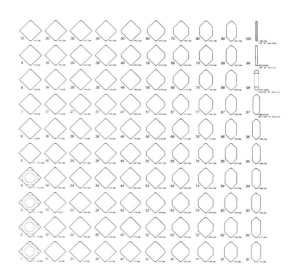

7

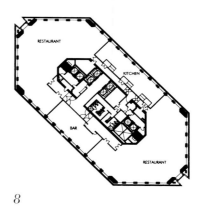

8

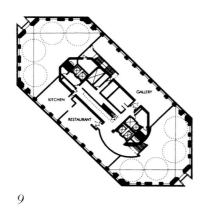

9

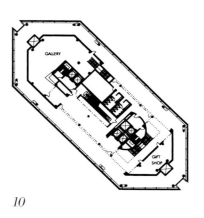

10

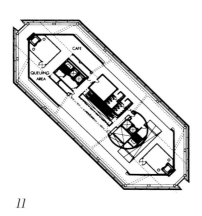

11

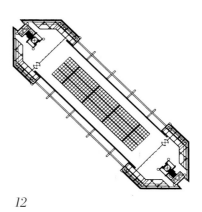

12

7   Typical hotel floor
8   Hotel restaurant floor
9   Observation deck restaurant and gallery floor
10 Observation deck
11 Observation deck cafe
12 Observation bridge

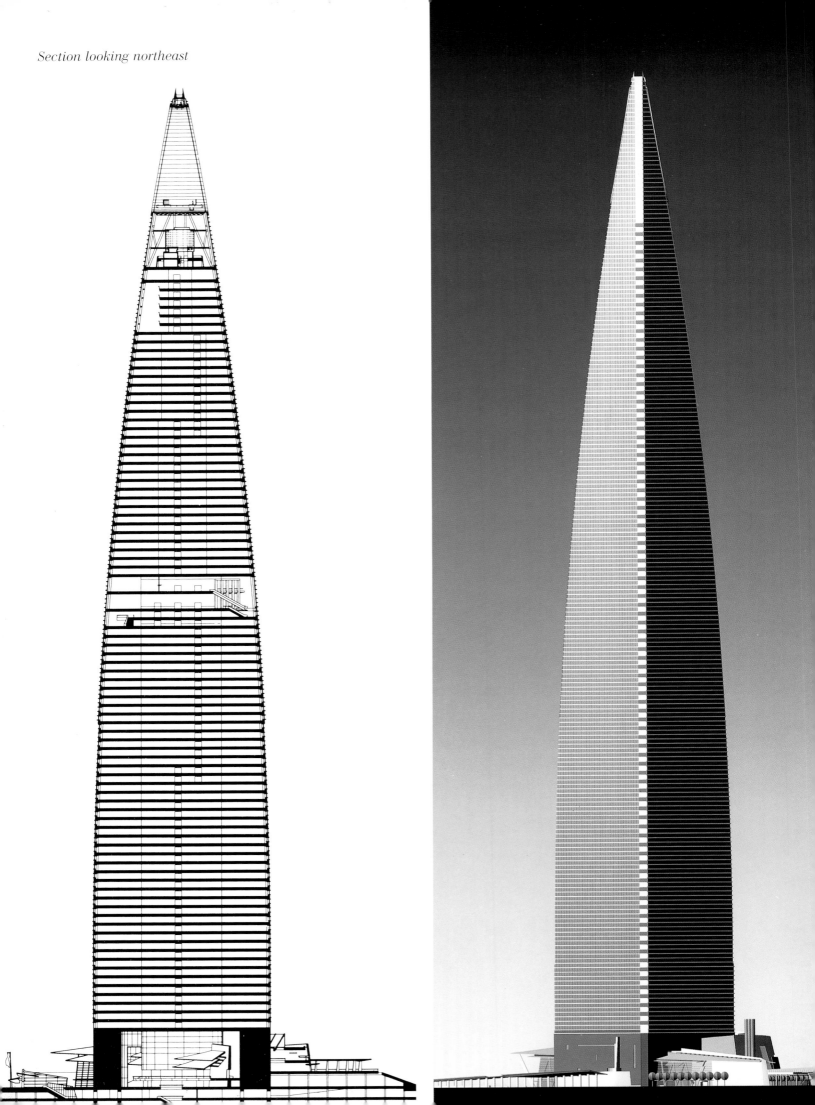

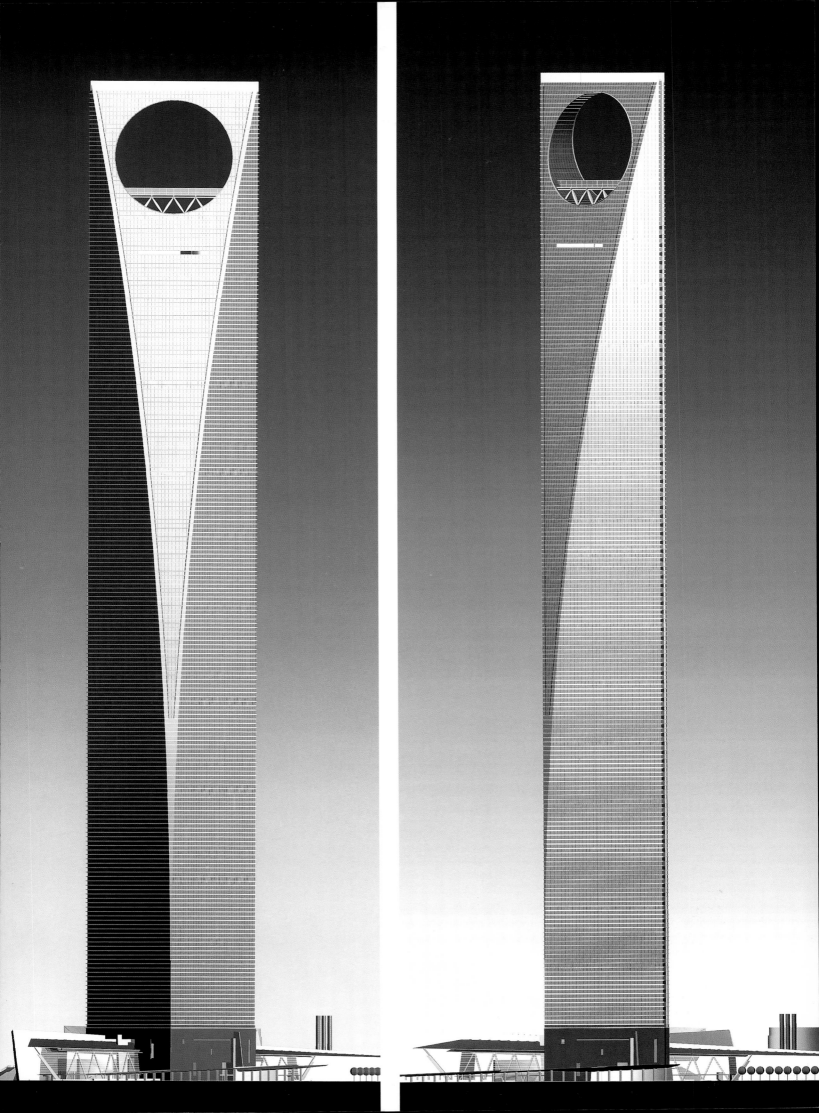

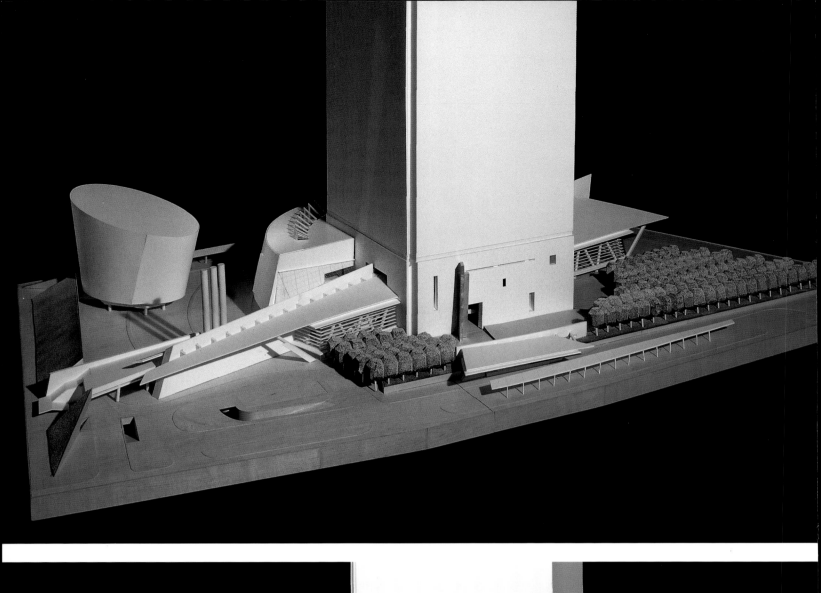

Thames Court

London, England
1995-1998

Thames Court occupies a highly sensitive, archaeologically rich site at Queenhithe, close to Southwark Bridge. To the south is the river Thames, with views across to historic Bankside, Shakespeare's Globe Theatre, and the Tate Modern; on the north is Upper Thames Street, a canyon-like urban highway lined with buildings of distinctly mixed quality. Tightly contained by the river and surrounding roads, the site was further constrained by strict controls on building heights imposed to protect the setting of Christopher Wren's St Paul's. A further problem was posed by the survival of a derelict (but listed) warehouse, for which demolition consent was given only after extended negotiations with the planning authorities.

The project therefore had to address a series of issues beyond that of creating an ideal working environment appropriate to the needs of international finance—the building was leased to a major Dutch investment bank. The client brief provided for a mix of internal spaces, including floors suitable for trading room use and more conventional corporate offices—the aim was to bridge the gulf between the office culture of London (where North American models dominate) and that of northern Europe, with its emphasis on environmental issues.

The use of a steel frame, combined with the reuse of some existing basement structures, ensured minimum disruption to the archaeological remains on the site. The structure is clearly expressed in the external elevations, where stone (from six British quarries) is used in an explicitly non-structural way to connect the building to its historic context; on Upper Thames Street, a dramatic stone portal frames the entrance facade and encloses a glazed screen mediating the noise and pollution of the street.

Steel, glass and stone are similarly juxtaposed in the interiors, which form a dynamic progression of spaces from north to south: the section is the key to the building. The heart of Thames Court is the skylit atrium with perimeter floors hung on 88-foot (27-meter) steel trusses to provide column-free space below—the louvered roof provides generous but controlled amounts of natural light. The energy efficient servicing strategy makes use of cool air drawn in from the river at basement level, while operable windows offer users a degree of control over their working environment. Transparency is a key theme in the scheme. The views across the river, where the building cantilevers across the extended public walkway, are spectacular.

Second floor plan

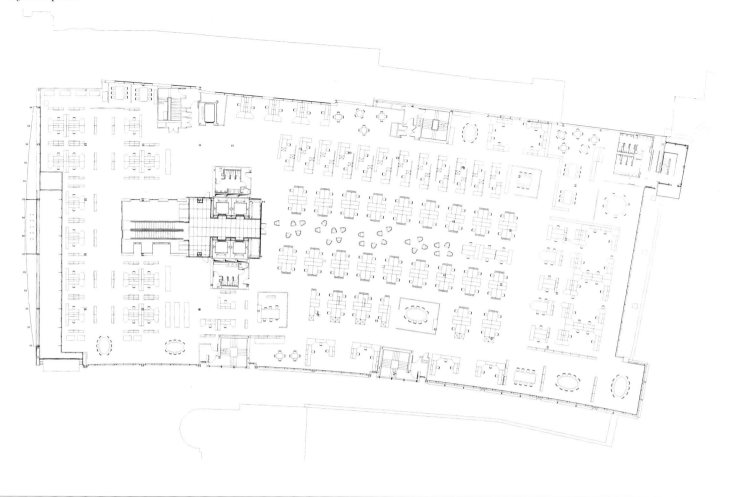

Ground floor plan

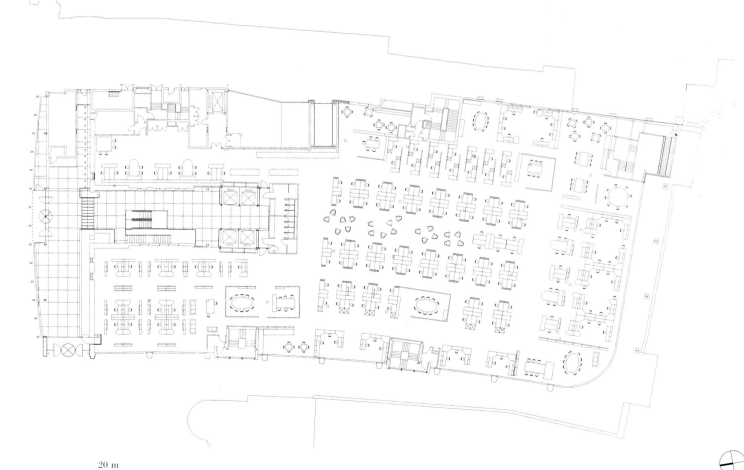

0   20 m

Third floor plan

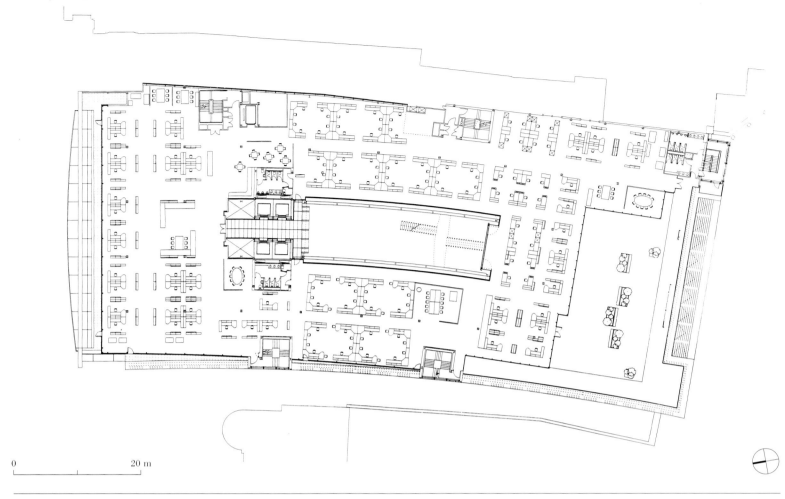

0   20 m

Axometric section of atrium

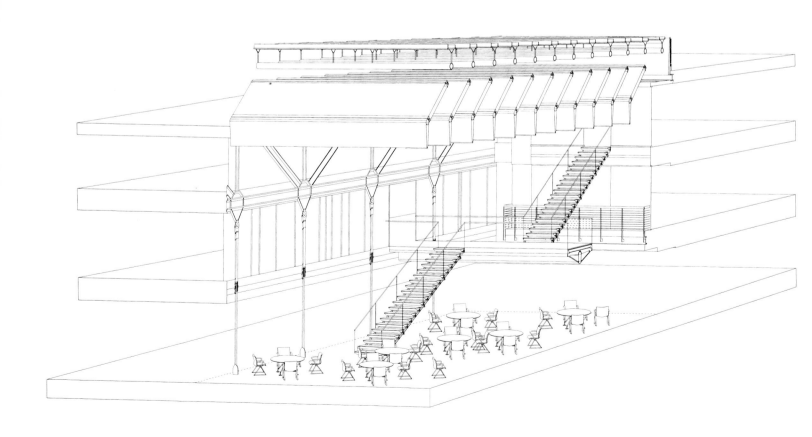

West elevation

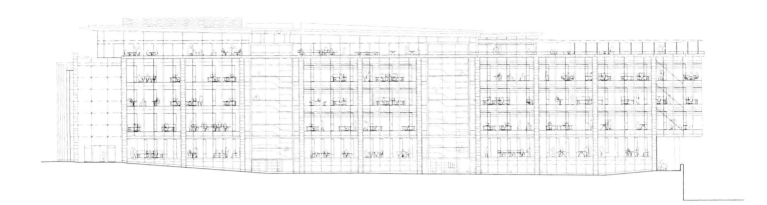

Section looking east

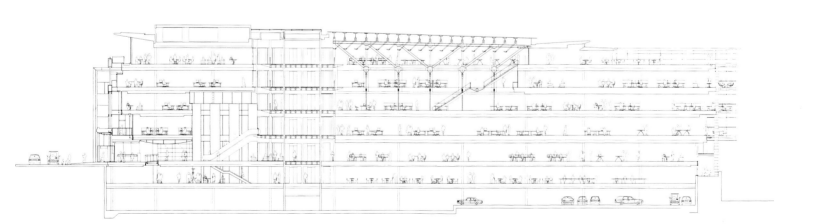

0   20 m

IBM World Headquarters

Armonk, New York
1995-1997

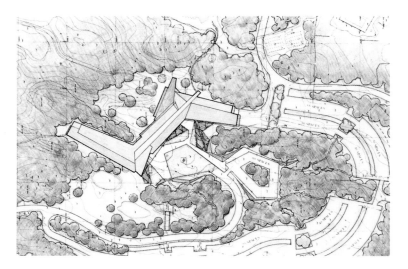

Nestled within a landscape of 450 wooded, rocky acres some 50 miles from Manhattan, the IBM World Headquarters exemplifies KPF's demonstrated ability to respond to the natural context and produce an innovative work of architecture. The building offers IBM a strong and dynamic image, embodying the aspirations of a client with a tradition of progressive architectural patronage while it addresses a complex operational and programmatic brief.

Completed in 1997, the headquarters is the centerpiece of an existing corporate campus in this rugged, wooded setting that is surprisingly dramatic in character, with deep ravines slicing through the landscape. A relatively low-rise development was inevitable, adapted to the contours of the site to allow the 280,000-square foot (26,000-square meter) building to be comfortably accommodated.

The form of the new headquarters takes its cue from the world of architectural experiment, yet offers enormous practical advantages. Designed to interact with its natural surroundings as much as possible the building has a generous provision of controlled natural light and excellent views out to the landscape, and open terraces for relaxation and informal meetings. The building assumes an extended, tapering Z-shape, which adapts well to both the existing site contours and to the open space program required by IBM as a significant change to their corporate culture. The central wing includes areas of enclosed space for executive offices and meeting rooms. The connecting wings maintain a highly functional core-to-wall depth to accommodate the open office workstations. The internal, irregular spaces within the plan are utilized for conference rooms, services and core functions.

The building is anchored to the ground by a base of natural stone, which stands in contrast to the dominant aesthetic of stainless steel, aluminum and glass. The roof is treated as a "fifth elevation"—the conventional distinction between walls and roof is abolished. The careful attention to materials and detail is evident in the two-story entrance lobby, where dark green granite is counterpoised by stainless steel and copper leaf, with a landmark "prow" bringing light into the heart of the building.

Third floor plan

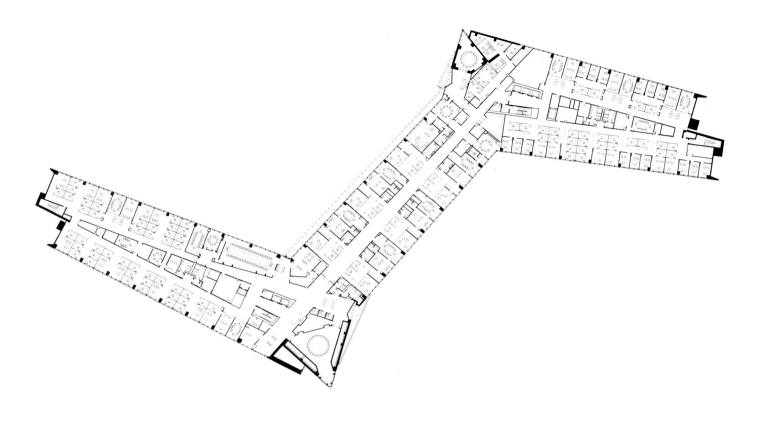

Ground floor plan

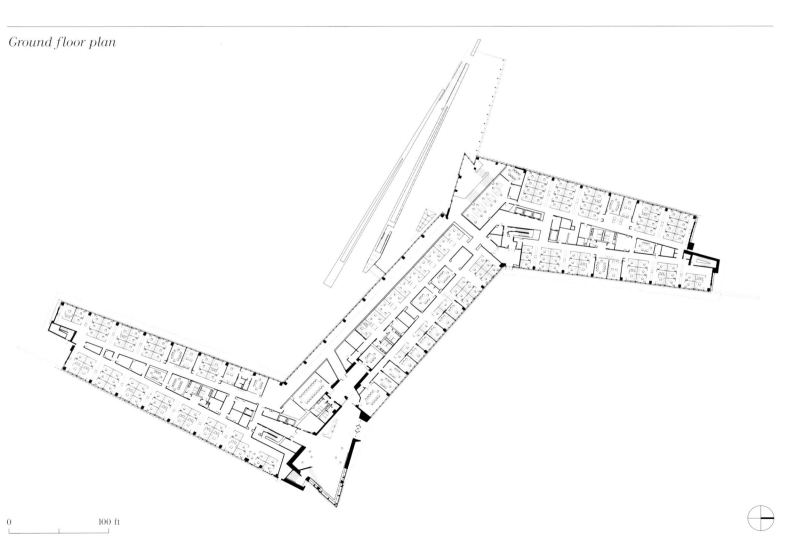

0   100 ft

ICEC/LKG Tower

Manila, Philippines
1995-2000

This 39-story office tower for the International Copra Export Corporation is located on a midblock site on Ayala Avenue in Makati City, a major commercial district within greater Manila. The scheme employs ideas found in Philippine architecture and decorative arts, combining them with modern planning strategies and building technology to create a building which is at once international and evocative of place.

The Philippine decorative tradition is a fusion of Malay, Spanish-Mexican, Chinese, and American influences. It finds expression in a culture of pattern making that favors delicate geometric or vegetal forms. Evident in the vernacular application of architectural details, loomed indigenous textiles and embroidery, these patterns employ fields of lightly contrasted texture and scale. In this project, a variety of these patterns have been interpreted in the development of the massing, the exterior wall, and the lobby elevations. The patterns created also define fields, which interact with each other to animate the form of the tower. At the same time, they help make the project a site-specific work by employing a repertory of formal devices familiar to its users.

Managing sunlight and maximizing air circulation are two key considerations in the design of the tower. Sunscreens and grilles are incorporated in the curtain wall system to supplement air-conditioning and tinted glass, while lower portions of the tower project forward to provide shade.

Roof plan

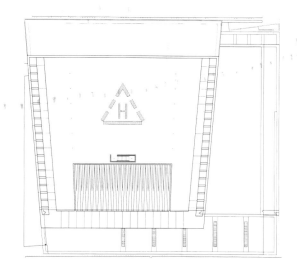

Typical floor plan

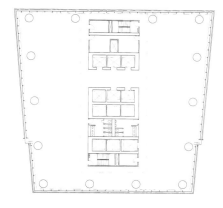

Ground floor plan

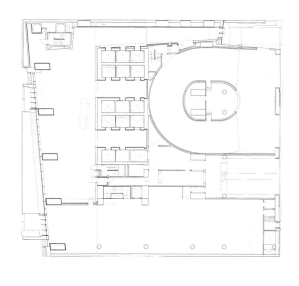

0   20 m

Section looking northwest

193

Rodin Museum
Samsung Headquarters Plaza

Seoul, South Korea
1995-1997

The Rodin Museum is part of a larger assemblage of glass interventions for the Samsung Headquarters Plaza in downtown Seoul. Situated along TaePyong-Ro, the city's historic axis, this small glass pavilion evolved from the placement of two famous works of sculpture by Auguste Rodin. The tension between the frontality of *The Gates of Hell* and the spatiality of *The Burghers of Calais* suggested an architecture of gesture and dance. In the design, this juxtaposition is interpreted as a *pas de deux* between two glass walls. Though similar in execution, the walls respond to different conditions of movement and enclosure.

To heighten the experience of the museum as a place of contemplation and spirituality, the space is cast in a diffuse light by constructing the walls and ceiling in glass with varying degrees of translucency. The all-glass roof, supported by steel columns, was conceived as an independent element in contrast to the organic forms of the walls. The space created by this confluence of material and form is characterized by the contrast between the serenity of the diffuse light and the fluidity of the dynamic walls.

East elevation

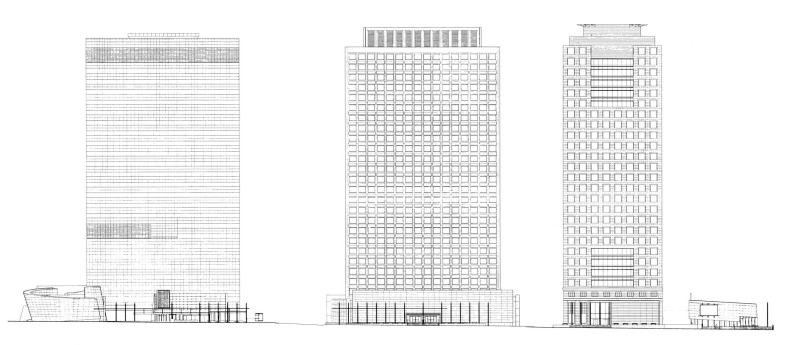

0   50 m

Site plan

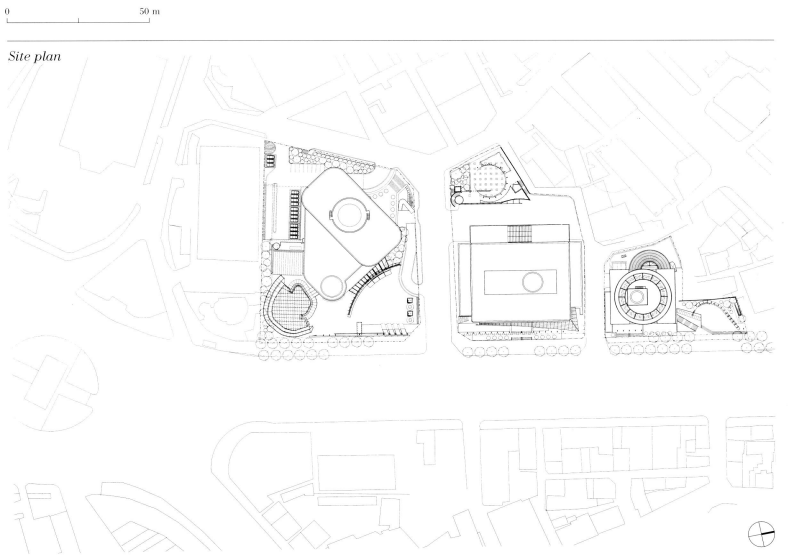

Section looking north

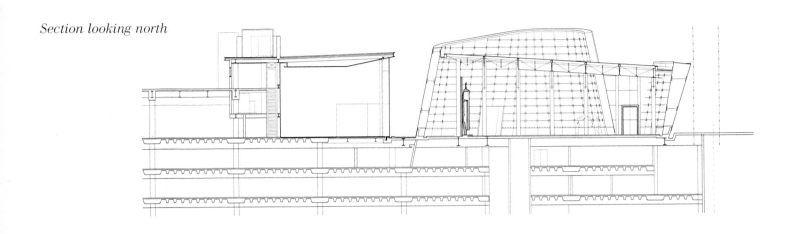

Section looking south   *Section looking west*

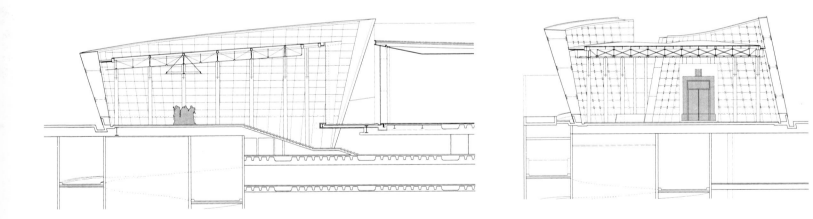

0   20 m

Ground floor plan

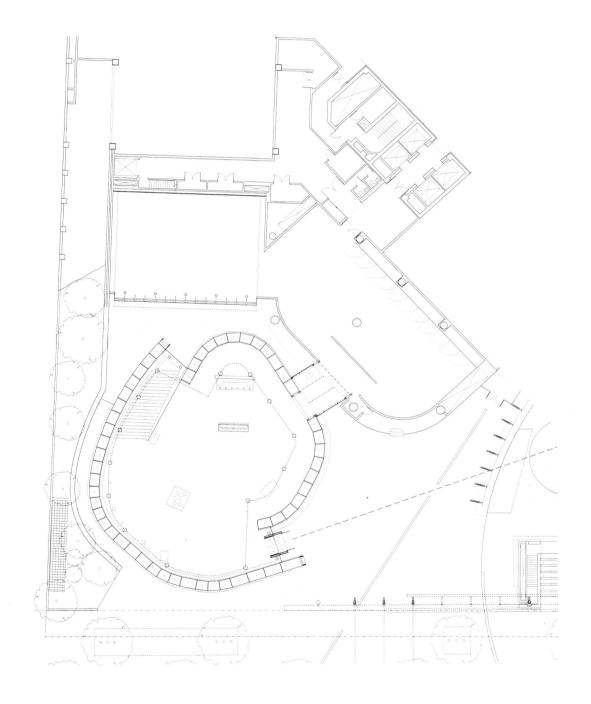

0   20 m

World Trade Center Amsterdam Renovation and Extension

Amsterdam, The Netherlands
1995-2002

The World Trade Center project is probably the most significant component in the emergence of Amsterdam's Southern district as one of the leading business districts in Europe. Set apart from the old heart of the city, the area was initially developed according to a master plan by H.P. Berlage which was somewhat compromised by post-1945 developments.

The existing World Trade Center consists of four multi-tenanted, mid-rise 1960s towers connected by lower structures and surrounded by open plazas, spaces that have been perceived as bleak and are consequently little used. The intensification of uses in the surrounding area, in which major road and rail routes are being covered with new office developments, provided an impetus to create attractive landscaped spaces with a much-needed conference center and shops and restaurants to serve the occupants of the World Trade Center and the wider public.

The key to the architects' proposals is a 323,000-square foot (30,000-square meter) freestanding, lightweight roof structure (designed in association with Guy Battle and RFR Paris) that wraps around the existing buildings to create a covered domain. The roof is far more than a cover: it incorporates opening vents and solar control panels to ensure comfortable conditions in the naturally ventilated spaces underneath. Fire control systems and acoustic panels are also incorporated into this innovative structure.

All the existing buildings are re-clad as part of the scheme— the benefits of the overall roof as an environmental buffer extend to the strategy for naturally ventilating the office spaces and shading the facades. To the east, in a second phase of the project, a new 25-story tower will provide an extension to the Center, facing the existing buildings across a new public square on the line of Berlage's axis. The use of timber screens and colored panels, set behind the glazing, adds a rich texture to this new landmark structure. The entire project demonstrates the way in which monocultural office districts can be transformed into mixed-use, round-the-clock city quarters.

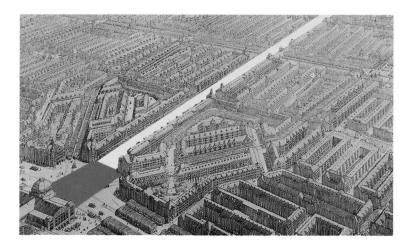

Site plan

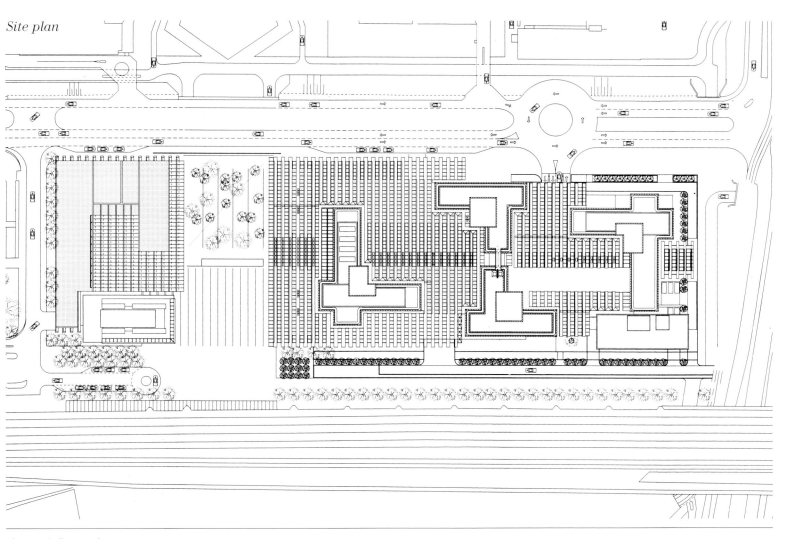

Ground floor plan

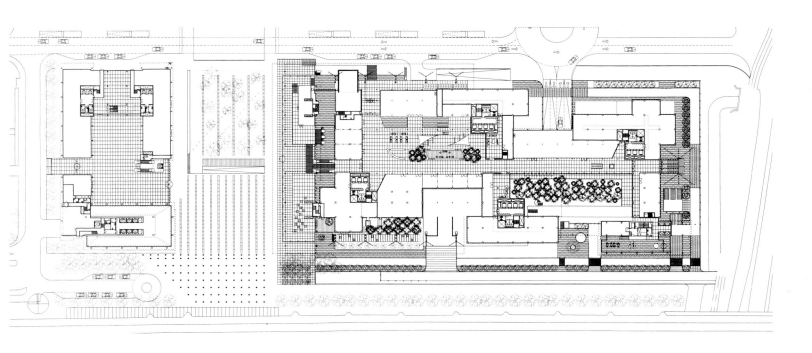

0   100 m

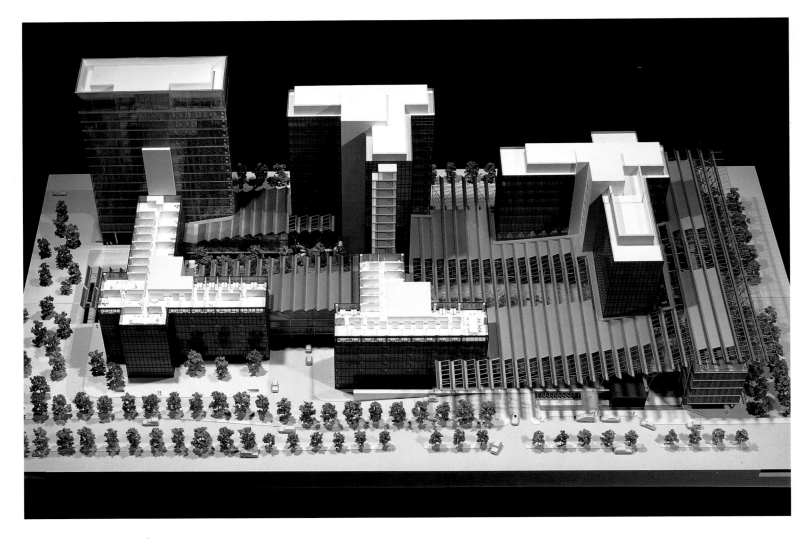

Section looking south

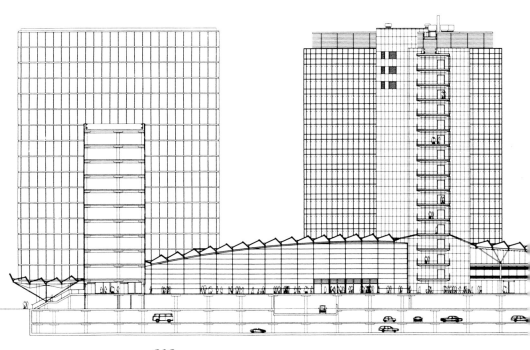

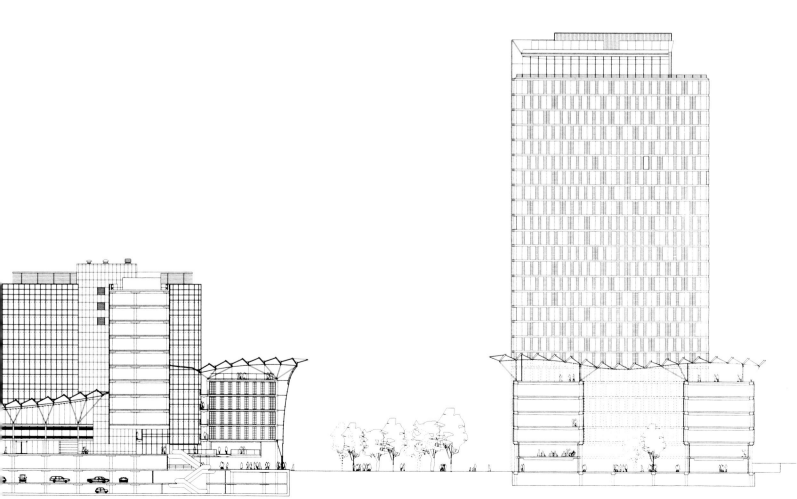

213

*East tower podium, exploded
axonometric diagram*

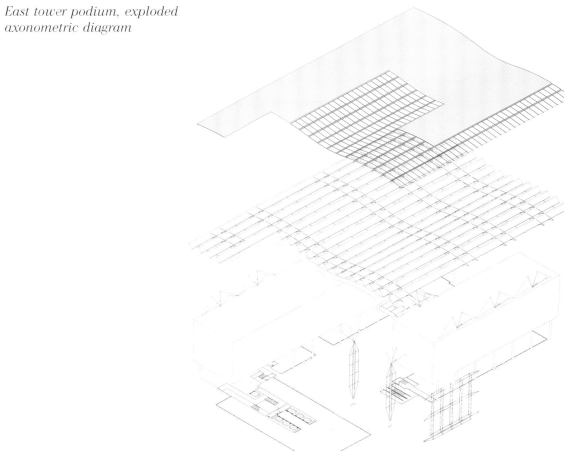

216

217

Baruch College Academic Complex
The City University of New York

New York, New York
1995-2001

This academic building for Baruch College occupies three quarters of a full block in lower Manhattan on Lexington Avenue between 24th and 25th Streets. Opposite the site is the University's recently completed Newman Library. Two blocks south on Lexington Avenue is the University's current academic facility.

The building is the center of Baruch's urban campus. At the heart of the building is a great central room that steps towards the sun from north to south. This room is a vertical interpretation of the traditional college quadrangle. The transformed quad connects three dominant pieces of the building: the business school, the liberal arts college, and the shared social amenities. The space functions as a central gathering space where students and faculty can meet and interact. The typical upper floors, linked by the common atrium, accommodate a variety of classrooms and offices. Large public assembly rooms and athletic facilities are located in the lower basement floors.

The massing of the building and the exterior wall systems address the zoning envelope and general context. The building envelope maximizes the building floor plate relative to the sky exposure plane and eliminates excessive setbacks and roofs. Each elevation responds to internal program and exterior context with a range of cladding materials and window sizes. The five-story brick and stone base relates directly to the library across the street and to the scale of the neighborhood. The high-rise component is broken into parts. Layers of corrugated aluminum wall panel, ribbon windows and curtain wall are detailed to define each elevation. Perimeter private offices typically have operable vents to regulate fresh air. Giant windows frame the central atrium on the north facade to provide a visual connection to the Newman Library and to bathe the public spaces in natural light.

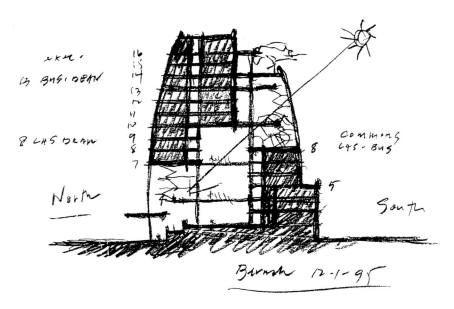

5th floor plan

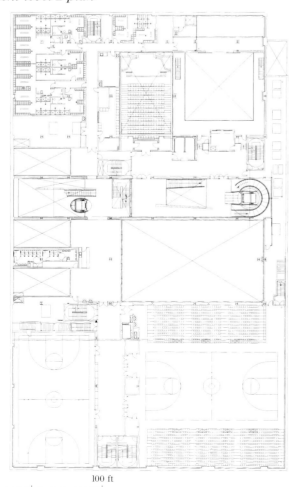

8th floor plan

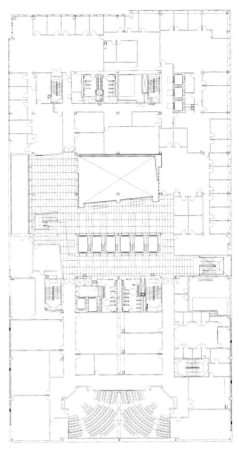

Basement level 2 plan

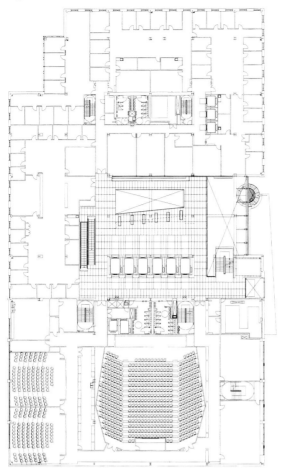

0   100 ft

Ground floor plan

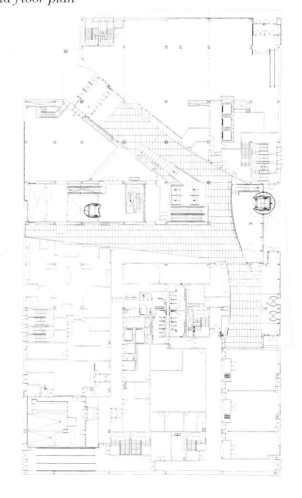

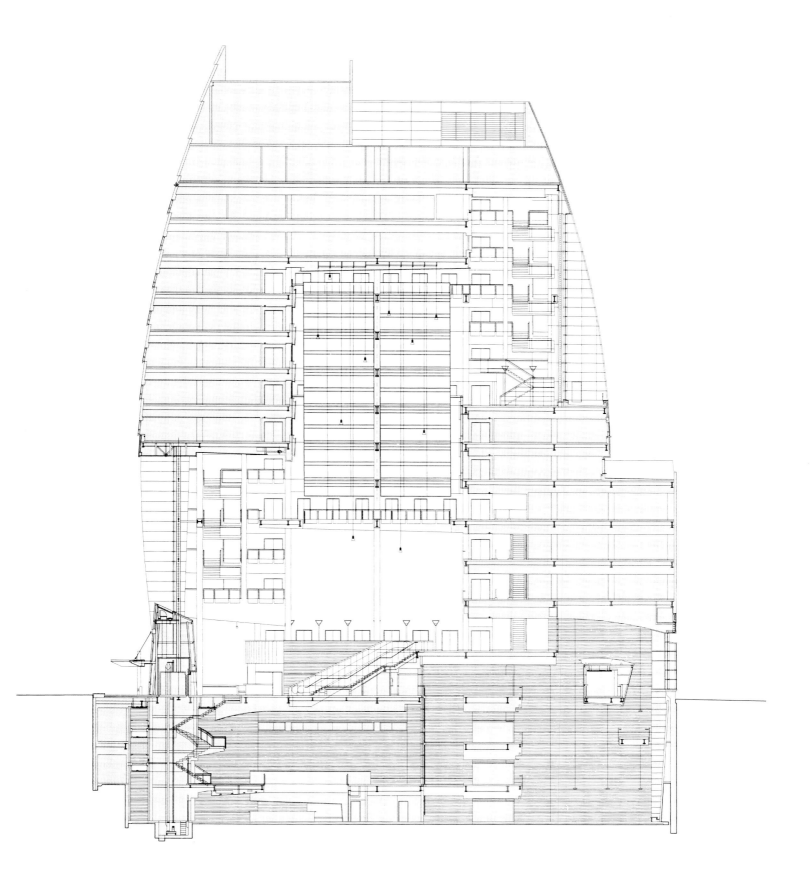

North elevation

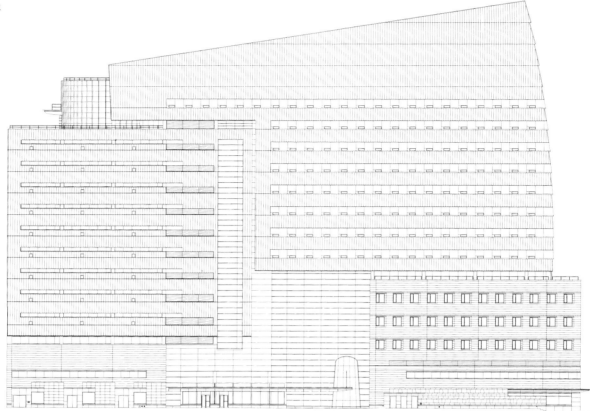

South elevation

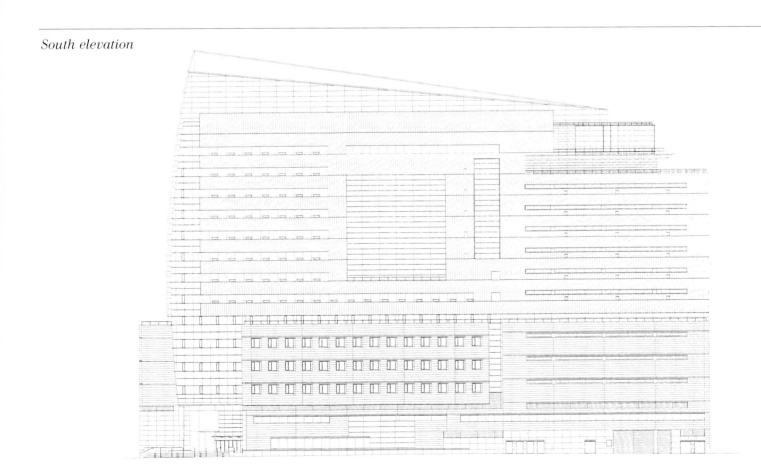

0   100 ft

West elevation

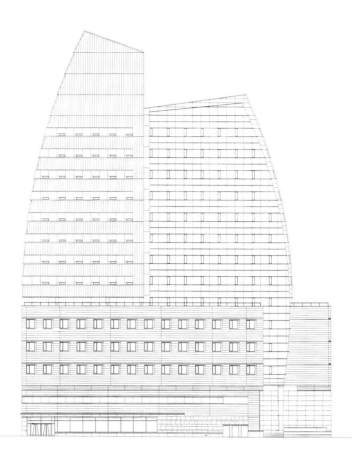

Section looking north

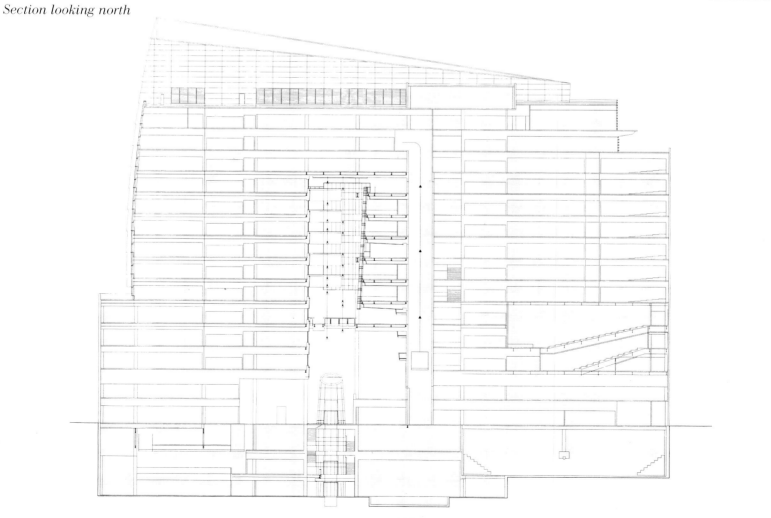

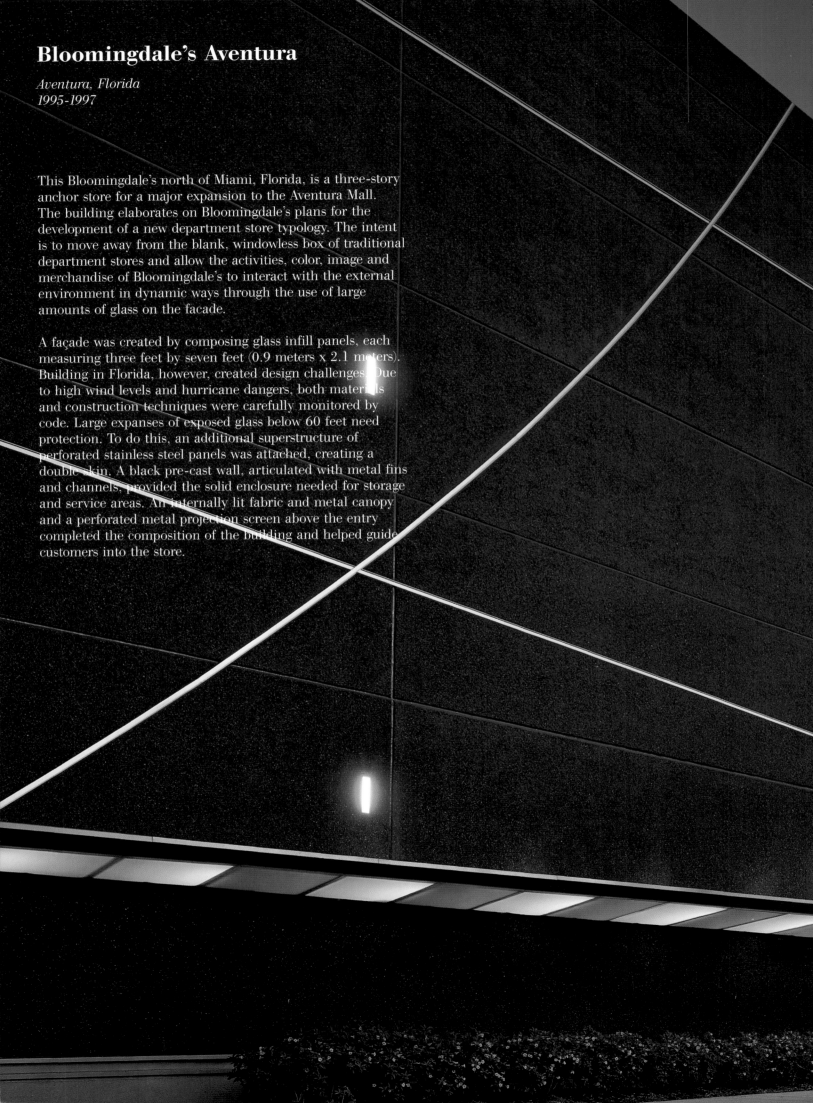

Bloomingdale's Aventura

Aventura, Florida
1995-1997

This Bloomingdale's north of Miami, Florida, is a three-story anchor store for a major expansion to the Aventura Mall. The building elaborates on Bloomingdale's plans for the development of a new department store typology. The intent is to move away from the blank, windowless box of traditional department stores and allow the activities, color, image and merchandise of Bloomingdale's to interact with the external environment in dynamic ways through the use of large amounts of glass on the facade.

A façade was created by composing glass infill panels, each measuring three feet by seven feet (0.9 meters x 2.1 meters). Building in Florida, however, created design challenges. Due to high wind levels and hurricane dangers, both materials and construction techniques were carefully monitored by code. Large expanses of exposed glass below 60 feet need protection. To do this, an additional superstructure of perforated stainless steel panels was attached, creating a double skin. A black pre-cast wall, articulated with metal fins and channels, provided the solid enclosure needed for storage and service areas. An internally lit fabric and metal canopy and a perforated metal projection screen above the entry completed the composition of the building and helped guide customers into the store.

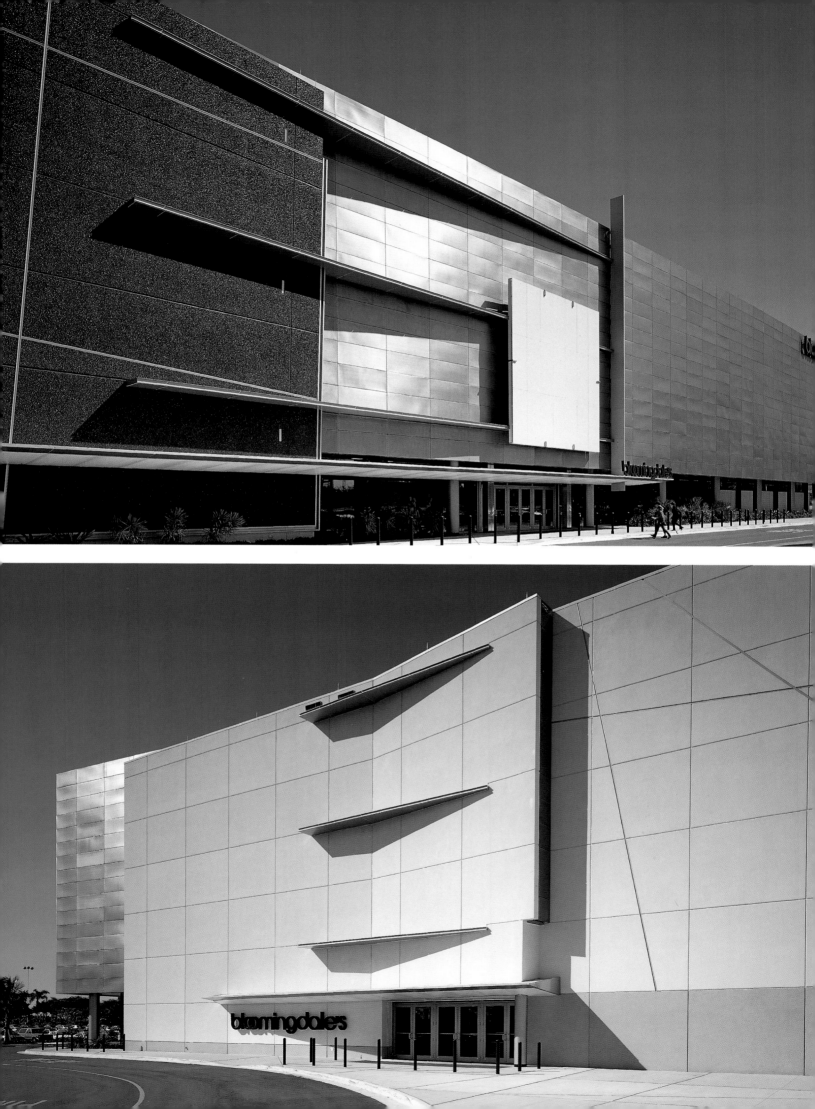

West section

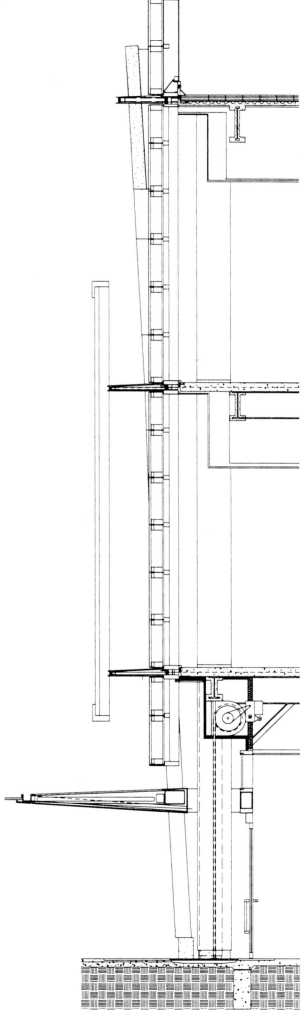

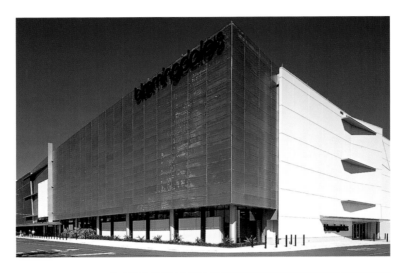

Dacom Headquarters Building

Seoul, South Korea
1995-1999

The Dacom Headquarters project occupies a gateway site just north of the Hang Gang Bridge, the principal link between the two halves of the city bisected by the Han River. At 26 stories, the design for the tower accommodates executive office suites, a business center, exhibition spaces, a health-club, a cafeteria, a 300-seat auditorium, telecommunications equipment and a satellite station.

The design is both figural and abstract, emphasizing ideas of simplicity in form and function in the midst of a cluttered architectural environment. On its west facade, the tower first responds to its context with a prismatic wall of a scale that firmly marks the presence of the client—a telecommunications company—in an area specifically zoned for high technology. This wall initiates a spiral composition of embracing straight and curved forms, terminating in a communications mast to the north. Heralded by a satellite dish, the leading edge of the tower is oriented to the south, announcing the building from the riverside.

Apart from the efficient enclosure of space, the building's green-tinted glass form was conceived primarily to respond to changing light conditions. Clad in slightly reflective vision glass, as much metal as possible is eliminated from the curtain wall to maintain a simple crystalline image.

The treatment of the building's base and entrance produces a human scale. A series of canopies and screen walls counter the smoothness of the building's curved prow. The landscaped portion of the entryway was developed to integrate the building form with the planting and the ground plane. The ground surface is composed of unfinished or patterned granite, and three pear-shaped berms create a unique vehicular sequence from the drop-off to the parking entry. Concentrated in a garden along the southern perimeter, bamboo is used to form a soft ring around the angular site.

Typical floor plan

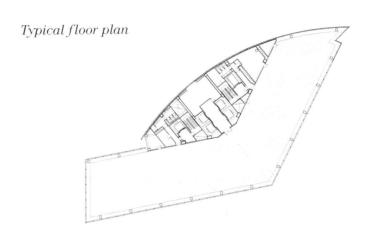

Ground floor plan

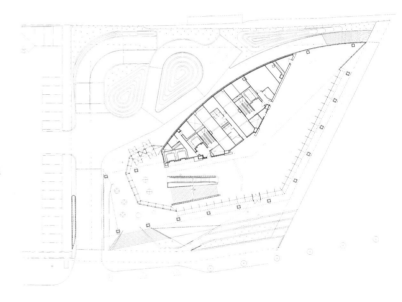

0   20 m

South elevation

North elevation

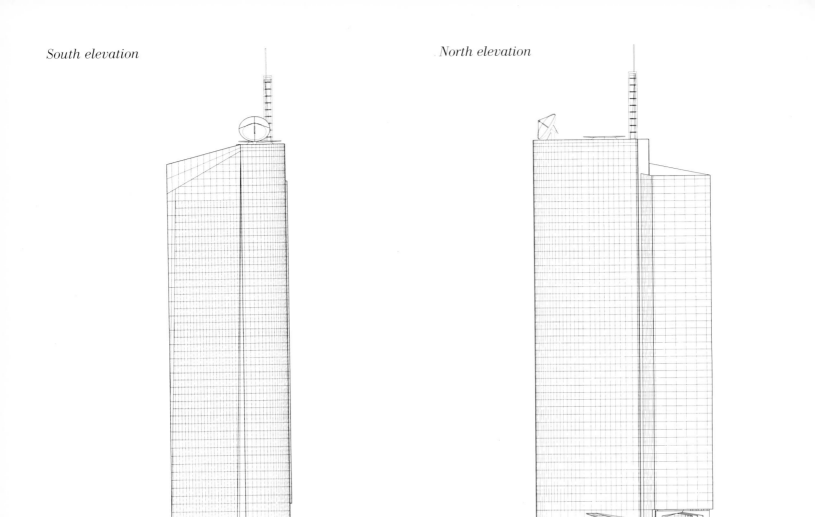

East elevation

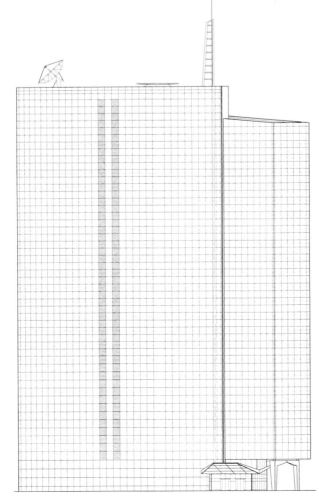

0   20 m

SBS Broadcast Center

Seoul, South Korea
1995

This project for the Seoul Broadcasting Company is located within a rapidly expanding neighborhood of TV studios and modern housing blocks surrounding Mok-Dong Park, and occupies a plot defining the northern edge of the green. Several parallel goals generated the design for this new thirteen-story building. In designing an efficient, state-of-the-art television and radio broadcast facility, an important consideration was to establish a sympathetic relationship between nature and technology.

The design explores the transmission of media from a central point. This idea of focused communication is expressed in the form of a circle. The circular form also describes an ideal or pure form as found in nature. In juxtaposition to a rectilinear form, the circle sets up a dialogue between nature and man. The dynamic between these two fundamental positions and their geometric representation—that of the circle embracing the square, or creativity cradling production—is then seen as the basis for a new culture of mass communication and information transfer.

The program for the new SBS Broadcast Center is divided into three primary areas: the television studios and related facilities, the adjacent offices and support areas and shared spaces such as the cafeteria, club, conference and seminar rooms. The juxtaposition of the orthogonal and the circular form generates the building's shape. Heightening this contrast is the combination of long-span, multi-story structure for the studio spaces, and short-span structure for the surrounding office space. A tall void separates the two spatial types and becomes the heart of the building's interior. Externally, the building spirals around the volume of the studio spaces. These spaces are terminated by a great community roof garden, for dining and lectures, sheltered by a south-facing glass enclosure.

Roof plan

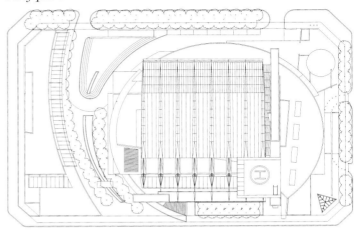

Ground floor plan

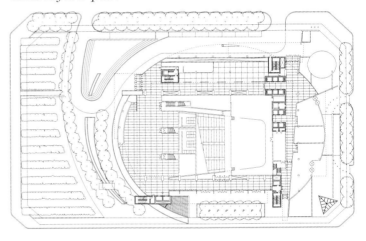

7th floor plan

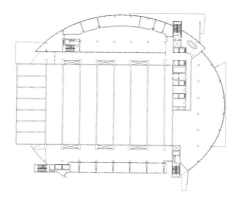

13th floor plan

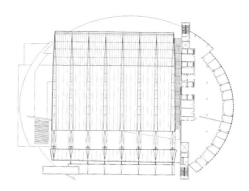

6th floor plan

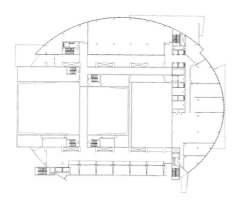

12th floor plan

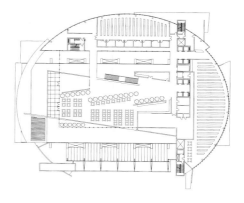

5th floor plan

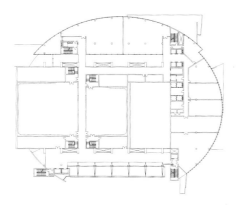

11th floor plan

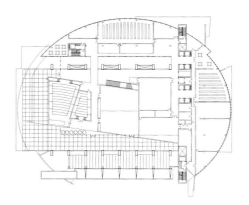

30 m

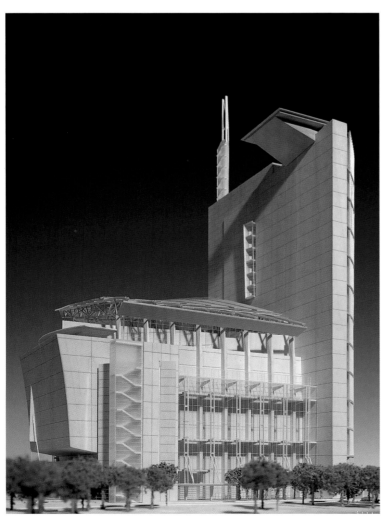

Samyang Mixed-use Building

Seoul, South Korea
1996-1999

The tablet forms of the Samyang building were generated according to the dimensional requirements of a mixed-use office and residential program for a key site in a commercial district north of the Han River. The scheme is composed of three slender structures and a public forecourt garden, all designed to strict open-space and building setback criteria.

The office space occupies the first eighteen floors of the tower. The first setback, located on the south side, punctuates the office volume while providing a terrace club level for the residential hotel above. These apartments take advantage of excellent views, north to the mountains, or south towards the skyline of Seoul.

The podium engages the site by utilizing a configuration of forecourts around entrances and gardens. Internally, the base of the tower provides specialized exhibition, retail and tenant spaces above and below grade. The entry courts to the office and residential lobbies are linked by a sweeping canopy along the east-west axis of the site. The resulting assembly creates a series of interior and exterior thresholds as one moves from public to private.

This layered organization becomes a vehicle for referencing and exploring the screen-like quality of spatial definition fundamental to traditional Asian architecture. An architectural language that suggests the limits of enclosure is employed, blurring distictions between interior and exterior zones. The layered density and scale of the various screens interact to create intentionally ambiguous spatial readings, obscuring the limits of public and private areas and the boundaries between interior and exterior.

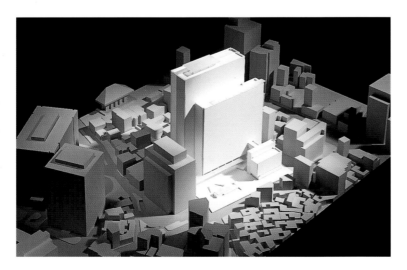

High-rise office plan

Residential/Terrace floor plan

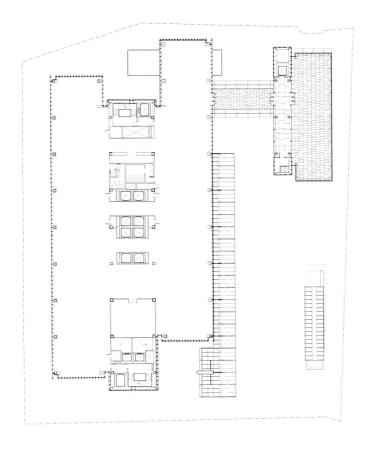

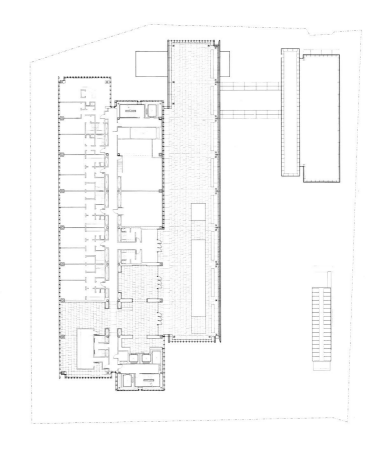

Ground floor plan

Low-rise office plan

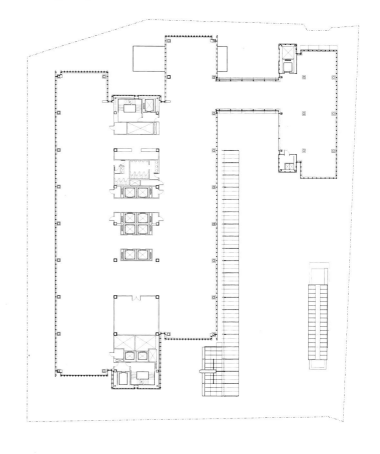

0   20 m

South elevation

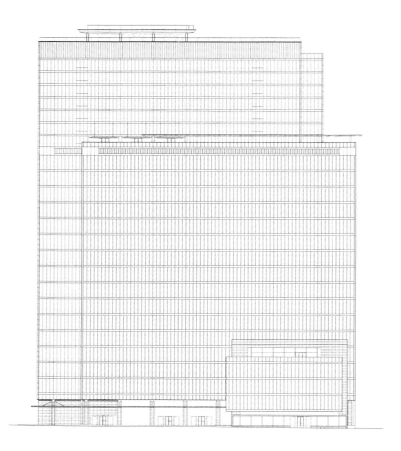

West elevation

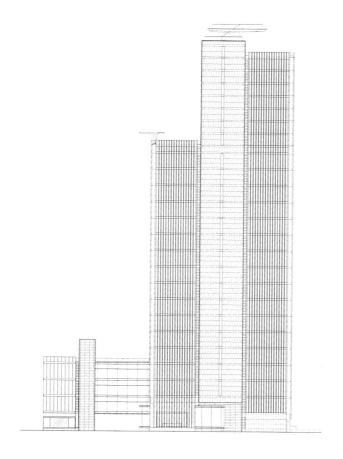

0   20 m

Suyoung Bay Landmark Tower
Daewoo Marina City

Pusan, South Korea
1996-1998

Designed for a site on the southern tip of the Korean peninsula, this 102-story tower is the focal point of a master plan for the Pusan waterfront. Set apart from the traditional downtown, the scheme establishes a magnet in the form of a grand retail, entertainment and cultural center on reclaimed land in Suyoung Bay. The tower accommodates prime office space, a hotel and serviced apartments, while clustered at its base are retail areas, a museum, a performing arts center, and a multipurpose hall.

Resembling a giant sail, the structure is shaped to respond to its site at the water's edge. Informed by formal motifs in Korean art and architecture, the extruded form of the tower is composed primarily of asymmetrically curved planes intersecting with an iris-shaped shaft. The dominant longitudinal axis of their form also creates a bridge between the sea and the mountains to the north of the city. The north-south axis of the site is further reinforced by its alignment with a major causeway crossing the bay.

On the ground, the tower form is met by a series of sweeping forms that contain the public space. Functionally, the lower levels of the tower provide flexible office space while the smaller upper floors, hollowed by a north-facing atrium, house a hotel. As the tower narrows toward the top, the internal atrium that connects the hotel floors opens the exterior, culminating in an observation level that offers magnificent views of land and sea.

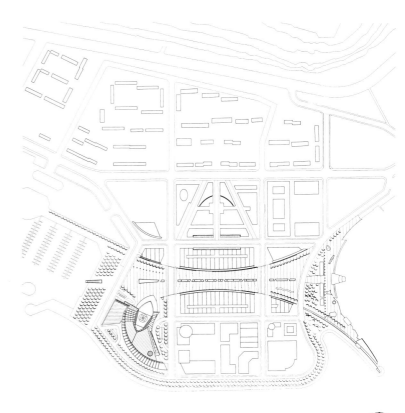

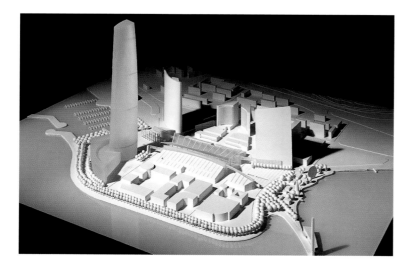

Level 3 plan

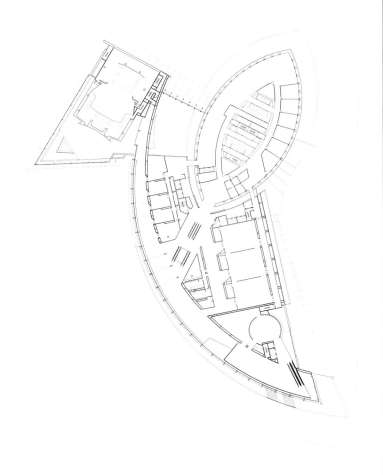

Level 5 plan

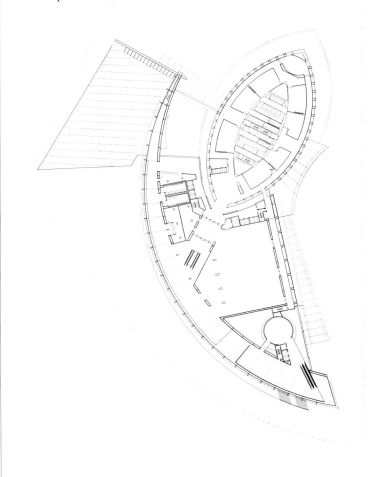

Ground floor plan

Level 2 plan

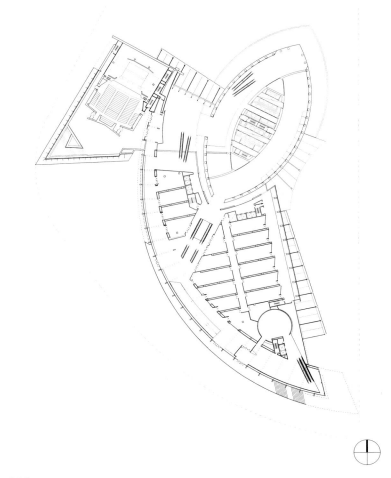

0   50 m

55th/Health club floor   *48th/Typical serviced apartment floor*   *42nd/Apartment common floor*

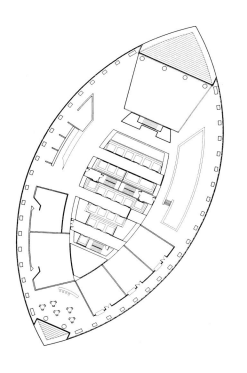
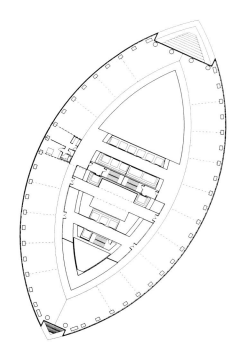
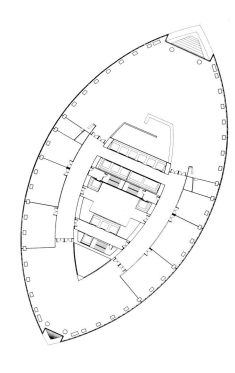

36th/Typical high-rise office floor   *31st/Mechanical floor*   *14th/Typical low-rise office*

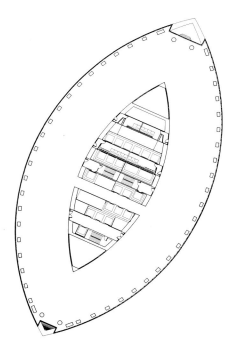
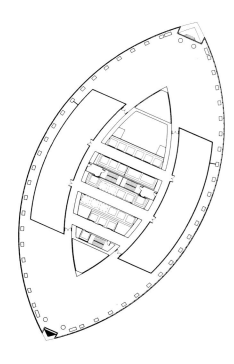
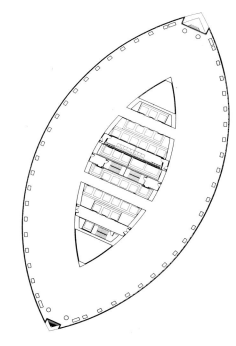

0   20 m

Observation deck

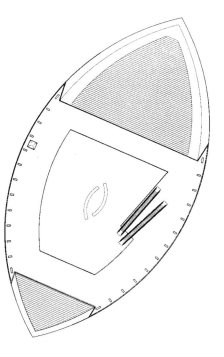

Skylounge floor

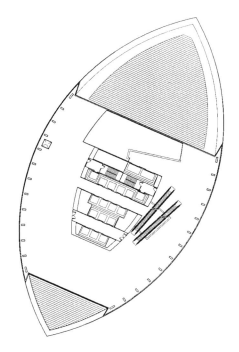

Executive hotel room floor

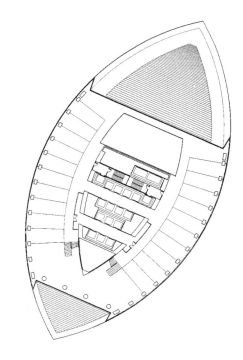

78th/Typical hotel room floor

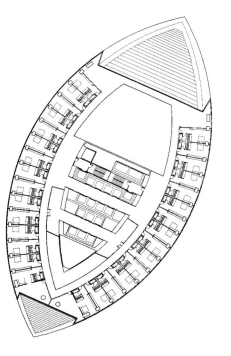

62nd/Hotel common floor

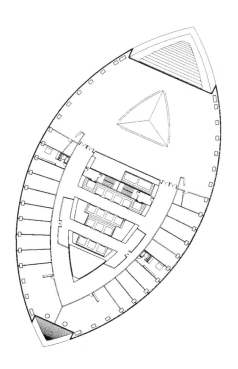

60th/Hotel lobby floor

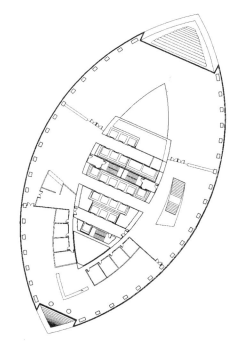

257

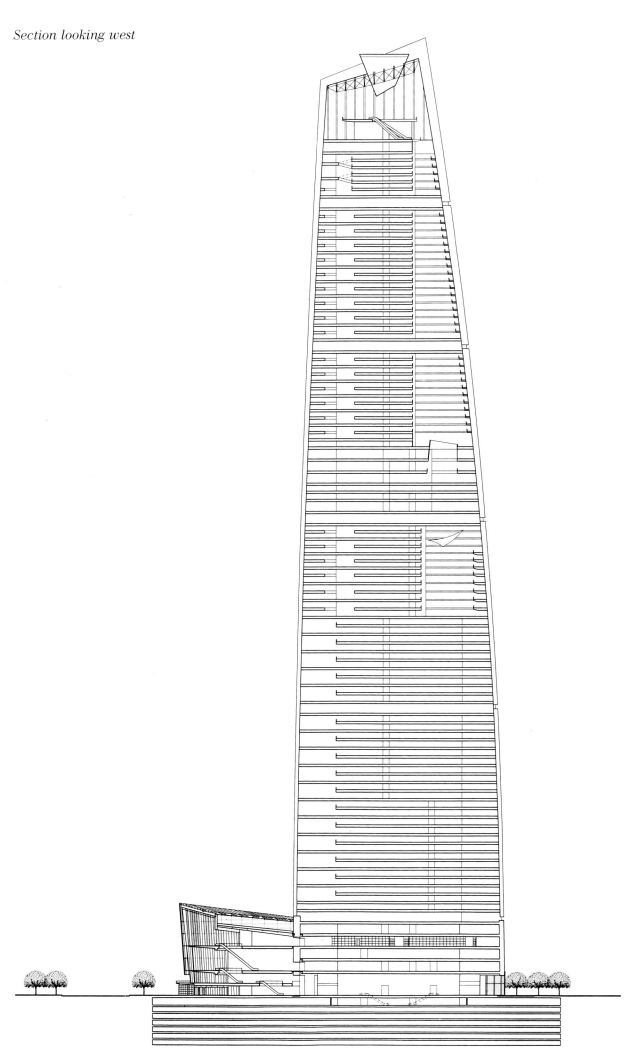

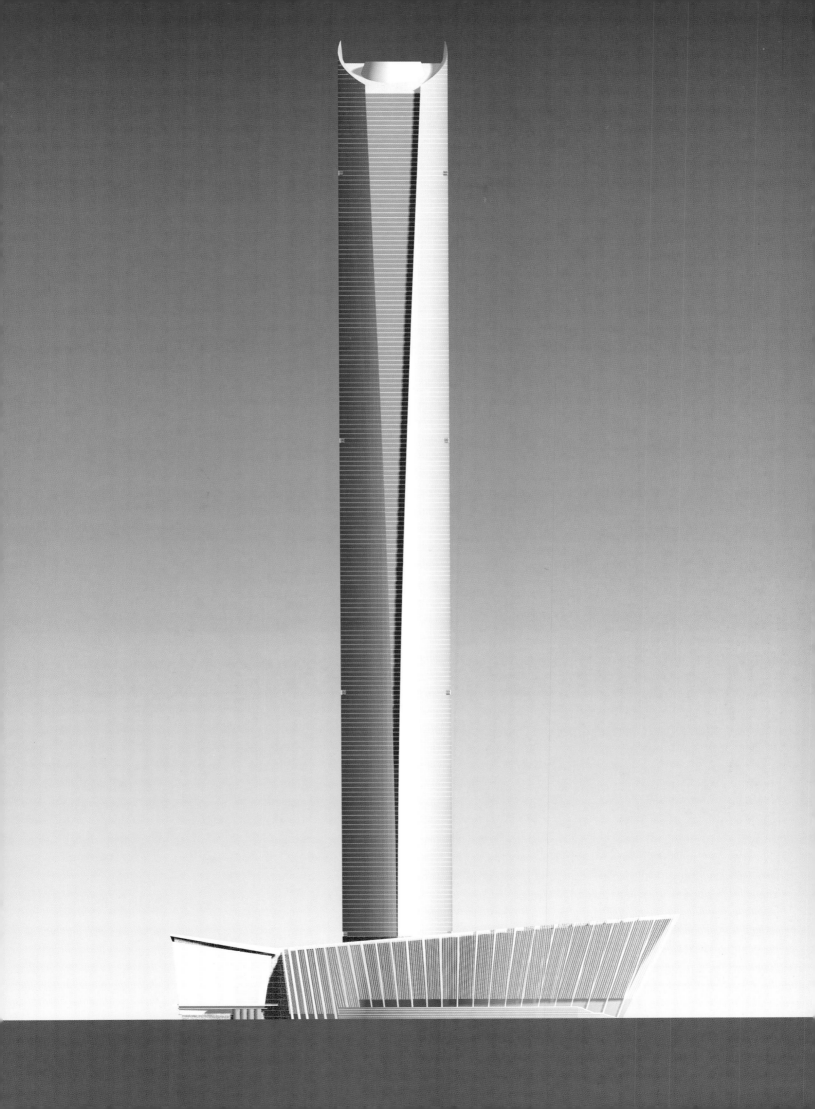

Hong Kong Electric Company
Head Office Redevelopment

Hong Kong SAR
1996-2001

The unique mid-level site on Kennedy Road overlooking
Victoria Harbor inspires the building's double-faced composition
of stone and glass. Articulating a dialogue between earth and
sky, the slope of the mountain behind the thirteen-story
building appears to pressure the solid limestone wall of the
south facade, folding the wall symmetrically at each end. This
compression bows the taut glass face of the north façade out
toward the sky, providing generous views of the city below.

Within the glass facade, asymmetric elements portray
activities inside the building. Three elements align to create a
vertical composition. Two and three-story conference rooms
are stacked over one another, defining the body of the figure.
These rooms occupy an interstitial space created by a small
interior concave glass wall and the larger convex glass facade.
Peeling away the reflective coating of the outer glass reveals
the presence of these rooms and marks the lobby below. Set
within an arching stainless steel roof, an observatory lantern
crowns the vertical composition. A depression in the facade
for a six-floor balcony creates a horizontal counterpoint.

Inspired by traditional Chinese garden architecture, a civic
plaza and garden wall gesture to the surrounding landscape
across the front of the building, locking it to the site. The
garden wall, with its integrated fountain design, provides a
synthetic backdrop for a picturesque allée of trees, connecting
the structure to Hong Kong's transforming landscape.

Site plan

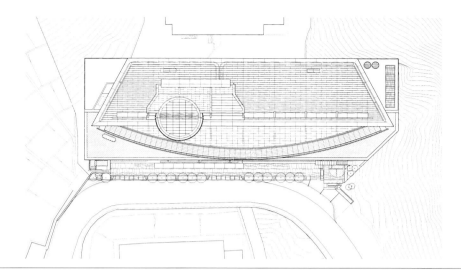

Typical floor plan

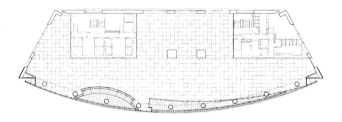

South elevation

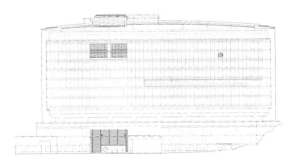

North elevation

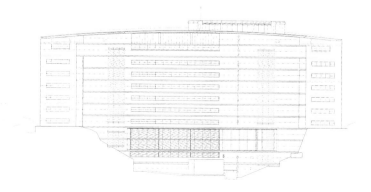

0   10 m

One Raffles Link

Singapore
1996-2000

This seven-story "groundscraper" is unusual in Singapore where the majority of office buildings are towers. One Raffles Link provides long span, column-free office floors ideally suited to the city's growing financial services sector. It sits on a pivotal site fronting the War Memorial Park and adjacent to the open space of the Padang, the colonial-era parade ground. To the east is Marina City, a commercial district on reclaimed land; to the west is the City Hall area, the civic zone that includes Parliament House, the Supreme Court, and St Andrew's Cathedral. To the south lies the central business district; to the north the International Convention Center. The development of this sensitive site completes Singapore's urban planning strategy for this district by providing the crucial link for a direct, climate-controlled, 492-foot (150-meter) retail tunnel to the MRT transit system.

One Raffles Link has a dual role—it completes the City Hall zone and it announces Marina City, a cluster of large, mixed-use projects including office, hotel and retail space. City Hall by contrast is made up of historic, low-rise buildings that create a formal sense of enclosure around public space. The building's design responds to this context. A more formal facade responds to the War Memorial on the west, while to the east the building reflects the abstract modernism of the Marina district. The compositional tension created by this bipartite design is resolved across the roofline where the static barrel-vaulted roof of the west facade is overlapped by the dynamic triangular-louvered roof of the east. The composition is balanced by a triangular volume that completes the plan at the north end. Because One Raffles Link is clearly visible from higher buildings, it was a planning requirement that the roof top mechanics be shielded from view.

Another planning requirement dictated the provision of a continuous covered arcade along the building's perimeter. A monumental granite wall stretches north-south across the site and supports the western facade with its attached, monumental sunscreen. This wall sets up a series of colonnades around the four sides of the building, bridging the colonial tradition represented in the civic center with the modern idiom of contemporary structures.

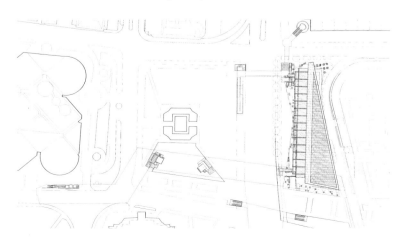

Typical floor plan

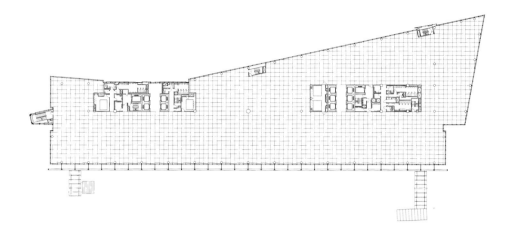

Second floor plan

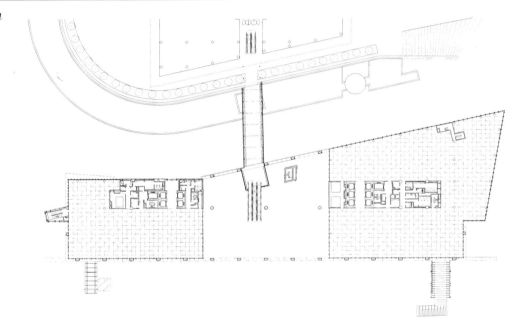

Ground floor plan

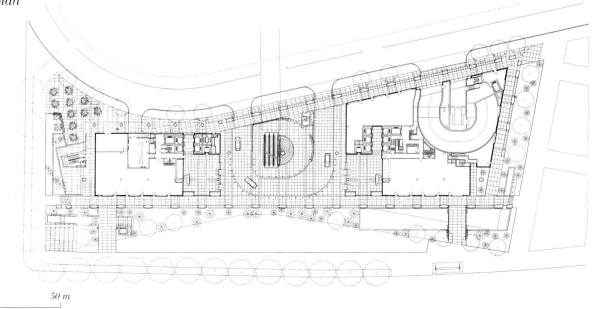

0   50 m

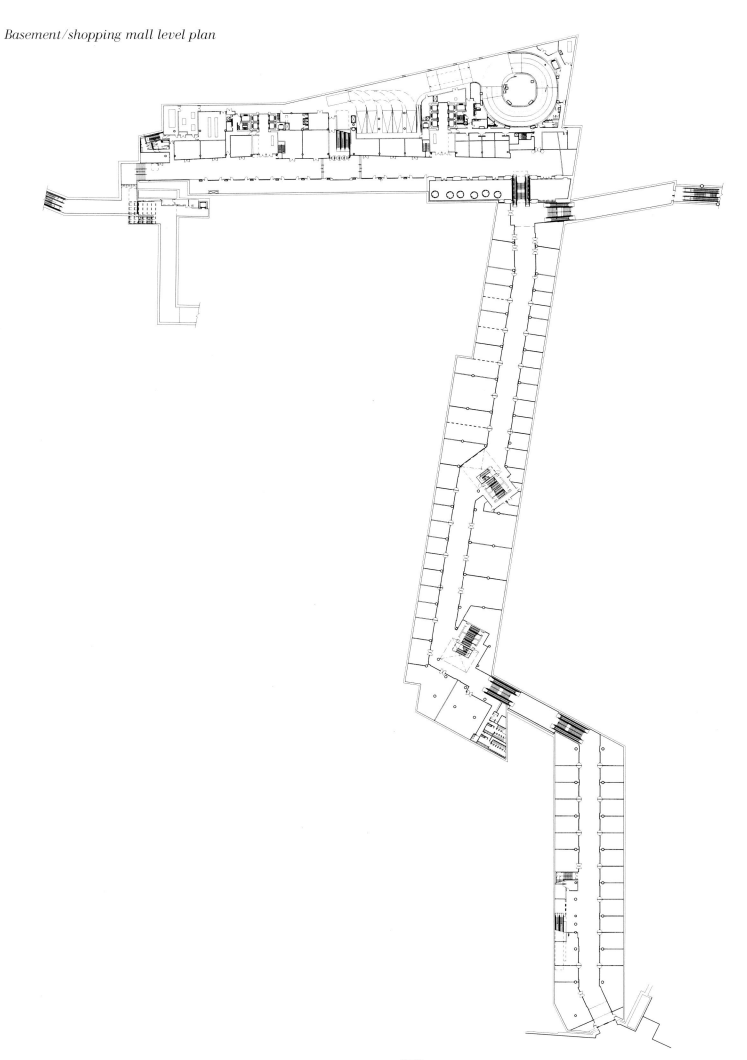

745 Seventh Avenue

New York, New York
1996-2001

Located between 49th and 50th Streets, the 745 Seventh Avenue project, initially designed for Morgan Stanley Dean Witter and later sold to Lehman Brothers, is a build-to-suit office building in midtown Manhattan.

The granite, metal and glass building rises through a series of alternating setbacks. The setbacks maximize floor area while complying with stringent New York City sky exposure requirements.

The ground floor contains retail space, two generous lobbies, separate entrances on Seventh Avenue, 49th and 50th Streets, a porte-cochere, garden plaza, subway entrance, and a pedestrian connection to the Rockefeller Plaza concourse system.

By integrating a block-long LED display within the curtain wall, the building satisfies the strict signage guidelines of the Times Square Business Improvement District. The signage connects the building, located at the northern "bow tie" intersection of Seventh Avenue and Broadway, to the heart of Times Square.

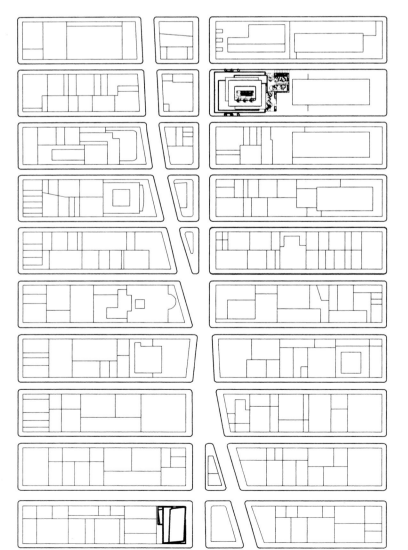

Typical floor plan

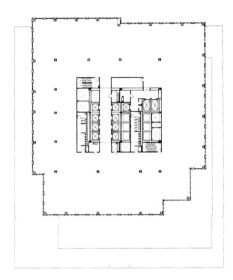

Ground floor plan

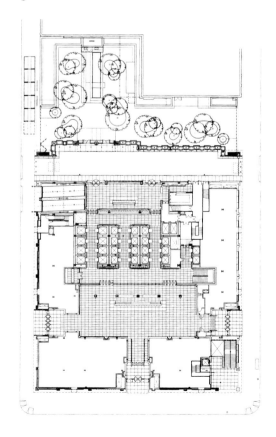

0   100 ft

Posteel Headquarters Tower

Seoul, South Korea
1996-2003

The Posteel Headquarters Tower is situated on Teheran-Ro, a principal financial street in the south section of the city. The client, Posteel, manufactures steel plate, and the design brief for the project interprets the tower as an icon to their product. The scheme is composed of various plate-like surfaces, sculpted to enclose the programmatic and public spaces.

The folds in the fenestration of the building reference an assemblage of metal plates. The varied triangular metallic plates undulate in a dynamic composition that rises to a height of 25 stories. The four facades are distinct responses to four diverse site conditions. The north facade along Teheran-Ro reinforces the frontality of the street wall, but also leads the eye to the entry corner where the massing of the building is most dynamic. At the eastern facade, the diagonal bracing is visible, reinforcing the parti. The stone wall that rings the site offers a more diverse palate to the composition, and provides visual weight to anchor the dynamic forms of the building's massing.

The public spaces at the base of the tower are clearly expressed from the exterior and are easily accessible. The lobby, exhibition space and auditorium are connected through a series of escalators and activate the building at street level.

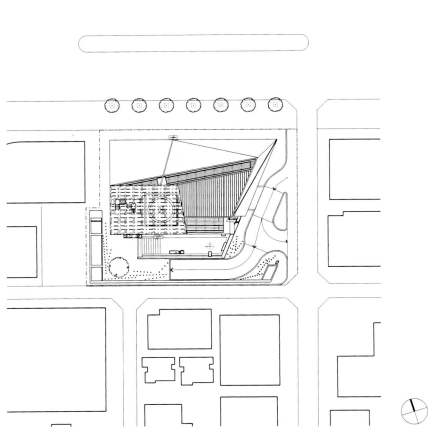

Typical floor plan

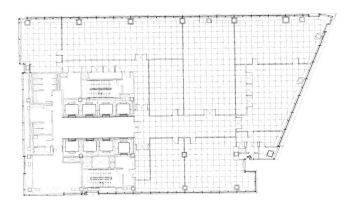

Second floor plan

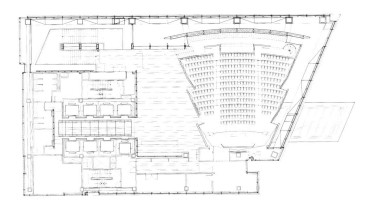

First floor plan

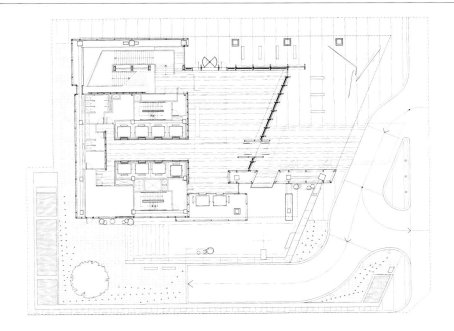

0   20 m

Section looking west

Section looking south

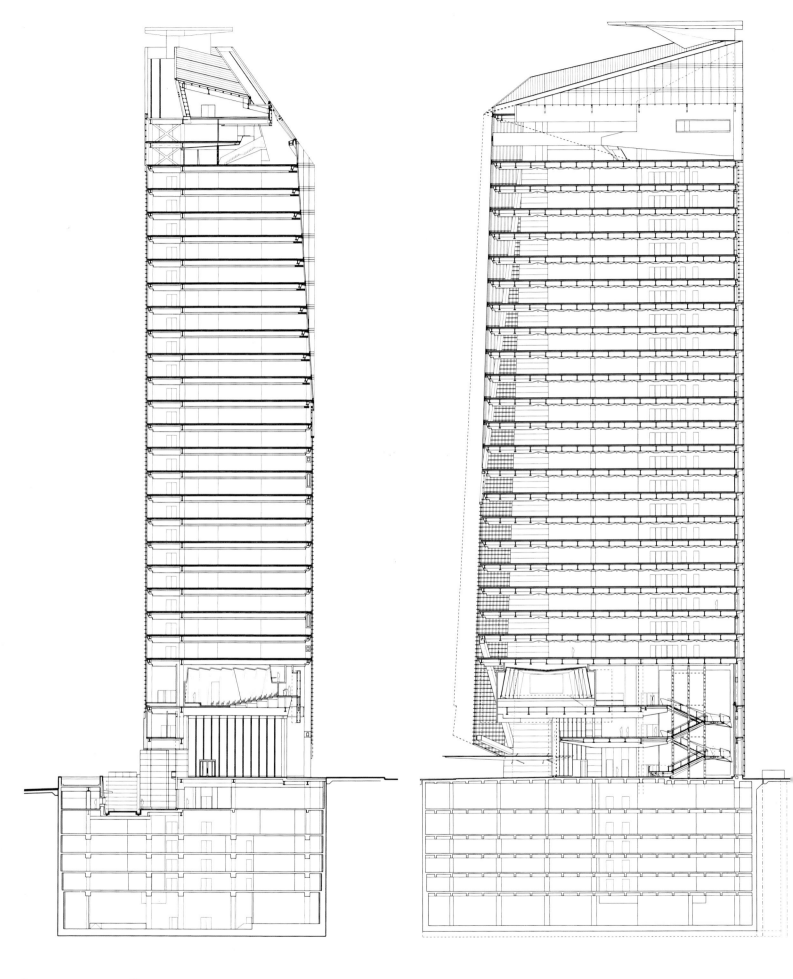

0   20 m

ADIA Headquarters

Abu Dhabi, The United Arab Emirates
1997-2004

The 42-story headquarters building for the Abu Dhabi
Investment Authority (ADIA) reflects the emergence of a
number of significant themes in the work of the firm's
London office; in particular, its rethinking of the tall office
building in a changing cultural, social and environmental
context. The scheme draws on lessons learned from unbuilt
tower projects of the 1990s, including the three "Wave"
buildings proposed for Bangkok and the Rotterdam Coolsingel
development. In each case, a dynamic and memorable built
form is generated from the interlocking geometry of curving,
highly-glazed planes. The parti of Coolsingel—two towers
"wrapped" with a continuous ribbon of glass and separated
by an atrium—was particularly influential.

The siting of the development, close to the sea in a green
fringe of the city, further influenced the designs—the
building opens up to the waterfront on the west, with
elevators and other services concentrated on the eastern, rear
flank. Its fluid form has an undeniably nautical flavor, but is
far from arbitrary. A prime objective of the client brief was to
demonstrate the potential for low-energy design even in the
extreme climate of the Gulf. A series of sky gardens, in tune
with the Islamic tradition of incorporating cooling green
spaces into buildings, punctuate the office floors and provide
an attractive outlook for the building's users.

ADIA provides a stylish benchmark for environmentally
responsible design in the Middle East. The use of clear glass
was seen as vital to obtain the requisite element of
transparency: generous daylighting in the offices (a mix of
cellular and open-plan spaces) provides significant energy
savings. The development of the low energy double wall is
brought to bear as part of an economical strategy—developed
in consultation with Buro Happold—for ventilating the
interior spaces. Stale air is extracted through the solid core of
the building using the thermal chimney effect.

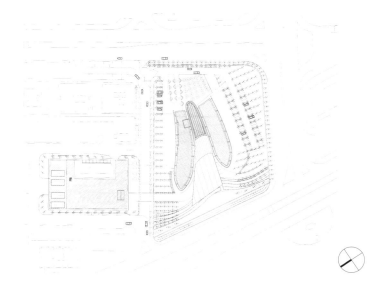

Typical floor plan

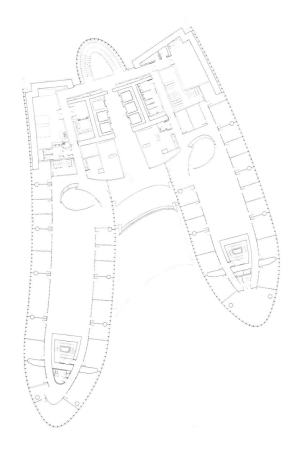

Ground floor plan

0   20 m

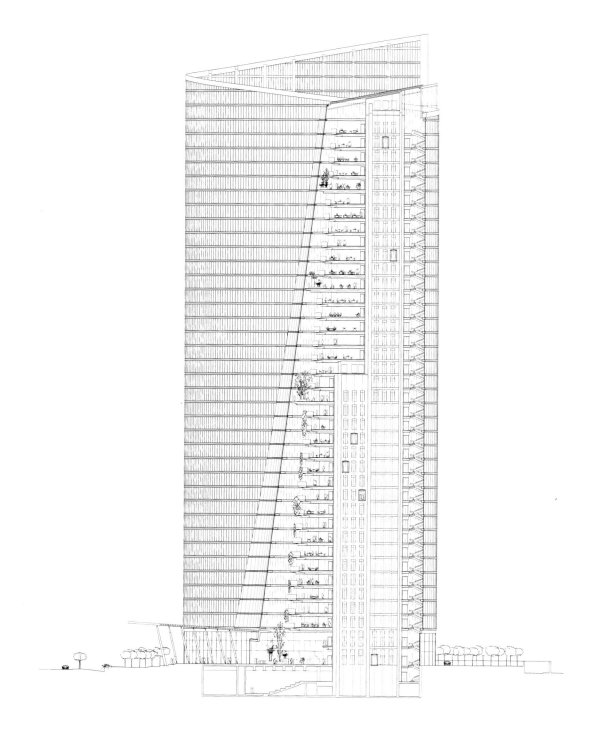

0   20 m

Roppongi Hills Tower

Tokyo, Japan
1997-2003

This fifty-eight-story mixed-use tower is the centerpiece of a 27-acre project in an important commercial and entertainment district in Tokyo. Located along the Roppongi Dori, an arterial highway, the building houses over 3 million square feet (280,000 square meters) of office space, a 550-room hotel, and a variety of cultural uses—including a 1200-seat theater at podium level and a large museum for contemporary art located at the crown of the tower. Upon completion, the tower will be the tallest building in Tokyo.

The form of the tower draws from traditions in Japanese design, where variegated natural forms are expressed in geometricized patterns. This interpretation creates a faceted curtain wall that unfolds as one moves around the project. The fragmentation created by the curving geometry of the tower, the folded base and top, and the shifting planes of the elevation combine to heighten this impression of constant change. The rooftop museum is intended to attract a high volume of visitors—an estimated 20,000 a day.

The lower masses of the hotel and the theater surround the tower. The design of the smaller buildings responds to both the central tower and the localized conditions at the periphery of the project. As one unit, the hotel and theater appropriate materials from the metallic palette of the tower and distinguish their forms with warm horizontal expanses of limestone. The tension generated by these opposing elements creates an angularity more pronounced as the structures come in contact with the street grid.

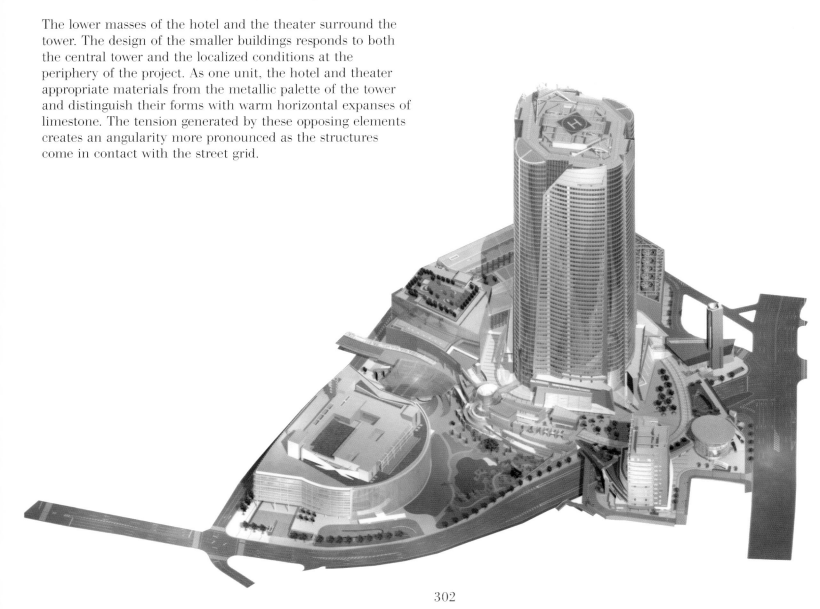

Ground floor plan

Second floor plan

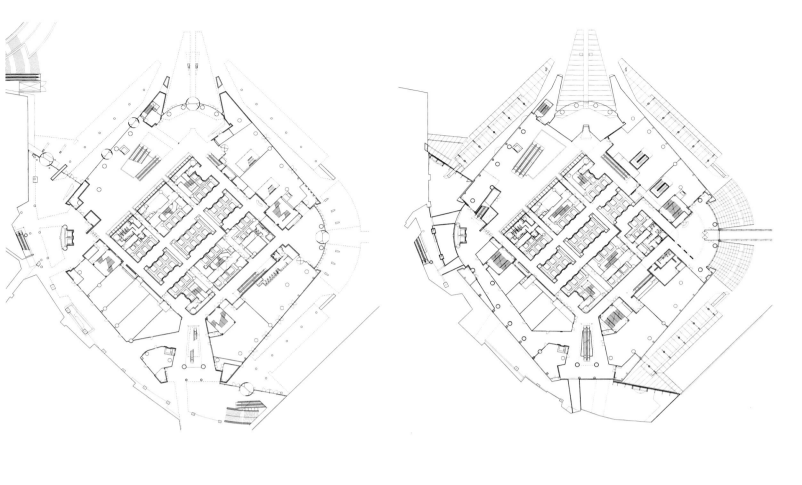

Typical floor plan

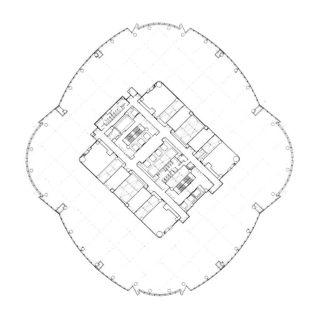

0   50 m

North elevation

South elevation

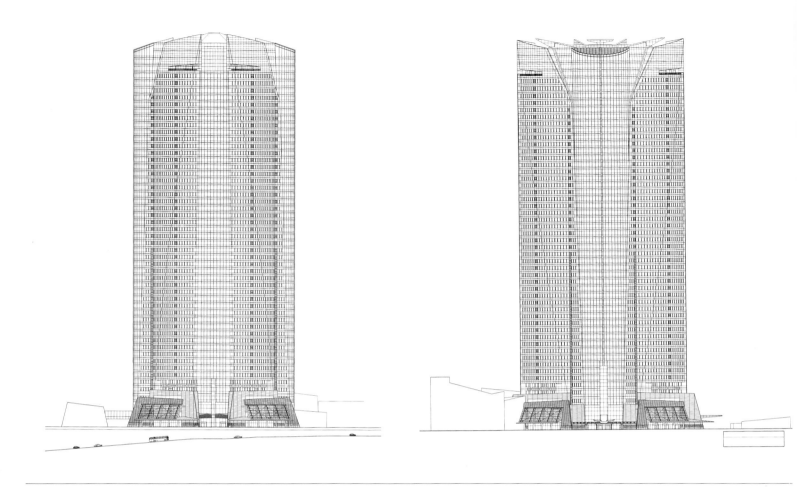

Section

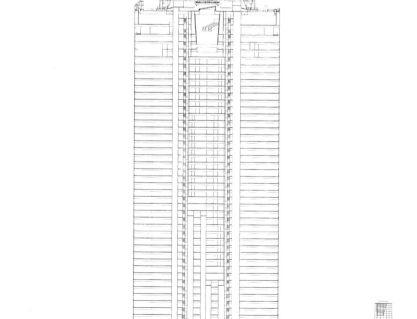

0   50

Sotheby's Headquarters

New York, New York
1997-2001

The design of the worldwide headquarters for the 255-year old auction house presented the challenge of adapting a four-story granite-clad structure to Sotheby's requirements for the 21st century. Located in Manhattan's Upper East Side and surrounded by high-rise apartment buildings, the six-story addition incorporated the existing building as a podium for new construction.

The client required a generous provision for natural light to best evaluate works of art. The resulting "light box" features a highly articulated curtain wall with glass engineered for maximum clarity and color rendition. The changing wall module and mixture of transparent and translucent panels express the differing functions on each floor.

The entrance on York Avenue is announced by an atrium extending the full height of the ten-story building in which Sotheby's will hang banners to herald their activities to the city. The main lobby provides access to all the public exhibition and sales areas via escalators rising at the center of the atrium, as well as to a group of four elevators servicing all levels of the building. The structure incorporates six floors of consignment storage, expert research, cataloging and exhibition areas for the various art and art object categories. The major Auction Sales room, accommodating up to one thousand bidders and spectators is located on the seventh floor. A grand gallery for contemporary art and special collector sales is located on the top level. A café and teahouse, as well as an outdoor terrace and sculpture garden—all open to the public—complement the grand gallery spaces and provide a welcome venue for food and refreshments for staff and public alike. Administrative offices are located on floors eight and nine, and post sales/pick-up and shipping areas occupy the lower ground level.

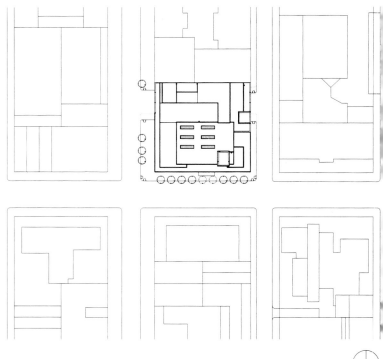

Second floor plan

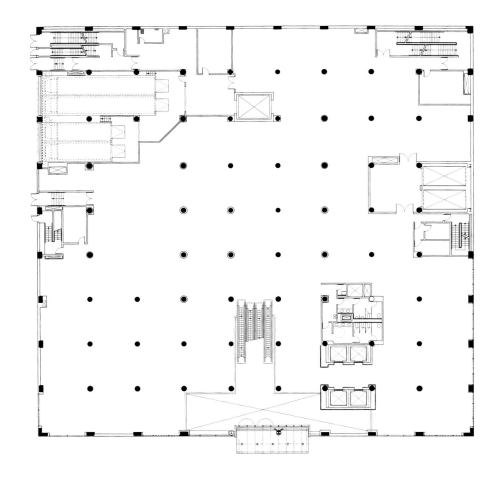

Ground floor plan

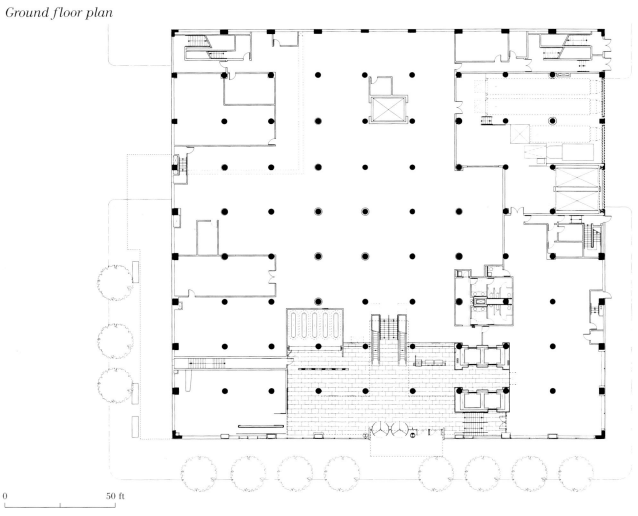

0   50 ft

Gannett/USA Today Corporate Headquarters

McLean, Virginia
1997-2001

The Gannett/USA Today Corporate Headquarters represents a thorough restudy of the office building. In its design, every aspect of the office environment was critically reconsidered, from the individual workstation, to the exterior form and cladding of the complex, to the ecology of the site. The resulting complex follows no familiar precedents. It is neither high-rise nor low-rise, provides consciously varied work settings, and looks unlike any other corporate headquarters. The client is a two-part corporate entity, comprising the headquarters of Gannett Co., Inc., a diversified news and information company, and USA Today, a national newspaper.

The 825,000-square foot (76,645-square meter) building is situated at the intersection of two regional arteries, the Beltway and the Dulles Toll Road. It consists of two mid-rise structures for Gannett and USA Today, spiraling up from a base of shared facilities that wraps around an exterior "town square" at the main entrance. The northwest portion of the 30-acre (10-hectare) site was judged most ideal for the U-shaped building. The southeast-facing entry court captures desirable sunshine and is shielded from the coldest winds, as well as highway noise.

Open in plan, the large floor plates easily support the primary functional requirement for newsrooms, production areas and corporate offices. The other half of the building is dedicated to auxiliary facilities and amenities such as a cafeteria, an auditorium, conference and training suites, a health club, a bank, a credit union, a concierge service and on-site retail. The lobby is a high space connecting the two elevator towers, with a reception desk from which both elevator banks can be observed.

The glazed corridors running along the edges of the central courtyard make interior circulation visible and foster a sense of community with the least interruption of the office floors. Pulling the elevators outside of the building volume and enclosing them in glass adds to the sense of activity as seen from both corridors and courtyard, while it reduces the obstruction of floor layouts that elevators typically entail.

Cladding is composed of glass for spandrels as well as vision glass, with closely spaced vertical glass exterior fins that modulate the appearance of the walls as one moves around the structure.

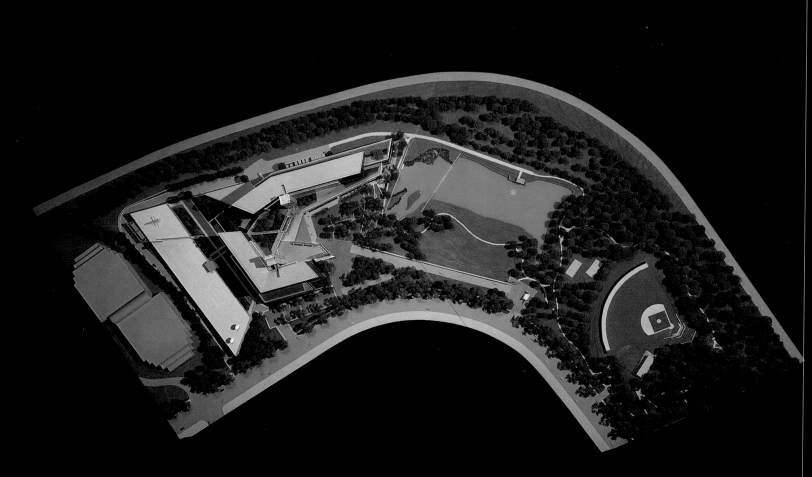

Typical office floor plan

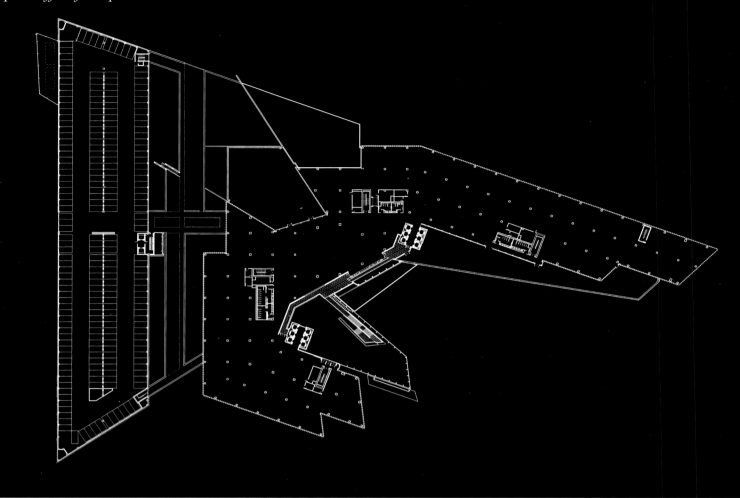

Ground floor plan

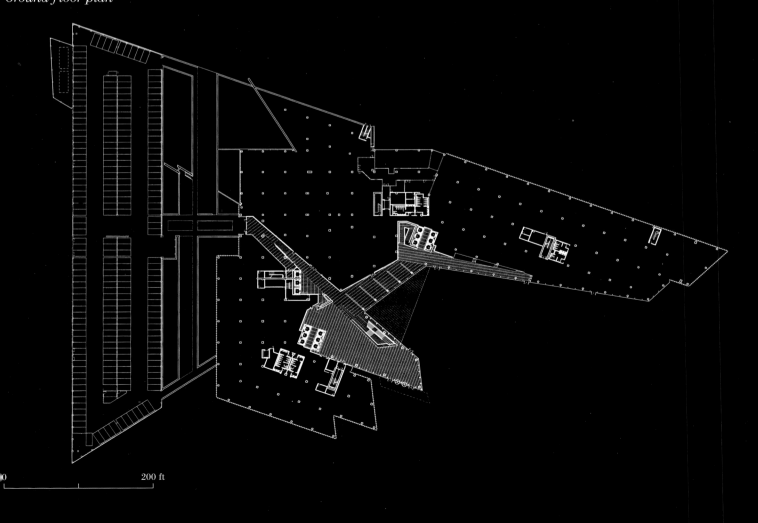

200 ft

North elevation

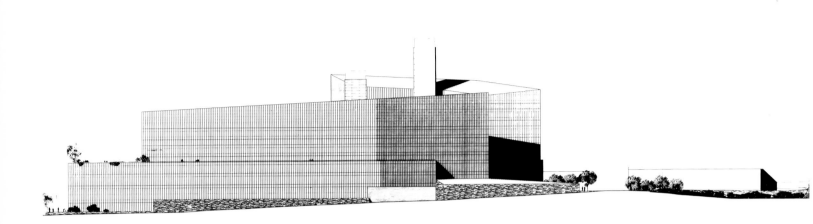

South elevation

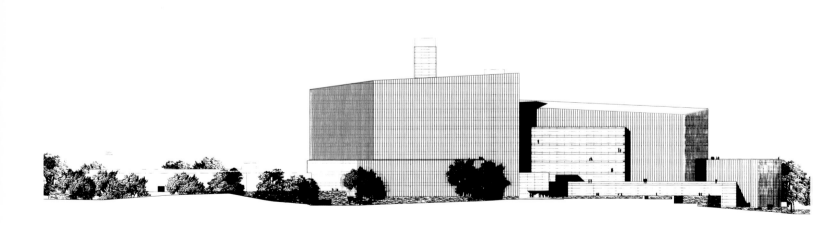

Section looking north

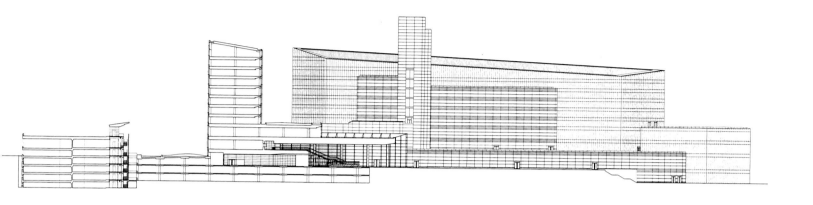

Section looking west

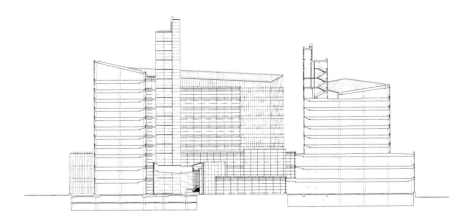

200 ft

30 Hill Street

Singapore
1997-2001

The 30 Hill Street office building is situated in the cultural district of Singapore, on a site previously occupied by the United States Embassy. The design was conceived as a response to two major factors: the immediate urban context and the desire to preserve open views while protecting the interiors from the intensity of the equatorial sun.

To the south, the building faces the lush garden of a nineteenth-century Armenian Orthodox church. An expansive glass façade opens towards the garden and serves as a clean backdrop against which the white stucco details of the church silhouette can be appreciated. In contrast, the east, west, and north facades respond to urban streetscapes—including the historical shop-house facades on the north side—with opaque materials such as aluminum and Jerusalem limestone.

In order to protect the building from the low sun angles of the east and west, deep vertical fins are employed as brise-soleils. On the north and south facades, high-performance glass and blind systems limit the penetration of vertical sunlight. Thus, the composition of the building as a series of planes running east to west supports not only an appropriate urban response, but also an effective environmental strategy.

Upper level plan

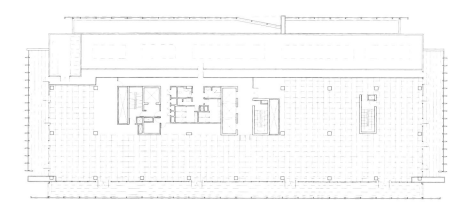

Typical floor plan

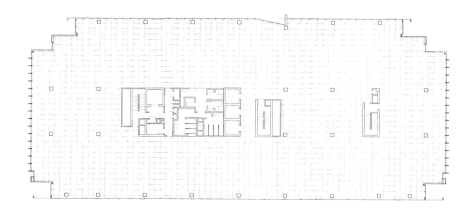

Ground floor plan

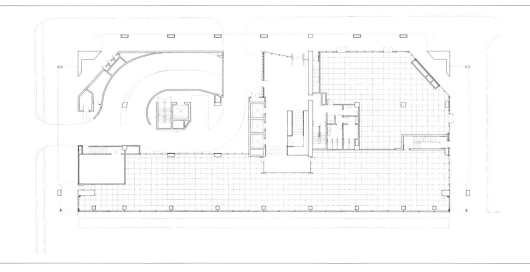

Section looking west

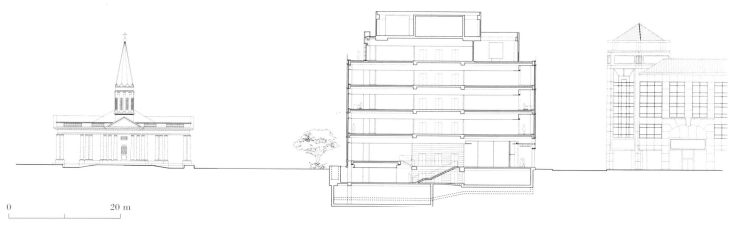

0   20 m

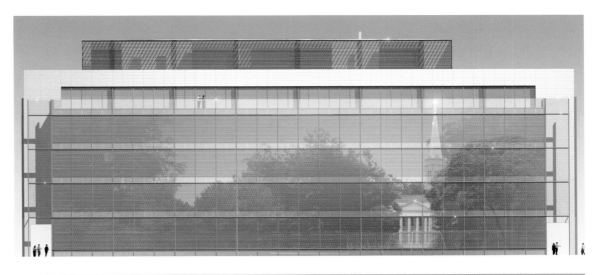

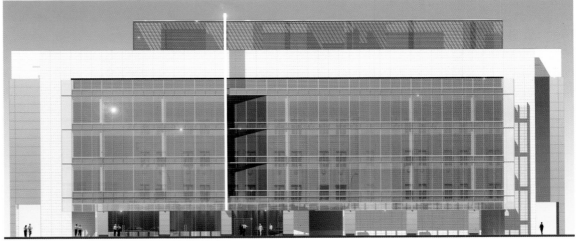

US Airways International Terminal One Philadelphia International Airport

Philadelphia, Pennsylvania
1997-2002

US Airways' International Terminal One is part of a phased expansion of the Philadelphia Airport System, initiated in response to increased passenger traffic. The facility consists of a four-level terminal with 13 new international gates. Situated on the western edge of the runway, the building is linked to six existing terminals arranged to one side of a roadway.

The project brief mandated a design that satisfies the operational and spatial requirements of a modern terminal facility, but the siting posed a particular challenge. Hemmed in to the north by the service road, the site area was originally conceived as a narrow rectangular band. This airside provision was ultimately insufficient, and to accommodate the demands of a complex program, Kohn Pedersen Fox proposed stretching the mass of Terminal One 190 feet (58 meters) over the roadway.

The novelty of this scheme is revealed in section. The approach to the terminal is defined by a large truss suspended 38 feet (11.6 meters) over the access road. All arrival functions—including baggage claim, a skylit arrivals hall, and the Federal Inspection Service (FIS)—are located on this level, one floor above the departure hall. This layout reverses the sectional sequence between arrival and departure, a transformation essential for a terminal conceived as an international gateway. Distinct from traditional air transport facilities, which feature sunlit departure areas but afford deplaning passengers less than memorable amenities, arrival areas here are given equal architectural significance.

The quality of the space underneath the span is key to the design solution. The soffit acts as a weather-protected drop-off zone for departing travelers. Passengers enter the building through revolving doors along a clear glass curtain wall, and proceed to a double-height lobby with ticketing counters along the south wall. This concourse opens up to the arrivals level above, allowing daylight into the hall from the south and uniting the principal components of the program into an integrated composition of light, transparent spaces.

Three roof types organize the spaces within the terminal. The lower shed roof slopes south toward the airfield; a higher roof is formed by a subtle curve upward toward the center of the building, bowing north. The lower roof form contains thirteen gate lounges along the south and west walls. A secure corridor runs parallel between the gates and the glass partition overlooking the ticket hall below. It was crucial to distinguish from one another the open, public concourse, the more enclosed security areas, and the intimate lounges at the gates. The interior and exterior of the new FIS facility are organized around an articulated saw-toothed roof. North-facing vertical clerestories span between the expressed metal-clad trusses, receiving uniform sunlight during the day, and illuminated from within at night.

WEST-BOUND I-95
EAST BOUND I-95

(291)

ARRIVALS

Second floor plan

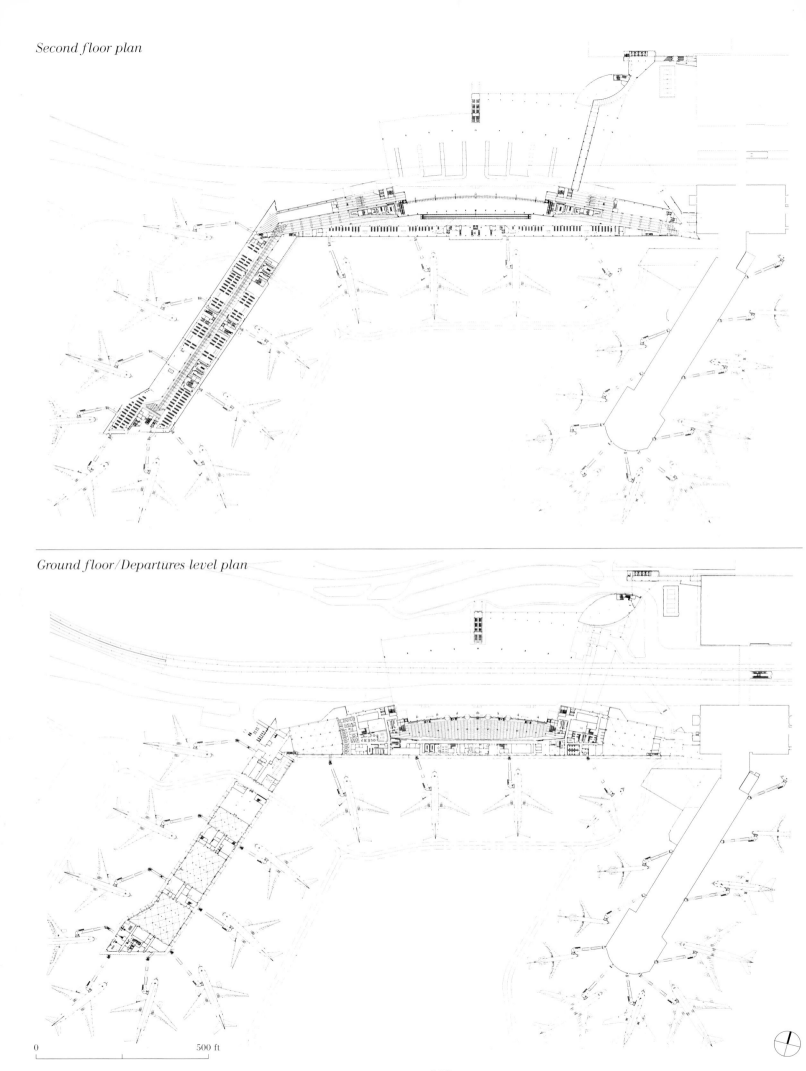

Ground floor/Departures level plan

0   500 ft

Third floor/Arrival level plan

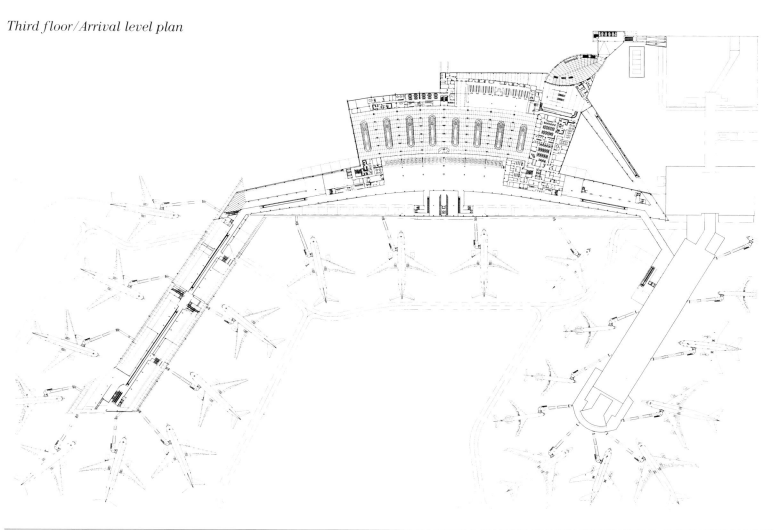

Roof plan

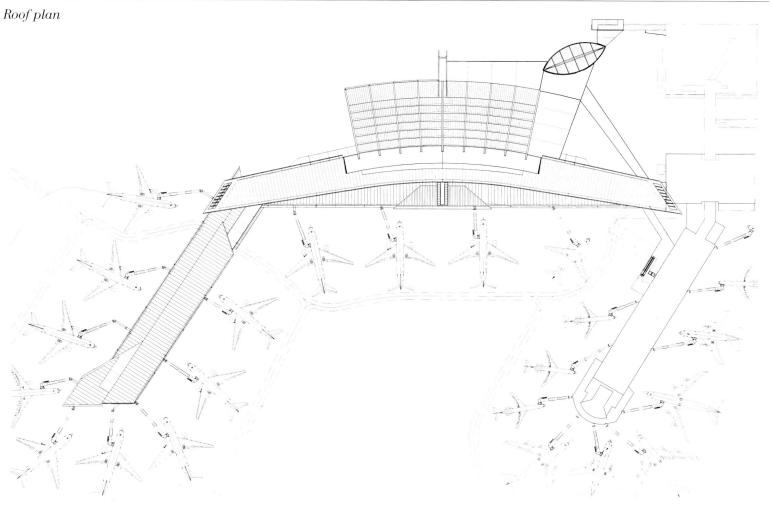

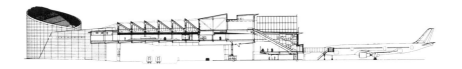

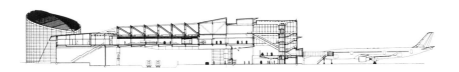

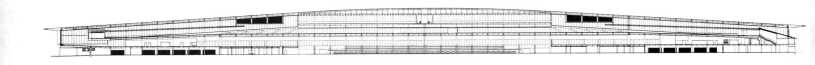

344

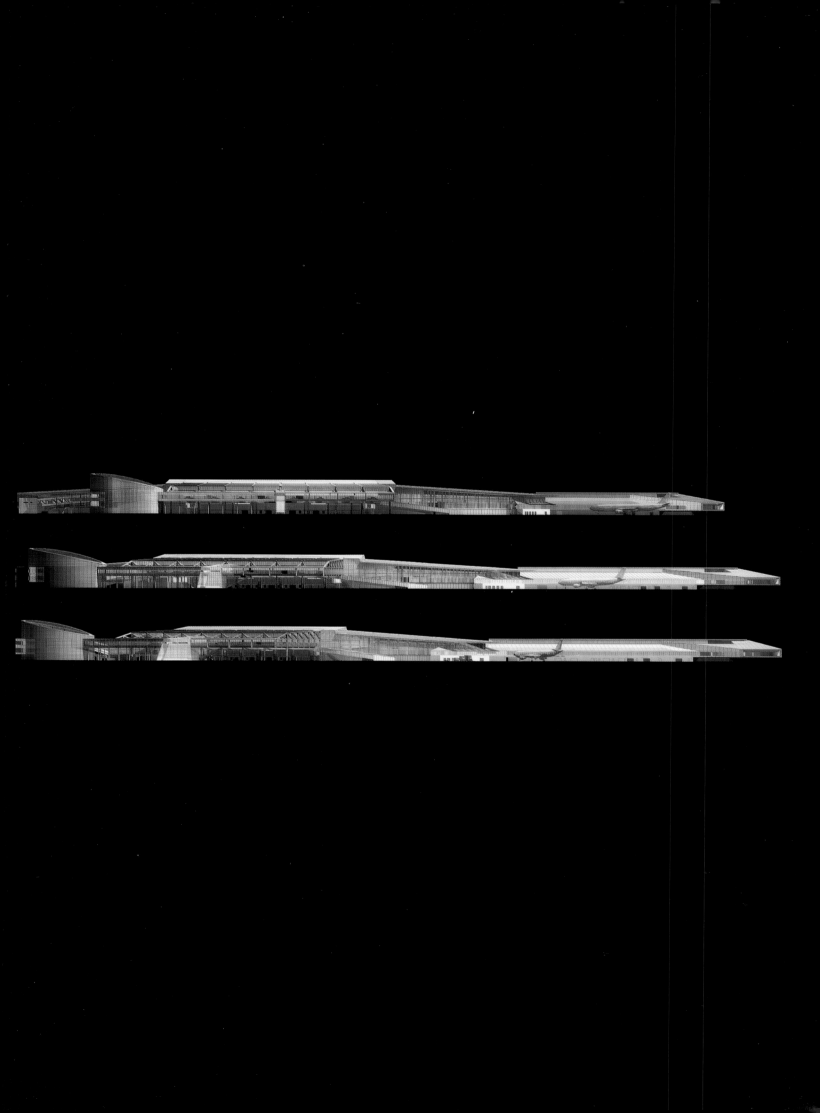

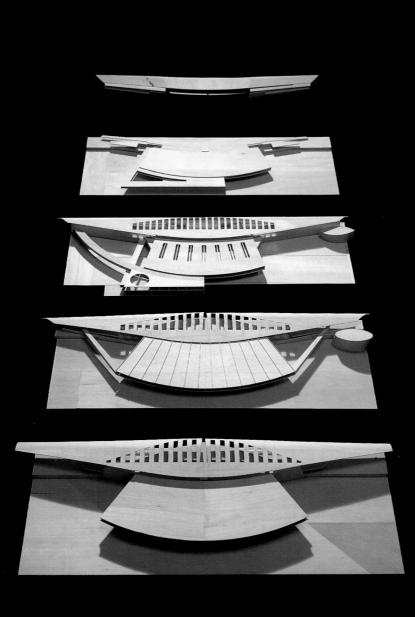

Engineering Centers Building
University of Wisconsin

Madison, Wisconsin
1997-2002

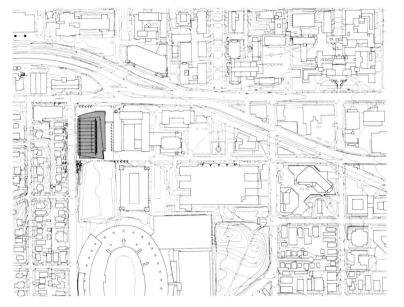

Located on the Madison campus of the University of Wisconsin, this project uses the building as a pedagogical tool. The program is defined as a series of student and research centers, intended to bridge disciplines and foster a new approach to learning and discovery. In addition to student workshops, group activity areas, meeting rooms and office space, the building provides large flexible engineering laboratories supported by a modular utility infrastructure.

The site, at the northwest corner of the engineering campus, serves as a transition between the institutional scale of the college and the residential neighborhood to the west. It slopes down to the east, where it terminates a pedestrian mall linking college facilities. Three principal gestures generate the design approach. First, a three-story skylit interior street opens up the center of the building. It gives access to all major program elements, brings daylight to interior spaces, and displays a translucent 'technology wall' which reveals the building's engineering systems—mechanical, structural, electrical, telecommunications and vertical transportation. It also opens into a student workshop area, where design projects, such as solar-powered cars, can be exhibited.

Second, to minimize the bulk of the building and reduce its scale toward the residential edge, the roof is treated as a sweeping metal curve enclosing the mechanical penthouse and forming the ceiling of the interior street, which emerges at the southeast corner to terminate the pedestrian mall. Finally, the north elevation curves to link the building to the existing campus facades while pulling back to reveal the First Congregational Church at the corner.

On the exterior, the facades are layered to reveal the means of construction. Brick is detailed as a non-load bearing screen wall cast integrally into precast concrete panels. By using materials sympathetic to local context, and detailing them to express the technology of construction, the building respects its environment while communicating the sense of innovation essential to one of the country's foremost engineering programs.

North elevation

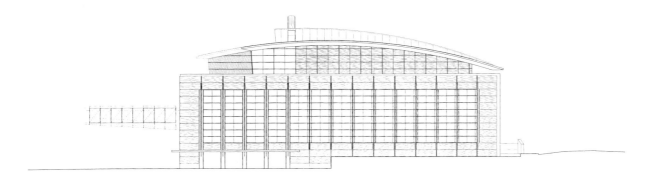

East elevation

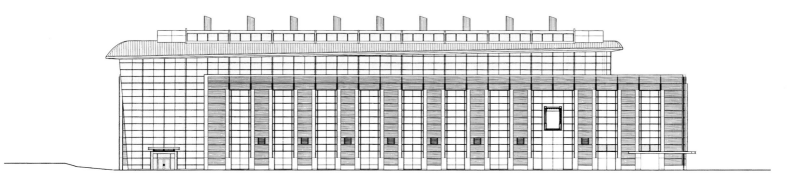

South elevation

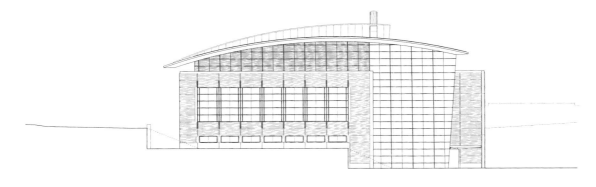

West elevation

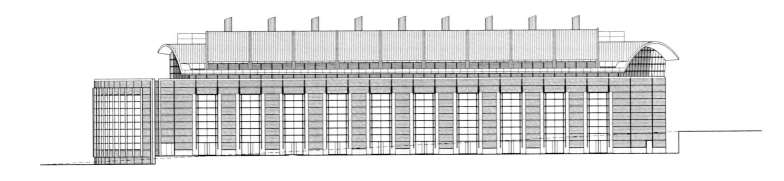

0   100 ft

Second floor plan

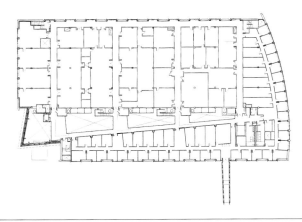

Mezzanine plan

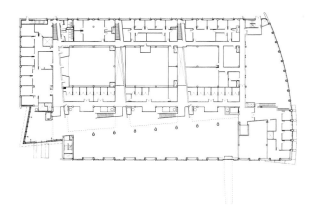

Ground floor plan

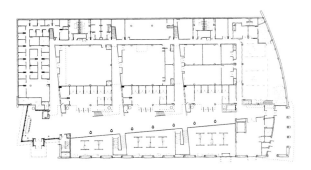

Basement plan

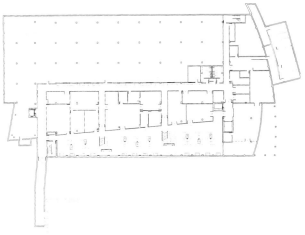

0   100 ft

Section looking west

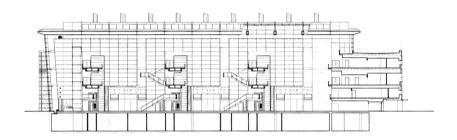

Section looking north

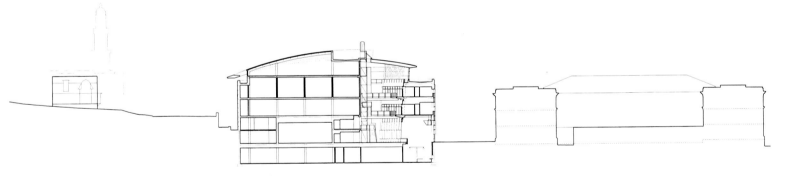

0   100 ft

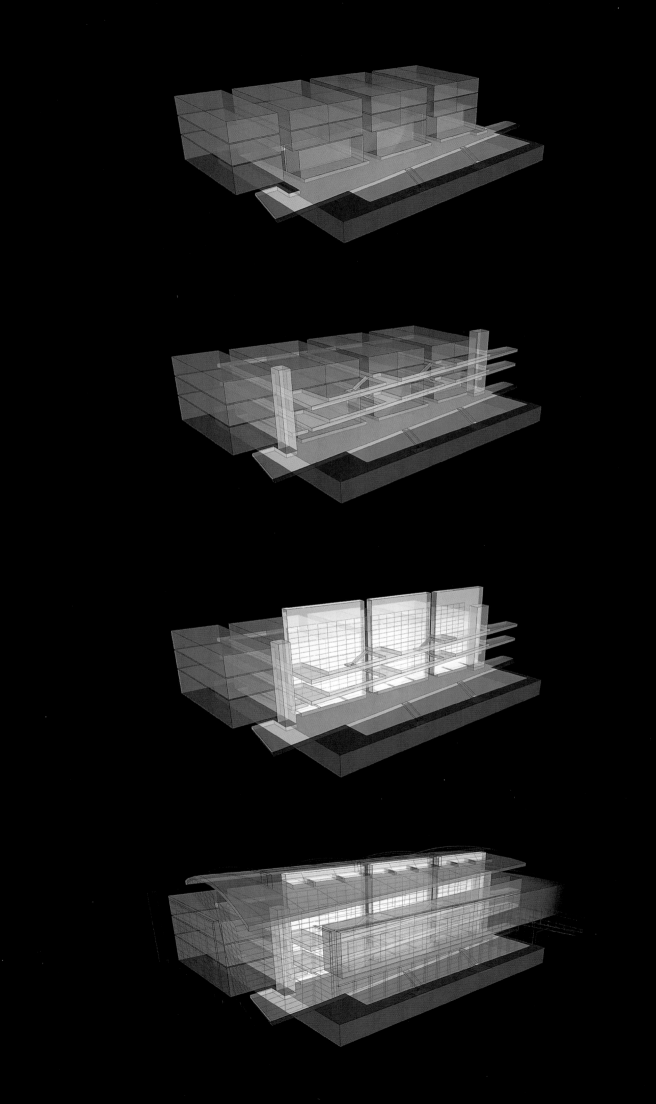

Espirito Santo Plaza

Miami, Florida
1997-2002

The new headquarters for the Espirito Santo Bank on Miami's Brickell Avenue addresses a highly varied urban context and provides a new public space while integrating the Bank's offices and a major hotel into a single memorable landmark.

The 37-story tower has as its neighbors on Brickell Avenue a series of late twentieth-century buildings unrelated in scale and style: immediately to the north is the 27-story Union Planters' Bank building, with sheer glazed facades, while to the south stands a fourteen-story block clad in a mix of glass and masonry.

The building makes a strong urban statement to the street; its concave western facade embraces a new paved and landscaped forecourt with a reflecting pool, and forms a rhetorical arch, rising 30 stories, which gives the development the character of a gateway and landmark. On the eastern flank of the tower, the ten-story hotel atrium, which rises from the 25th floor level is clearly expressed—there are spectacular views out to the ocean.

The plan of the building focuses on the need for a clear route through from Brickell Avenue to the parking areas on the rear (east facing) side of the site; the route from the latter is via a garden walk lined with retail units serving office workers and the public. Parking is concentrated in an eleven-story building accommodating one thousand cars, with additional berths for service trucks. The roof of the garage has been generously landscaped and used as the location for a health club with swimming pool and tennis courts—these facilities can be accessed by hotel guests via a dedicated link bridge from the hotel elevators.

Striking in its formal imagery, the tower provides a model for mixed-use, high-rise development in which new public amenities are integrated into a broadly commercial agenda.

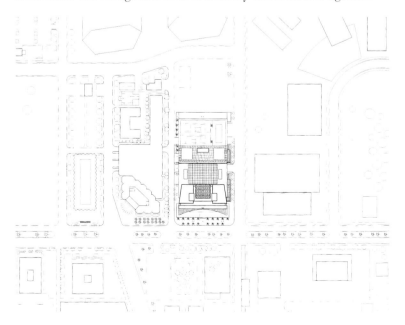

Second floor plan

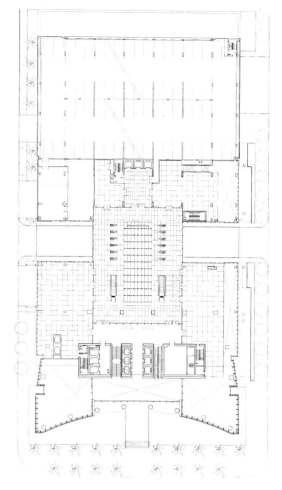

Typical condominium floor plan

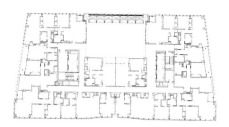

Hotel/Skylobby floor plan

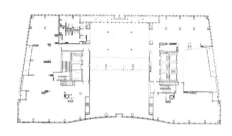

Ground floor plan

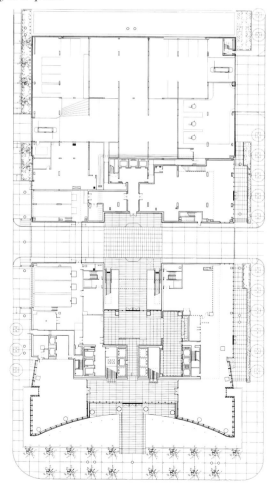

Typical hotel floor plan

Typical office floor plan

0   100 ft

361

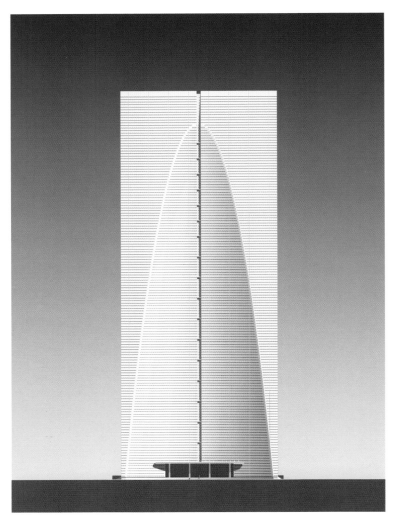

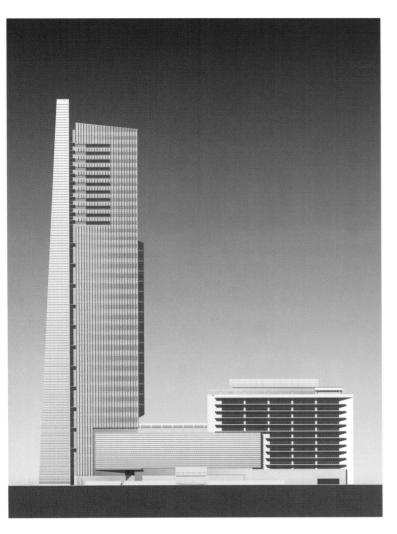

Section looking north

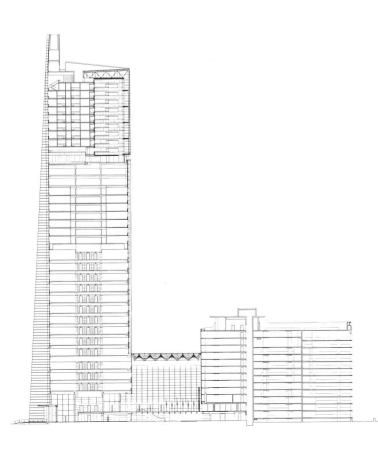

5 Times Square

New York, New York
1997-2001

Located at the core of Times Square, this 38-story tower combines prime office space with a base of retail enterprises. The location of the building on 42nd Street required that the retail areas be lively and engaging at the pedestrian level and that the tower focus on the intersection of 42nd Street and Seventh Avenue. The primary office entry occurs mid-block on Seventh Avenue; subway entrances are located at 42nd and 41st Streets. The historic New Amsterdam Theater is situated immediately to the west of the site.

The faceted, asymmetrical form of the building responds to the dynamic street grid of the Times Square crossing of Seventh Avenue and Broadway. The planar moves and setbacks of the facades address the neighboring structures. The exterior cladding uses two types of pewter-tinted reflective glass and bright silver horizontal mullions; the aim is to catch and reflect streetscape, light and sky. Further development of the facade elements, particularly overlays aimed at breaking up the scale of the major planes, were developed in response to requirements of the 42nd Street Development Project, the state agency charged with 're-visioning' the Street.

Consistent with the mandated guidelines, commercial signs jostle for position on the first three stories, rising to the seventh at the primary corner. Articulated structural elements at the east and west facades, and lighting elements at the north and south facades and at the cornice support the complexity of building elements.

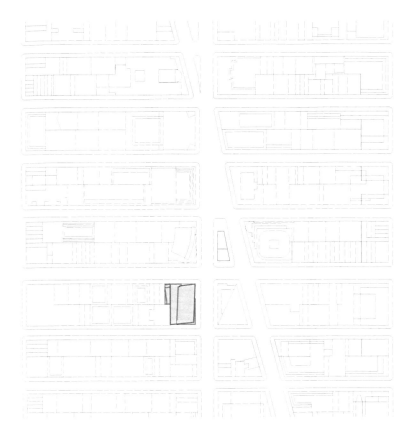

East elevation

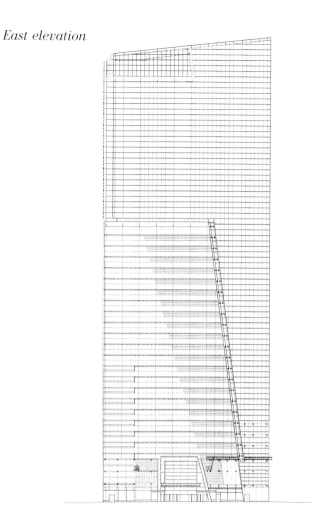

North elevation

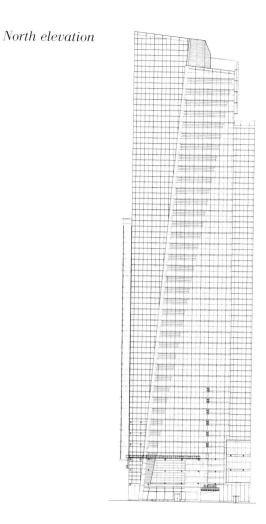

West elevation

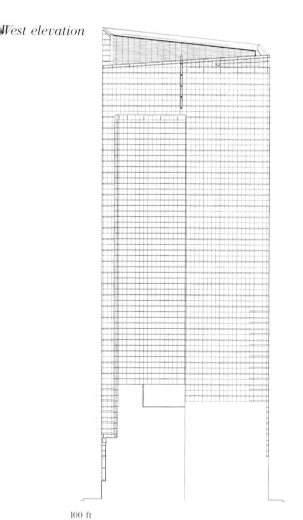

South elevation

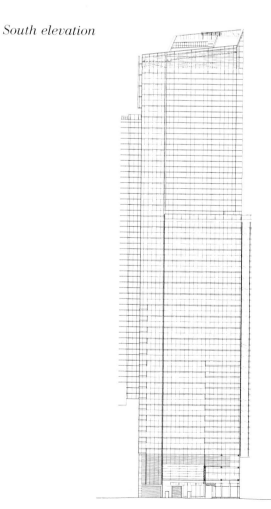

100 ft

Typical mid-rise floor plan

Typical high-rise floor plan

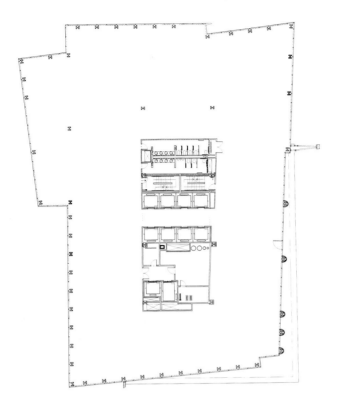

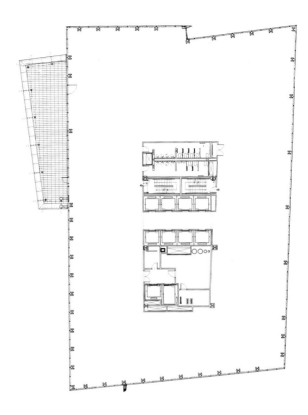

Ground floor plan

Typical low-rise floor plan

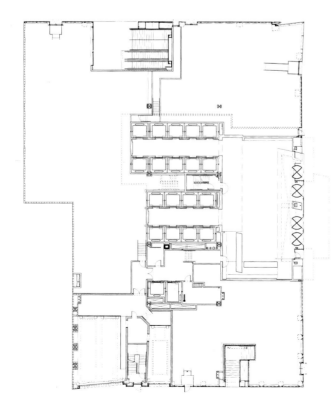

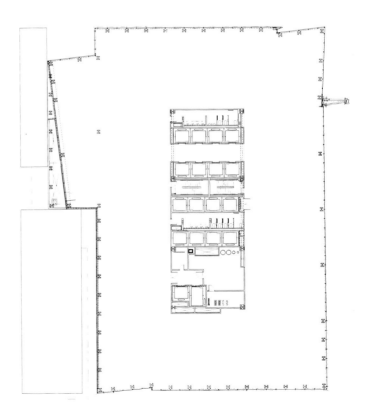

0   50 ft

The Sloan School of Management Massachusetts Institute of Technology

Boston, Massachusetts
1997

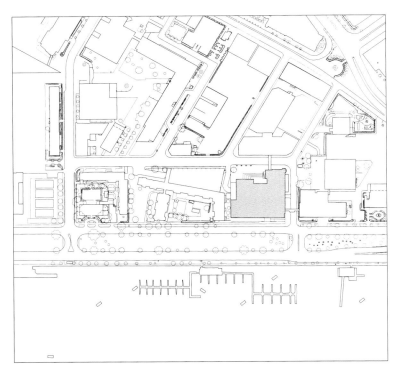

In 1997, Kohn Pedersen Fox participated in a limited design competition for a major addition to the Sloan School of Management at the Massachusetts Institute of Technology. The proposed building consists of 127,000 square feet (11,800 square meters) of new construction adjoining the Tang Center and linked to the Sloan Building on Memorial Avenue by a pedestrian walkway.

Located between Amherst Street and Memorial Drive, the site affords the building two principal elevations: a public facade visible from across the river during the day and night, and an internal, less formal facade on Amherst Street. Other urban gestures expressed in the scheme include the definition of a pedestrian connection to buildings east of the campus; a forecourt in front of the building entry on Amherst Street, and a massing that unifies existing structures and the new building visually as well as functionally.

The brief specified the creation of spaces that could integrate cross-disciplinary activities, and promote a sense of community. The primary building organization revolves around a central gathering space between the Tang Center and the new wings to the south and west of the site. The bulk of the classrooms and student activity areas are located off the main entrance plaza; faculty offices are located along the south façade. A five-story glass atrium stretches the length of the river facade. This "deck" facing the Charles River provides a vertical connection, linking faculty on multiple floors. A split-level scheme blurs the vertical separation between floors, encouraging interaction.

This design incorporates state-of-the-art technology, in the building systems as well as within the classrooms and interior spaces. The vertical atrium space created at the south facade employs a system of natural ventilation that reduces energy usage, with louvers bringing in air at the lower level, and exhausting it out at the top of the building. A further layer of surface articulation is formed within the space as a series of louvered pivot doors opens onto the atrium, modulating light and privacy in the offices.

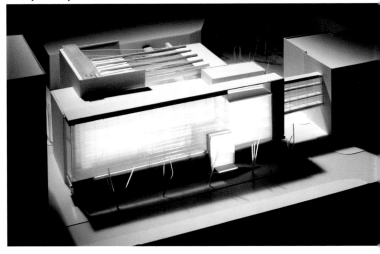

Elevation

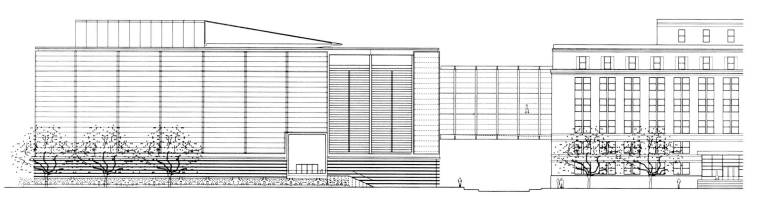

Ground floor plan

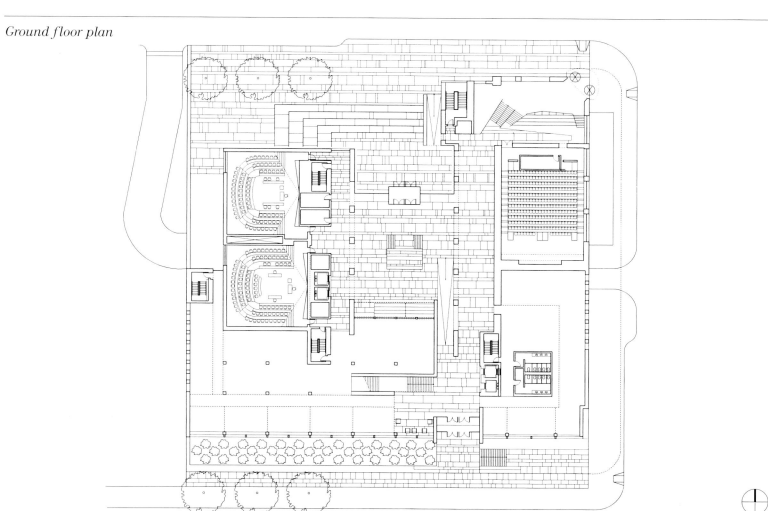

Section looking west

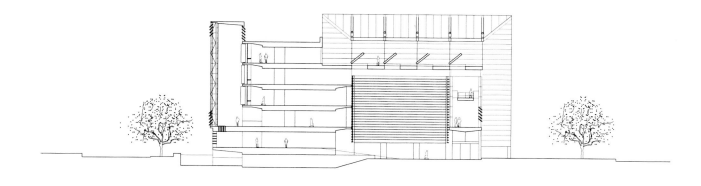

50 ft

Children's Hospital of Philadelphia Facade Remediation and Expansion

Philadelphia, Pennsylvania
1997-2002

Erected in 1974, the present exterior of the Children's Hospital of Philadelphia, on the corner of 34th street and Civic Center Boulevard, has had a myriad of technical problems that have not been successfully resolved. The firm's involvement started in 1998 with a conceptual design study for the replacement of the facade and a facility master plan for future expansion. The current scheme incorporates the facade remediation project and the phased construction of two entirely new buildings linked to the main wing. The design intent was to mitigate the problems of the existing building envelope and to transform the hospital into a campus of allied elements; strengthening its image as a major civic institution in the city of Philadelphia, and as one of the top children's hospitals in the United States.

Facade remediation generally involves the removal and the replacement of the glass and metal panels that comprise the existing building's envelope. The most difficult aspect of the project was the requirement that the re-cladding process not interrupt hospital operations. The solution proposed a transparent glass curtain suspended twenty feet in front of the patient rooms. The existing enclosure remains behind a decorative screen of illuminated glass fins.

The addition of 300,000 square feet (28,000 square meters) of new construction on the west and south sides of the existing building maximizes the zoning potential. Creating space for 150 more patient beds and a new emergency and treatment facility, the new wings join inpatient and outpatient functions in the adjacent building. In reconfiguring the site, an entry sequence is clearly defined, with logical access from surrounding city streets; parking access is also clarified, and emergency traffic is separated from other traffic flow.

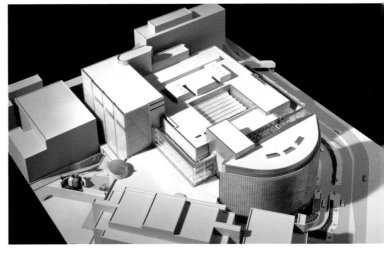

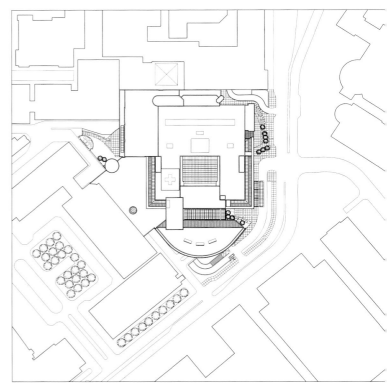

Section through sleeve

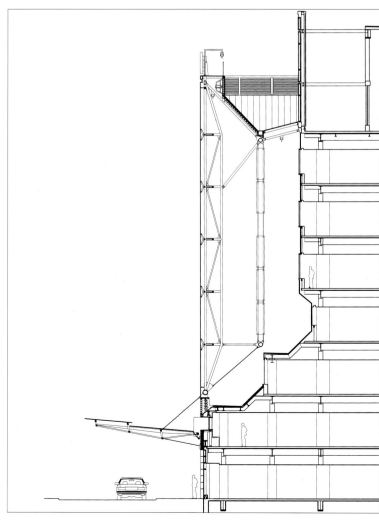

*Sectional diagram
through atrium*

Four First Union

Charlotte, North Carolina
1998-2000

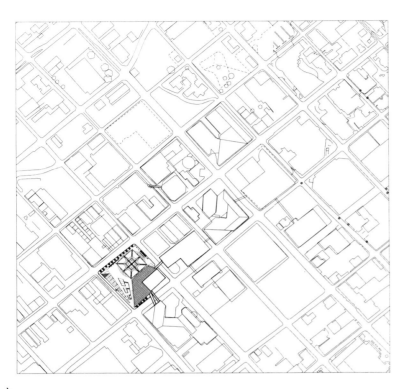

This 84-story skyscraper is the focal point of a corporate headquarters complex occupying a full-block site in downtown Charlotte. Bound by East Third Street, South College Street, East Second Street and South Tryon Street, the 1,250-foot (381-meter) tall tower stands in the northwest corner of the block with a plaza and public atrium space to the southwest. The existing Two First Union tower defines the eastern edge of the block and is connected to the tower through the atrium space.

Square in plan and curved in section, the largest floor plates for the tower are found in the middle of the building. The upper levels, which are half as large in area as the middle office floors, contain the executive floors. The top 300 feet of the tower is a public observation deck and mechanical penthouse enclosed in a stainless steel spire. The facades are articulated with a serrated curtain wall. Clear and taut, the glass and metal curtain wall cascades down the curve of the tower.

The structural concept for the building is a tube within a tube. Four "super columns" in the corners carry the outer load, while a braced core is found in the center. The two systems are tied together at the mechanical floors. With fanned columns 85 feet (26 meters) tall, the tower loads are transferred to the corners, freeing the entry of columns.

2nd floor plan

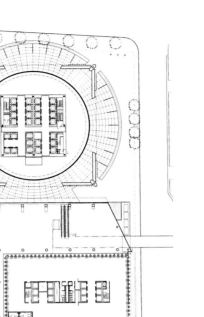

Roof plan
Observation deck
Executive floor plan
Mid-rise floor plan
Low-rise floor plan

Ground floor plan

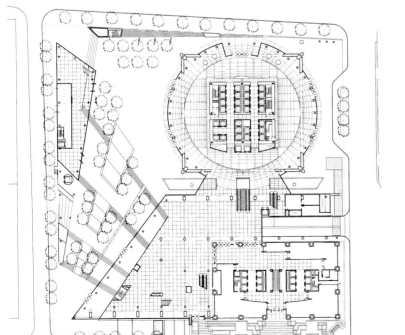

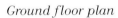

0   100 ft

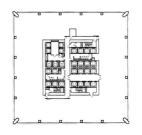

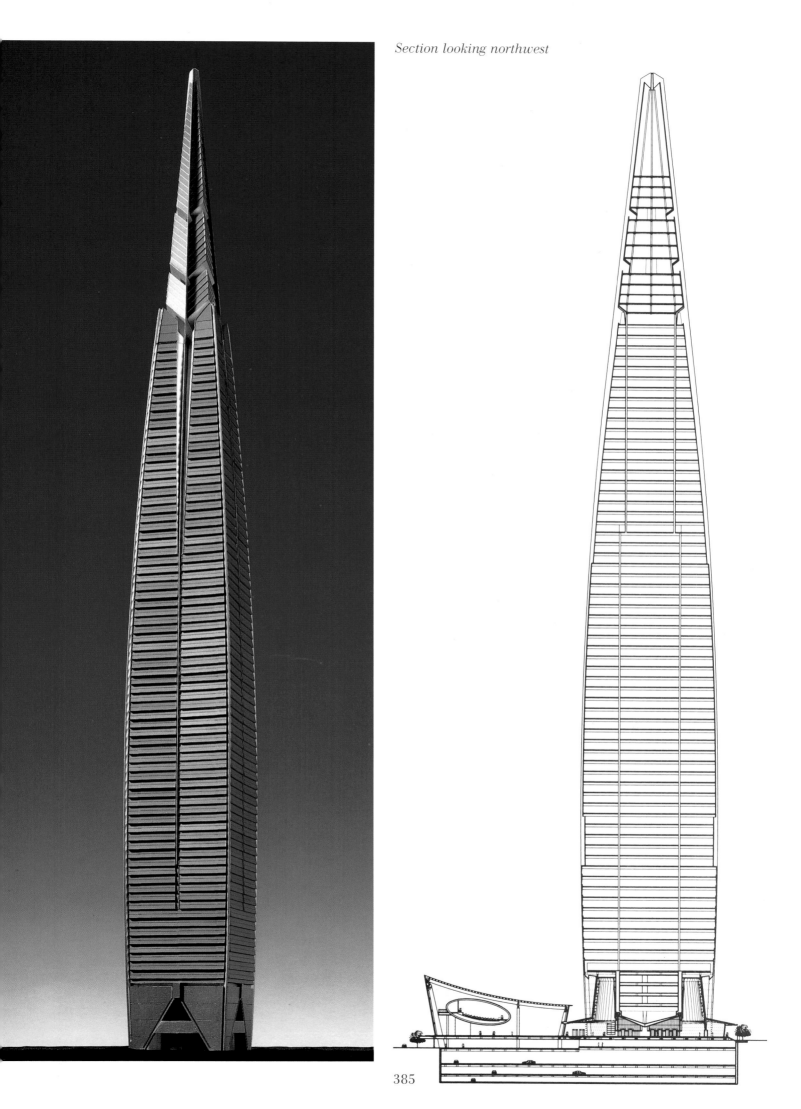

385

Mid City Place

London, England
1998-2002

Mid City Place was designed, to a strict budget, as a speculative office development. The 376,700-square foot (35,000-square meter) building was conceived as a highly flexible space, adaptable to the requirements of a wide range of potential occupiers. It also addressed the perceived problem of high construction costs in the UK market.

The site is located on High Holborn, an historic east-west route connecting the City of London with the West End and linked to Cheapside to the east and Oxford Street to the west. Over the last two centuries this route has been characterized by the development of a series of commercial *palazzi*—for example, Alfred Waterhouse's monumental Prudential Assurance, a landmark of the Gothic Revival, and the recent Holborn Circus development by Norman Foster. The Mid City Place site was formerly occupied by a sixteen-story 1950s office slab, demolished some years ago.

In contrast to its predecessor (which was prefaced by an open plaza) Mid City Place occupies the entire site, with a maximum height of ten stories. On High Holborn, the lower section of the building is designed to accord with the prevailing pattern of development along the north side of the street. Behind, a dramatic curved roof caps the main volume of the development—a bold compositional device that acts as a marker for the scheme.

The U-shaped floor plates, with elevators and services concentrated in a core adjacent to the central atrium, are designed with adaptability in mind. The aesthetic of the building is predominantly that of the metal and glass curtain wall, but with masonry applied at lower levels to ground it to the street.

Mid City Place balances commercial imperatives with a commitment to quality of construction and detail, resulting in a dignified, contemporary addition to central London.

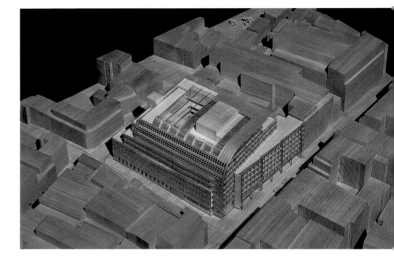

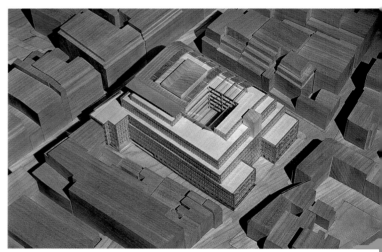

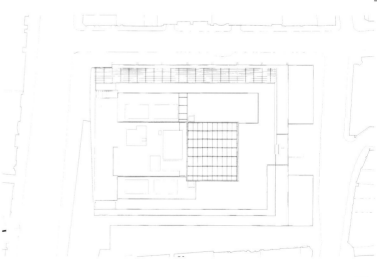

Typical floor plan

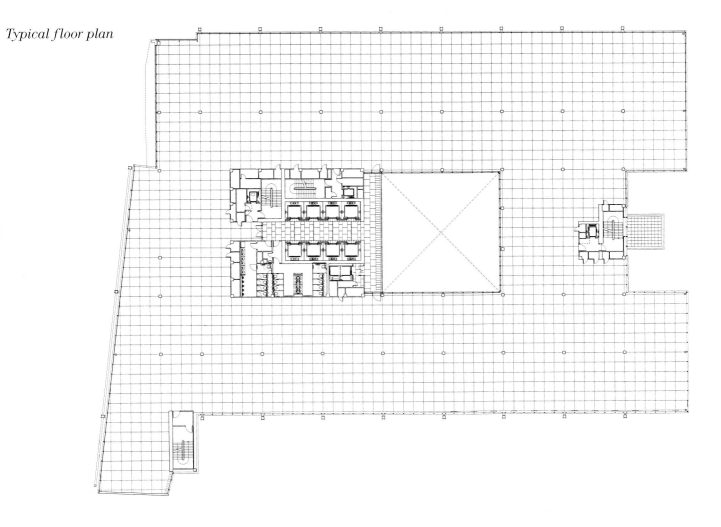

Ground floor plan

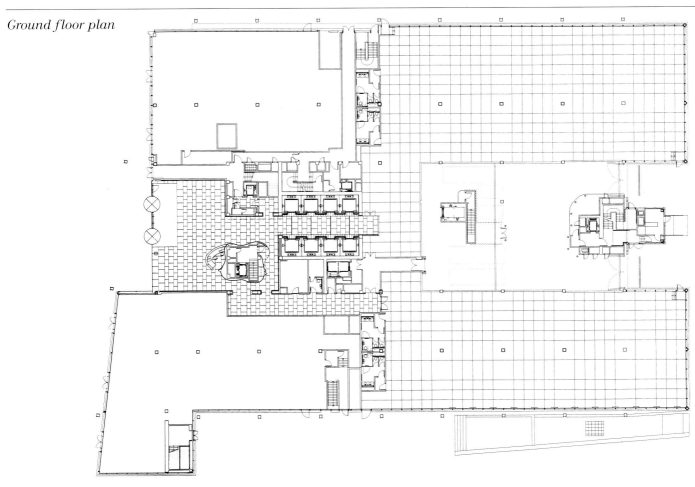

0   20 m

North elevation

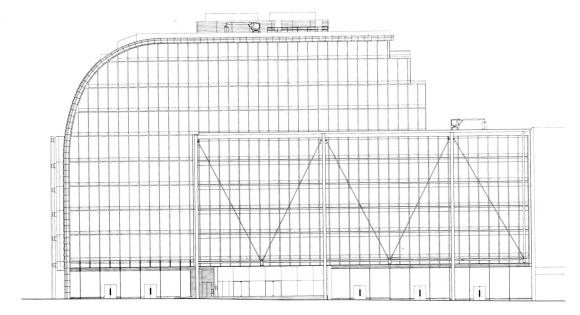

East elevation

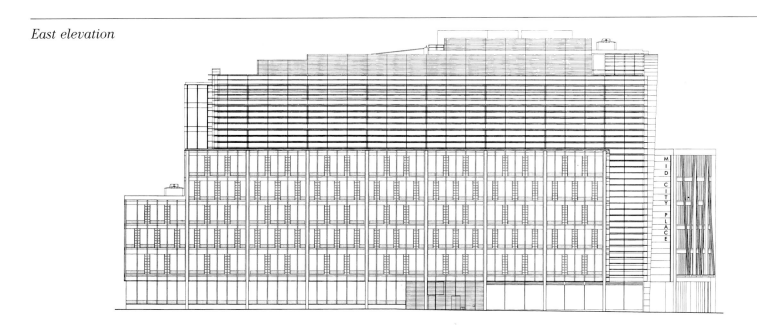

Section looking east

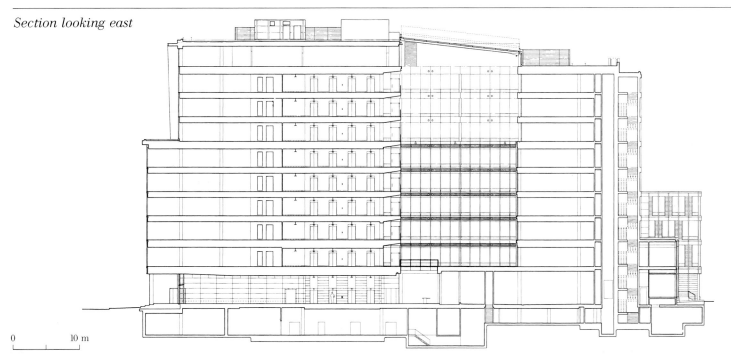

0   10 m

Chater House

Hong Kong SAR
1996-2002

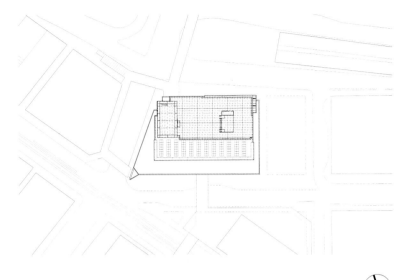

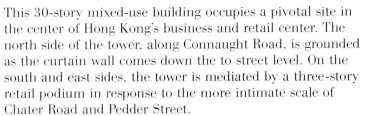

This 30-story mixed-use building occupies a pivotal site in the center of Hong Kong's business and retail center. The north side of the tower, along Connaught Road, is grounded as the curtain wall comes down the to street level. On the south and east sides, the tower is mediated by a three-story retail podium in response to the more intimate scale of Chater Road and Pedder Street.

Housing 23 floors of office space, the tower massing is driven by leasing depths for financial tenants. The office entrance on Pedder Street and Connaught Road allows for the strong vertical gesture on the corner, where the curtain wall is modified to articulate a three-story light box above the office entrance. A semi-transparent vertical mass by day, the corner structure transforms into an urban lantern by night. In contrast, the body of the tower is clad in a reflective glass curtain wall. The graphic patterning of the mullions creates a reading of layered grids. The layering of silver, white and gray mullions creates a sense of depth within a relatively flat wall.

The three-story retail podium houses fashion and lifestyle brands and is linked to adjacent properties by way of four pedestrian bridges. The bridges link to the north to Central Station and the Airport Express line. Pedestrian traffic is expected to reach 6,000 people per hour through the bridge network, creating an elevated pedestrian ground plane and an interior shopping street. The exterior podium elevations consist of stone plaques applied to a taut glass curtain wall. Large display windows provide opportunities for the display of supergraphics. The composition of several stone plaques allow different tenants a level of customization within the framework of a single building facade.

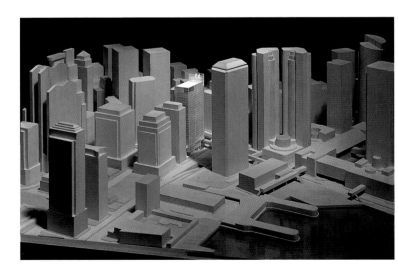

Typical floor plan

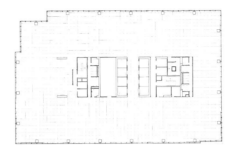

Second floor plan

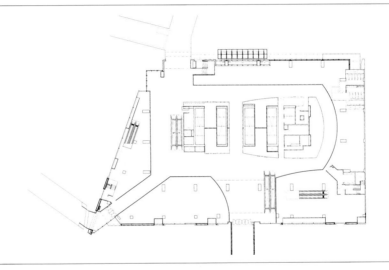

Ground floor plan

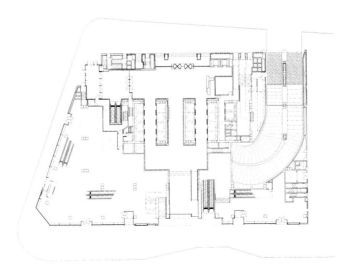

0   20 m

110 Bishopsgate

London, England
1999-2005

The Bishopsgate project is designed for a site on the eastern edge of the historic City, close to the busy Liverpool Street rail terminus. The scheme replaces several nondescript 1970s office buildings and forms part of a cluster of high buildings in this quarter of London.

The 42-story tower addresses London's clearly identified need for modern office space and is designed for multi-tenanted occupation, providing space for international companies of variable size and widely varying operational needs. Flexibility and a high degree of user choice were clear objectives in the scheme. The building is an efficient envelope within which corporate tenants can choose from more than one services option—chilled beams, for example, could be connected to the central cooled water circuit or more conventional air conditioning installed.

The environmental agenda of the building is expressed in its elevations and sections. To the south, the concentration of double-deck elevators, stairs and services provides a baffle against the sun but equally ensures that working spaces are unobstructed, with maximum flexibility. The east and west elevations are designed as double-thickness, ventilated facades. The building opens up to the north—from Bishopsgate, it is legible as a series of office "villages" grouped around vertically stacked atria. The use of clear glass ensures a high degree of transparency—the dynamism of the interior is apparent from the street—as well as daylit working spaces.

One of the most significant features of the project is its contribution to the public realm. The closure of an existing street provides room for a new piazza that focuses on the Georgian church of St. Botolph. The lower floors of the building are dedicated to retail and restaurant use, creating the first truly public lobby space in London —where lobbies are generally barred to all but building users. A public restaurant with its own dedicated elevator tops the building, offering panoramic views of London.

Typical office floor plan

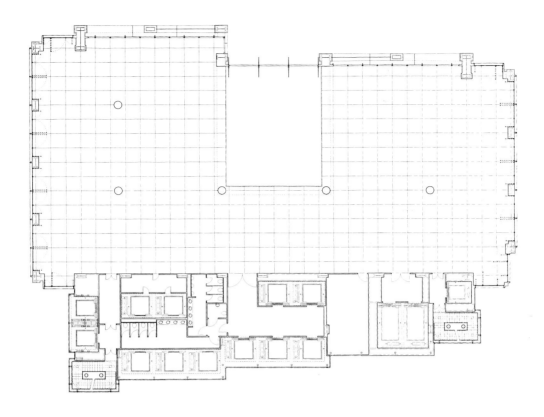

Typical trading floor plan

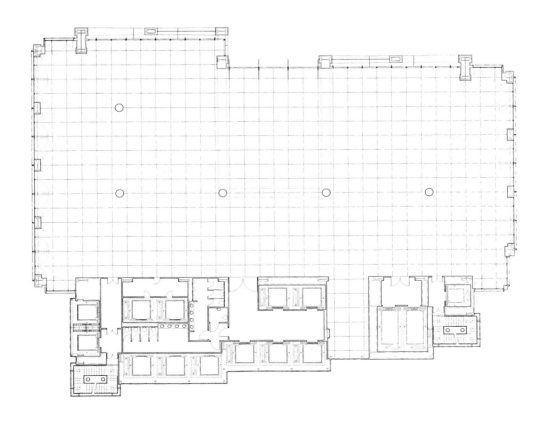

0   20 m

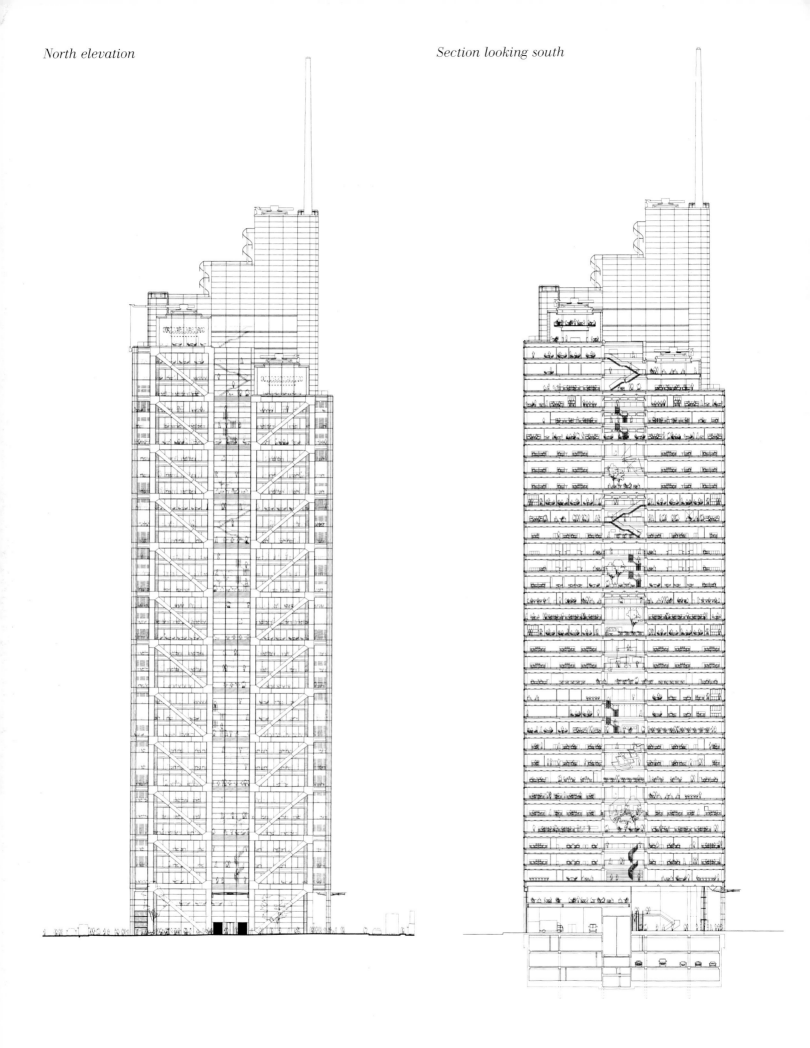

0   50 m

Heron Quay Site 5, Canary Wharf

London, England
1999-2003

This 33-story headquarters tower for the international law firm Clifford Chance commands a central position at Heron Quay, the second phase of development at Canary Wharf. The project overlooks Jubilee Park to the west and the south docks to the east and south. A six-story low-rise podium is linked to the tower by a five-story atrium facing the park. The glass and anodized aluminum curtain wall provides floor-to-ceiling views of the park, the buildings of Canary Wharf, the river Thames and the London skyline.

The building is fully attuned to the program and technology demands of an international law firm headquarters. The complex includes below-grade parking, a ground floor auditorium, two floors of conference rooms, a cafeteria and dining area, a fitness center with a skylit swimming pool overlooking the water, and a roof terrace with a tented outdoor reception space. A number of public amenities connect the office facilty to the Canary Wharf neighborhood, including a waterfront promenade with retail space, an underground shopping mall, and a link to the Jubilee Line.

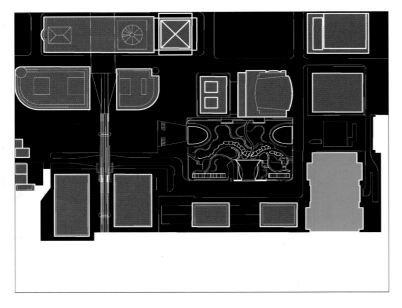

Typical floor plan

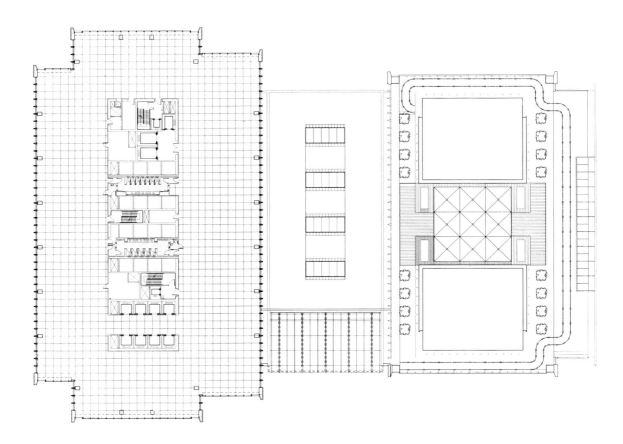

Ground floor plan

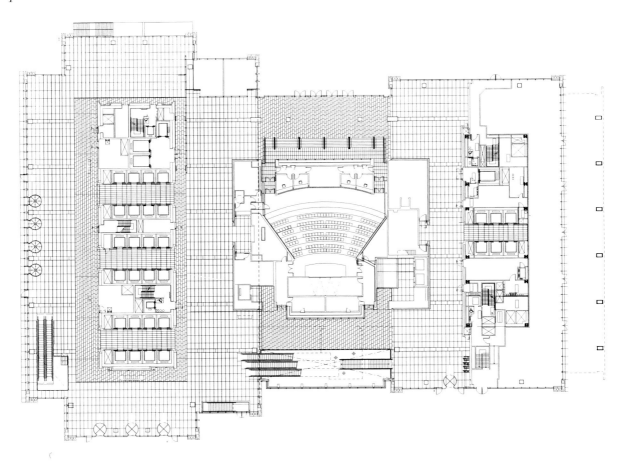

0   20 m

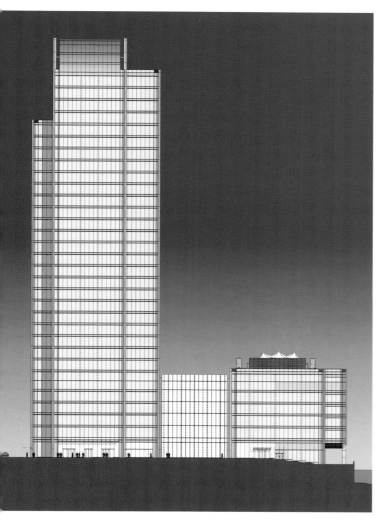

Section looking east

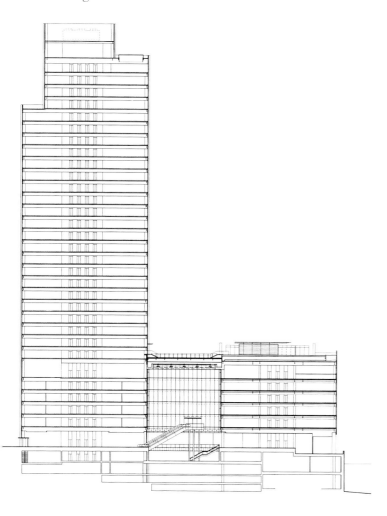

Institute for International Economics

Washington, D.C.
1999-2002

The new headquarters building for the Institute for International Economics occupies a prominent site on Massachusetts Avenue just off of Dupont Circle. Located on a block protected by a historic preservation board, this four-story facility provides office space, research facilities, and a 250-person conference center for an influential think tank specializing in research on international trade and monetary policy.

Devised as a modern *palazzo*, the building consists of two volumes, one containing the service core, and another larger volume housing the workspace. The office volume—whose façade is similar in proportion to that of the adjacent Clarence Moore House (now the Embassy of Uzbekistan)—cantilevers over a stainless steel and glass entrance canopy. The canopy itself is intricately detailed, in keeping with the elaborate ornamental metal canopies prevalent on Massachusetts Avenue's older Beaux Arts buildings. Both the core volume and the office volume are clad in a stainless steel and glass curtain wall, the relative lightness of which is balanced by the use of Jerusalem limestone at the base of the building. These heavier elements establish a relationship between the new structure and the historic masonry of the surrounding neighborhood.

The ground floor is devoted to a conference center and a terraced sculpture garden, which can open into each other by means of operable walls. The three-story box above houses the workings of the Institute. Within this area, the diversity of materials and architectural configurations of the project strive to express a balance between the openness of a community in search of knowledge, and the contemplative privacy of a monkish cell. Fifty offices and workstations are oriented in a U-shaped formation around a skylit atrium, at the center of which are a terraced reading room and a triple-height staff lounge. Extending from the second floor to the skylight is an information wall containing bookcases and storage units, as well as several display areas for works of art.

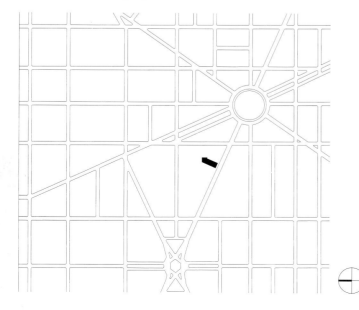

Fourth floor plan

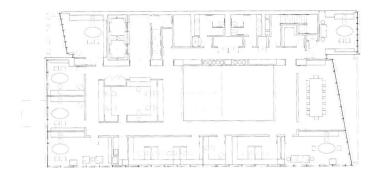

Second floor plan

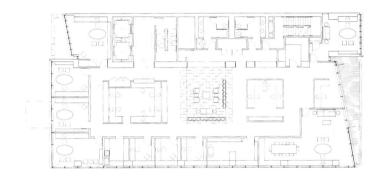

Ground floor plan

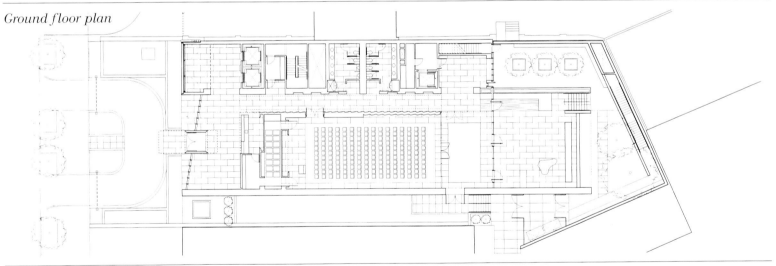

Section looking east

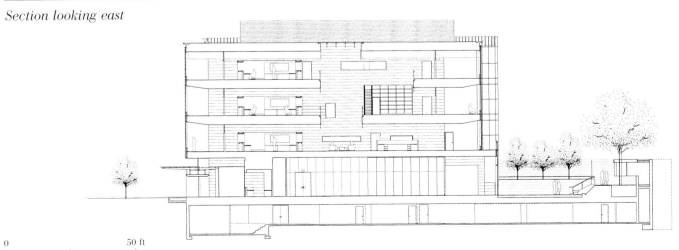

0   50 ft

River City Prague

Prague, The Czech Republic
2000-2004

Prague, one of the great historic cities of Europe, is now developing as a dynamic business center. The River City project responds to the identity of the city while reflecting the need for regeneration in Prague's increasingly rundown industrial fringe.

The site is east of the old core, close to the river Vltava, and within walking distance of the city center. Though developed from the eighteenth century onwards as a residential suburb, it was later engulfed by huge railway yards and factories.

The master plan for the area includes a first phase of seven buildings, four of which are being designed by Kohn Pedersen Fox. The river, to be spanned by new bridges, is to one side of the site, a principal highway into the city is on the other. A new central boulevard forms the spine of the development. Two of the blocks address the highway, and glazed atria are used as buffers to its noise and pollution. Offices look directly into the core of the site or the river, where there is a tree-lined public promenade. The atria are naturally ventilated spaces of an essentially public character, animated by banks of elevators. Roof structures, developed with engineers RFR and Battle McCarthy, have a multi-purpose role in both enclosing and servicing internal spaces.

The architectural language of the project mixes natural stone cladding with areas of curtain wall—the aim is to demonstrate continuity with the local tradition. The scheme acts equally as an urban marker and a gateway to the city center and has a dignity in keeping with that role.

Typical floor plan

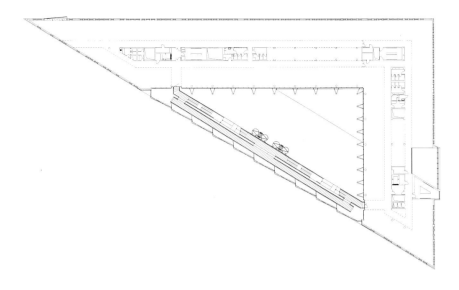

Level 1 plan

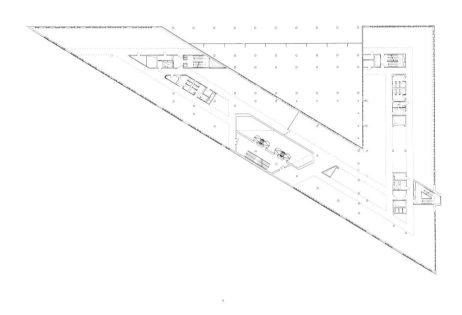

Ground floor plan

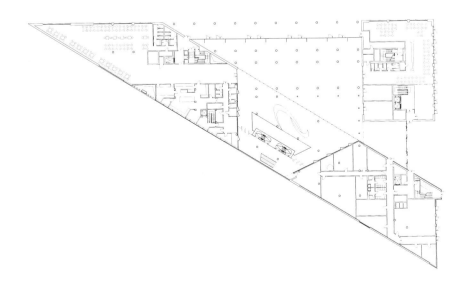

0   20 m

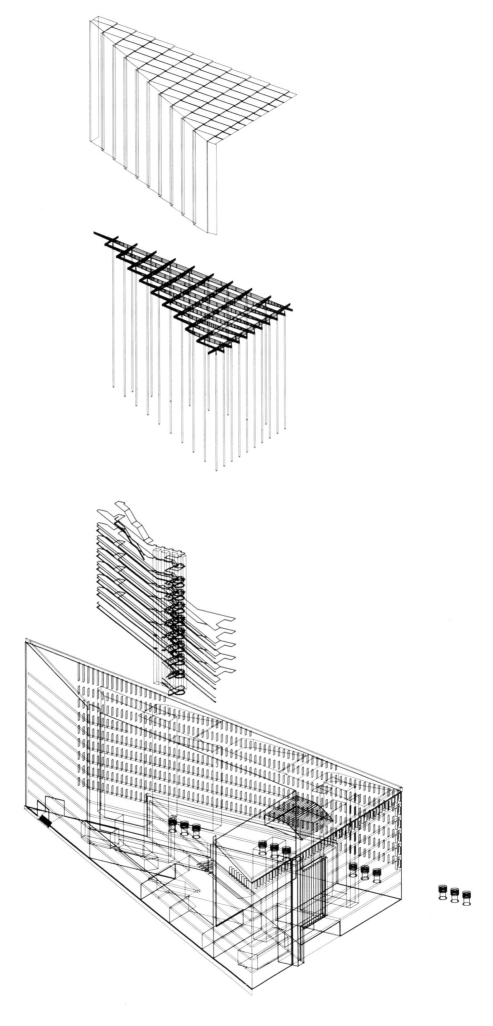

North elevaion

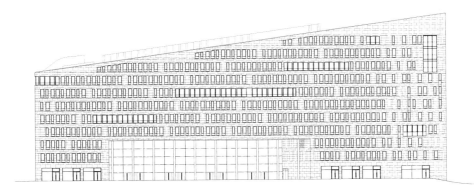

East elevation

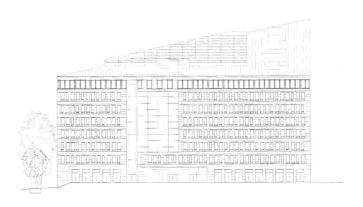

Southwest elevation

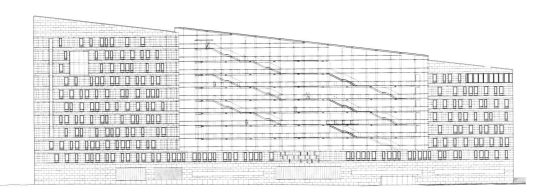

0   20 m

Tour CBX

Paris, France
1999-2003

The design for the CBX Tower is driven by a concern for the delicate context of this prominent site located along the major east-west thoroughfare linking old Paris to the modern commercial district of La Défense. Spatial constraints and view corridor restrictions influenced the design for this project. Rather than occupy the total site, the building takes an asymetrical blade form that changes dynamically according to the viewer's orientation.

The tower's sculptural form stands at the gateway between the verticality of La Défense and the dominant low-rise character of central Paris. The curved face of the tower addresses the north-south axis. The blades at either end of the curved facade run parallel to the Boulevard Circulaire in a gesture that connects old Paris to the modern landscape of La Défense.

The apparent weightlessness of the tower contrasts with the weighty masses of neighboring buildings. The glass and metal curtain wall is delicately articulated to provide an elegant addition to La Défense. The tower's dramatic profile provides a distinctive backdrop to the Parisian skyline.

Thirty-three floors and a double-height plaza level rest on a four-story podium that houses public and service spaces for the building. The ground floor contains a lobby/drop off, loading facilities and mechanical areas. A cafeteria and kitchen occupy the second floor. These levels are served by two banks of six elevators, as well as an escalator connecting the ground floor to the plaza.

Twenty-six floors of office space float above an elevated plaza level that contains a double-height main lobby space and provides a view to the skylit cafeteria below. This open space meets with the mandated view corridor requirements.

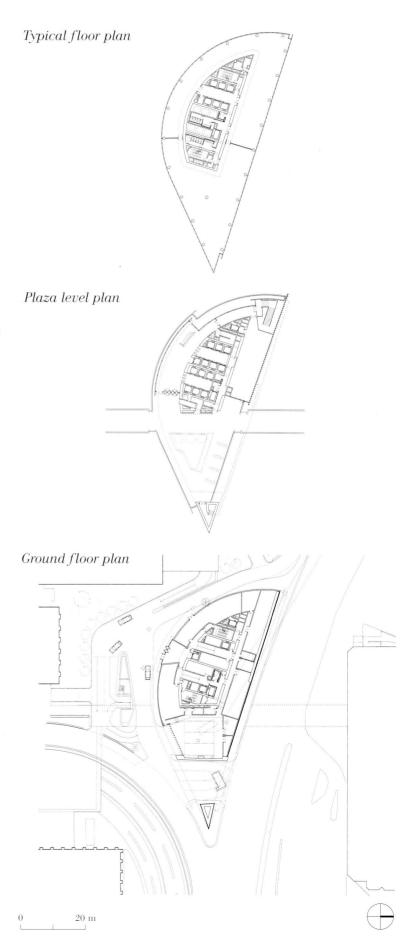

Typical floor plan

Plaza level plan

Ground floor plan

0   20 m

South elevation

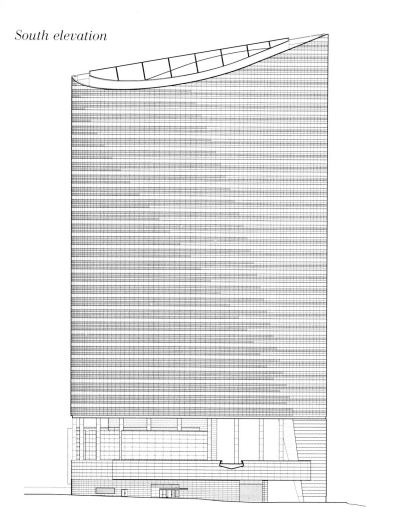

East elevation

North elevation

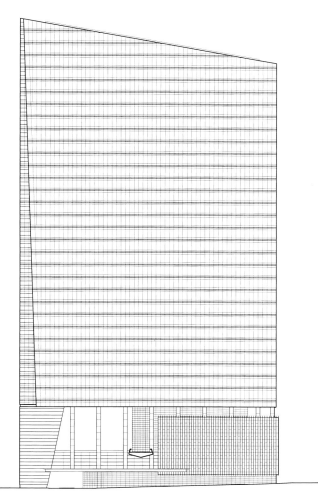

West elevation

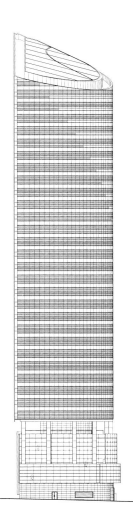

Tour CB16

Paris, France
1999-2002

The CB16 project revisits one of the original office towers at La Défense. Dating from 1971, the existing structure could no longer meet the requirements of modern financial services, and site pressures from subsequent construction demanded a redesign of the interior and exterior of the building. From this brief, a two-part tower massing emerged, evolving into a series of more elongated and elegant proportions.

In contrast to the mass of the original pre-cast structure, the detailing of the aluminum and glass curtain wall reflects a delicate sensibility. Pushing the curtain wall skin in front of the existing structure increased light and floor area dimensions, facilitating a state-of-the-art mechanical system. The windows, at 2.7 meters (9 feet) wide, reflect the planning module of the building. The top of the building culminates in an illuminated crown, with a sculptural mechanical enclosure seen through the uppermost translucent glass panels.

A reconfiguration of the lobby takes advantage of the project's enhanced natural lighting and increased floor areas—unwanted mezzanine space was replaced with a public-scaled stair serving a restaurant-club and the floors below. Lobby materials include limestone, wood, and a blind system of stainless steel and glass.

Typical office plan

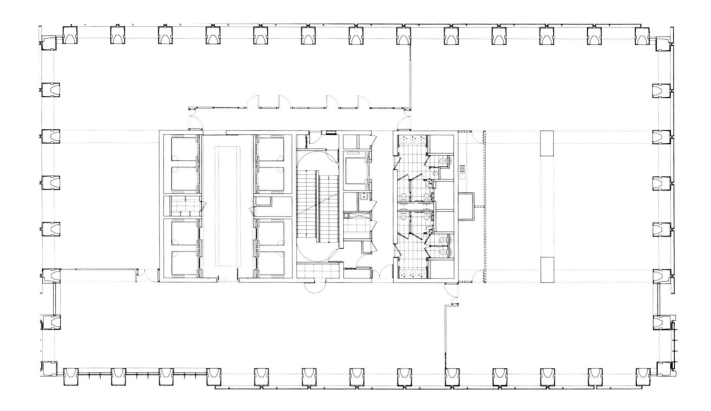

Ground floor plan

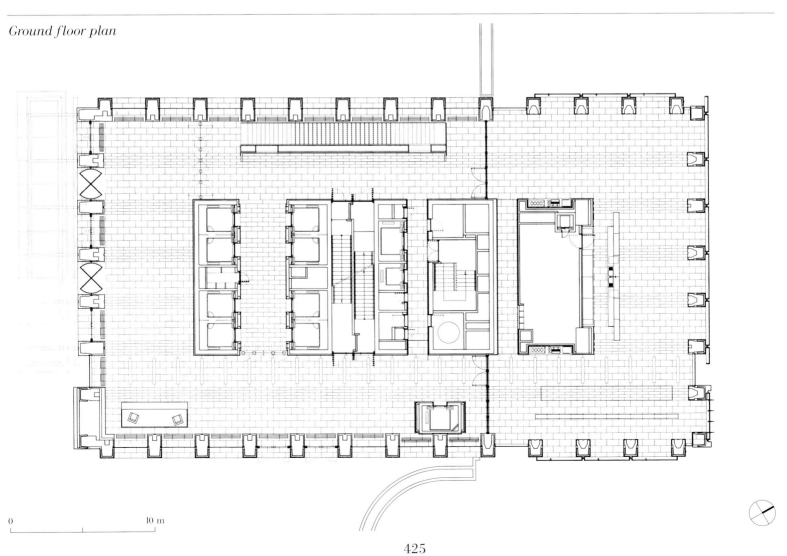

0   10 m

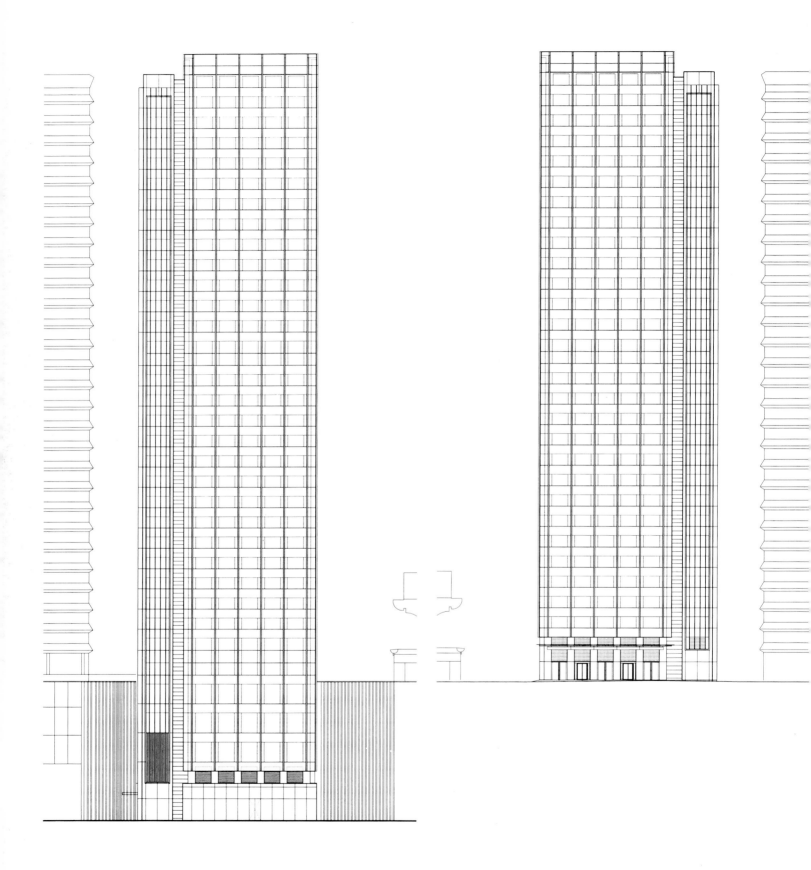

Endesa Headquarters

Madrid, Spain
1999-2002

The winning entry in an international competition, the Endesa project was seen by the client—a major national electricity utility—as an opportunity to mark its commitment to low-energy design and the development of a sustainable approach to building services. This agenda was addressed alongside a functional brief—to bring together several subsidiary companies previously scattered across a number of sites and creating a more efficient and interactive working environment. The site is on the edge of Madrid, in a new industrial and commercial quarter close to the M40 orbital roadway.

The scheme brings together operational and environmental objectives to memorable effect under a characteristic "big roof," a theme seen in other low-rise office projects, including Thames Court in the City of London and the unbuilt KBB project in Dusseldorf. As at Thames Court, this 86,000-square foot (8,000-square meter) "fifth elevation" has a multi-functional character, acting as social space, environmental buffer and as an active "lung" for the building, expelling stale air and drawing in fresh. The extremes of the Madrid climate allow for the use of night cooling to counter the effect of very hot summer days. Louvers and shading devices ensure comfortable conditions in the atrium, while maintaining evenly daylit conditions. The atrium is seen as a public and communal space, open to all. A clear symbol of the ecological thinking behind the scheme, it also makes financial sense since the facades which it encloses are internal, thus reducing construction costs. Photovoltaic units attached to the roof contribute significantly to meeting the building's energy needs.

The offices are arranged as a series of 59-foot (18-meter) deep bars, with five levels of office accommodation above ground. Extensive parking areas are located on two basement levels. The design of external facades has been carefully tailored to meet the exigencies of the climate, baffle glare and solar gain. The whole project marries environmental concerns more typical of Northern Europe with the Mediterranean typology of the sheltered courtyard.

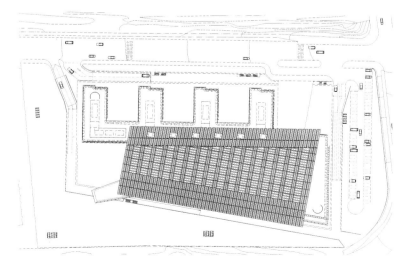

Typical floor plan

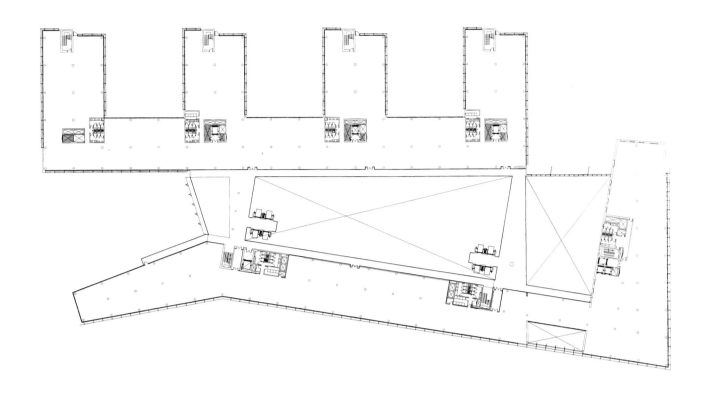

Ground floor plan

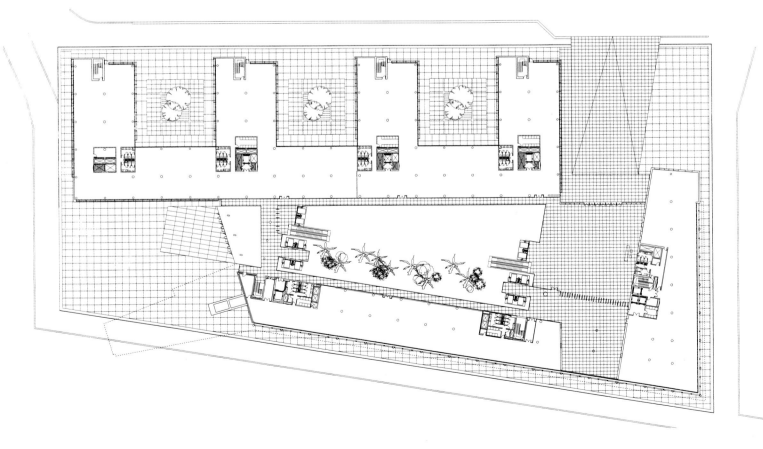

0   50 m

431

West elevation

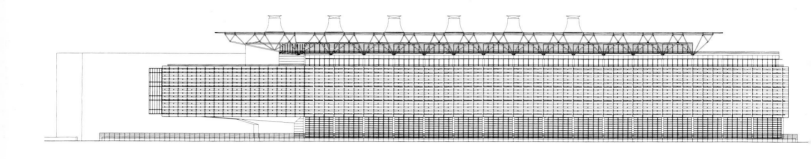

Section looking north

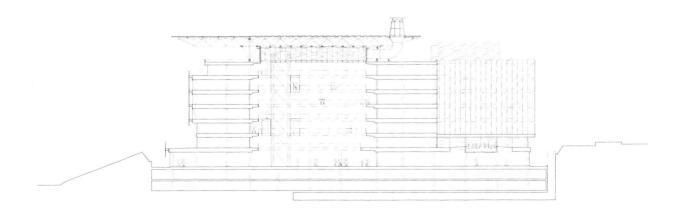

0   100 ft

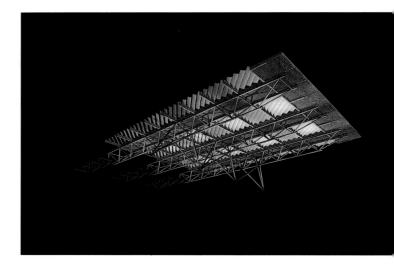

434

Columbus Learning Center

Columbus, Indiana
1999-2003

The Columbus Learning Center is a multi-tenant education
facility and community resource center in Columbus,
Indiana, a small industrial town with a population of 37,000.

The two-story building sits between two existing buildings
that house Indiana University Purdue University Columbus,
Purdue School of Technology, and Ivy Tech State College
Columbus. The new facility acts as a bridge to reduce the
physical and psychological distance among these educational
institutions. The three buildings form a college campus
centered on a large landscaped green. The design is influenced
by the simple forms of the many factories, farmhouses and
silos that dot the landscape. Each program component for the
new facility is housed in a distinct brick and glass form.

The building is approached from Central Avenue, the main
artery linking the site to downtown Columbus. The strong
forms of the building present a recognizable identity important
for a community resource center. The interior opens to the
landscape with a glass-enclosed public street that links the
lobby to all the services within the building. Along this light-
filled spine are reception areas for the various tenants.
Lounges are distributed throughout to encourage student life
and the spontaneous interaction that does not occur in the
existing institutional buildings. Major destination points are
provided at both ends of the public street to facilitate
campus-wide interaction.

Flexibility is built into the architecture. As program changes
and develops, spaces can be easily reconfigured without
significant alterations to the building's support system.

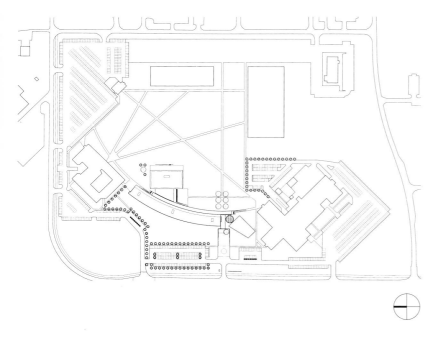

Second floor plan

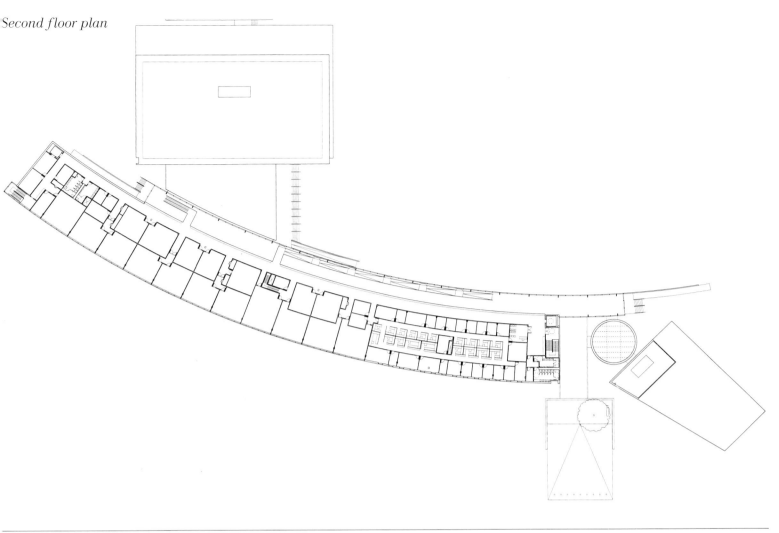

Ground floor plan

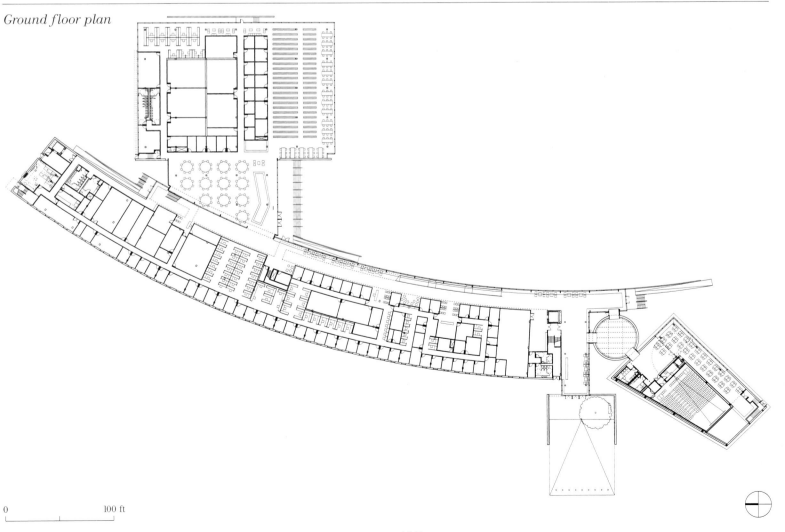

0   100 ft

Section through lobby looking north

Section through auditorium looking southeast

Front South

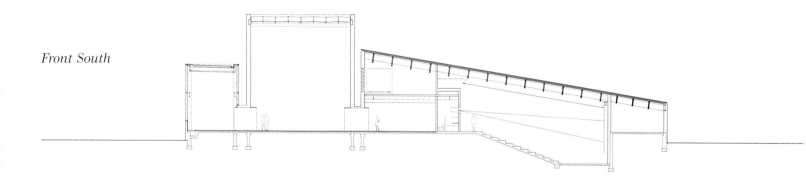

Section through library looking north

Front East

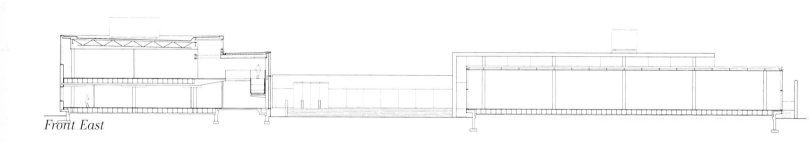

Section through library and connecting walkway

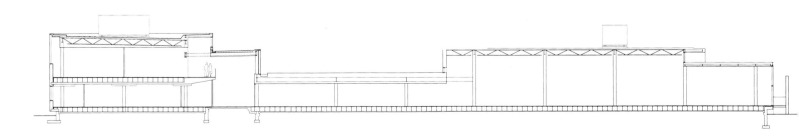

0   50 ft

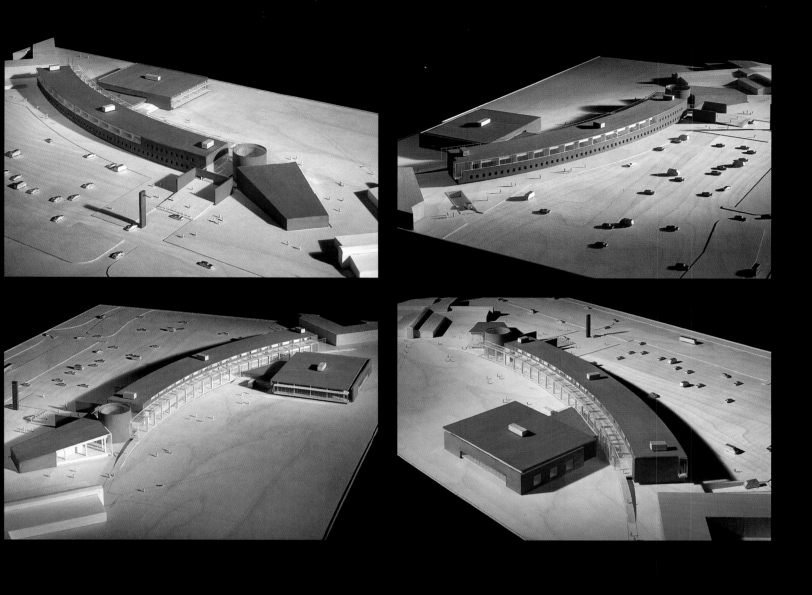

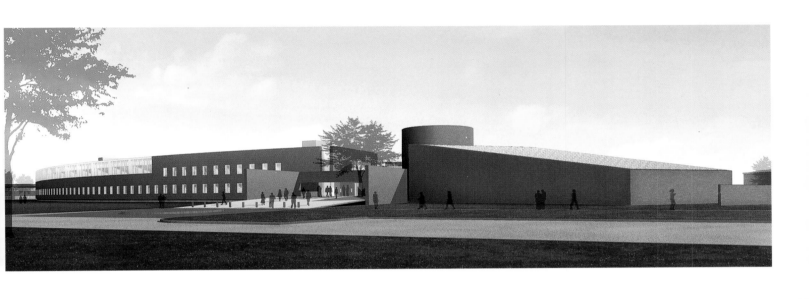

Beukenhorst Zuid

Hoofddorp, The Netherlands
1999-2002

The Hoofddorp development was conceived as a dramatic new gateway to Amsterdam, close to Schiphol Airport in one of the most exciting new business quarters in the Netherlands. Just as Amsterdam marries its role as tourist destination and cultural capital with that of a twenty-first century commercial and financial center, so the Hoofddorp successfully addresses issues of history and local identity alongside its practical response to the needs of commercial development, generating new public spaces and seeking to integrate the expanding city fringe into the historic urban fabric.

The master plan area is well served by existing road and rail networks—a main railway line runs through the site—and is adjacent to the historic Geniedijk, a massive dyke built as part of Amsterdam's defenses against invasion from the south and now designated a World Heritage Site. The area of the Geniedijk is protected against development and is used for grazing sheep and as a popular city "lung" where Amsterdamers come to walk. A majestic line of trees creates a strong natural border and forms the western perimeter to the site.

Kohn Pedersen Fox's master plan provides for a series of spaces linked together on an east-west axis. The scheme encompasses both east and west developments, each with different clients. A new linear road follows the line of the dyke on the eastern edge of the site, then develops into a crescent-shaped pedestrian square in front of the new Southpoint, The Avenue and Zuidtoren office developments that form the core of the new area. It continues below the railway tracks and reconstructed station, with its fast link to Schiphol, to a new square west of the station around the 269,000 square foot (25,000-square meter) Pharos Tower.

While the latter building is seen as a marker, other new buildings are mixed in scale with Southpoint, envisaged as a series of low-rise blocks around a new, tree-lined square overlooking a newly created lake. The Zuidtoren is designed, with the Pharos Tower, to form bookends that frame the station and create a memorable image for the development.

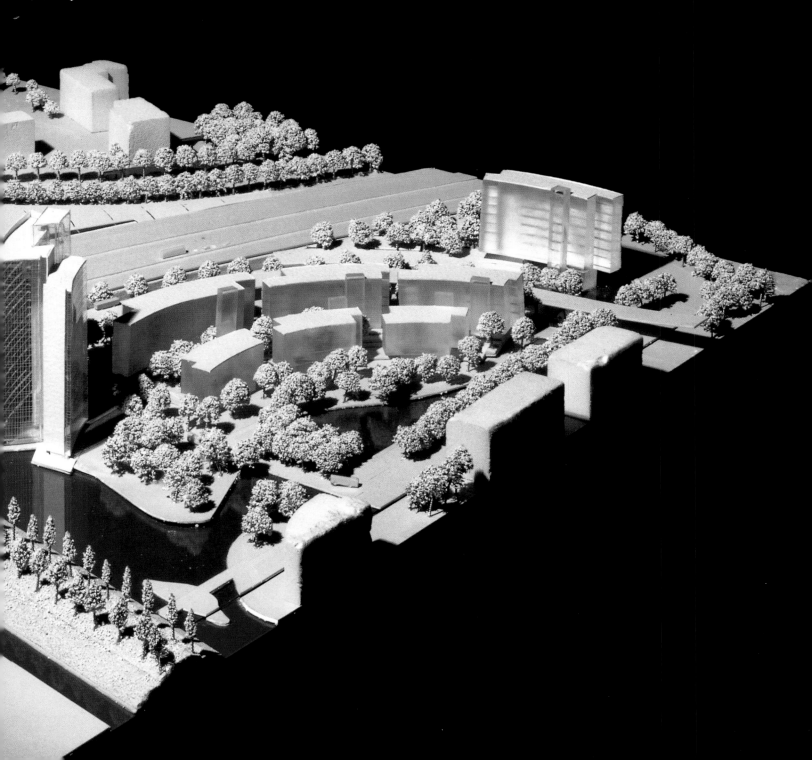

Site plan

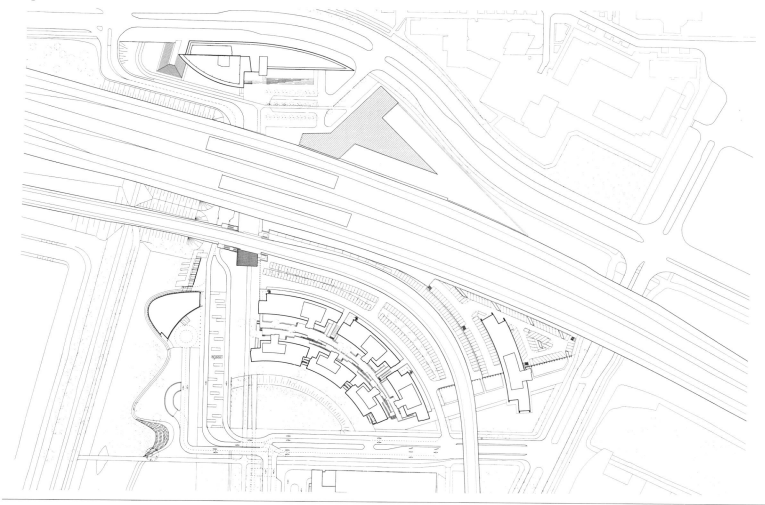

South elevation

Zuidtoren   *Southpoint*   *Avenue*

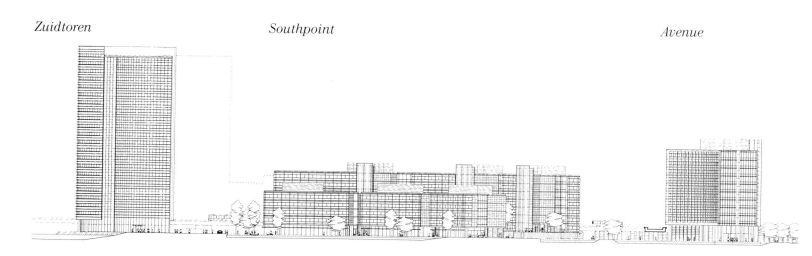

0 _____ 20 m

444

Section through Southpoint looking east

Typical floor plan, Southpoint

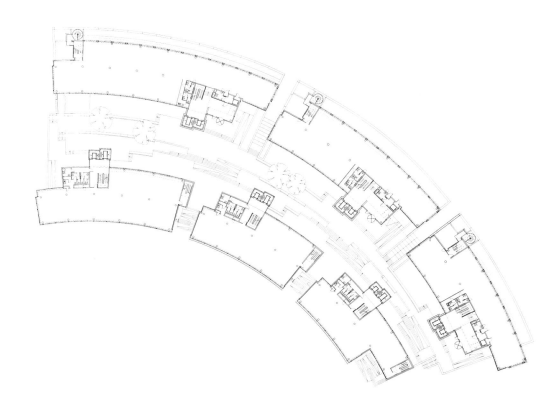

0   20 m

South elevation, Zuidtoren

East elevation, Zuidtoren

Typical floor plan, Zuidtoren

Ground floor plan, Zuidtoren

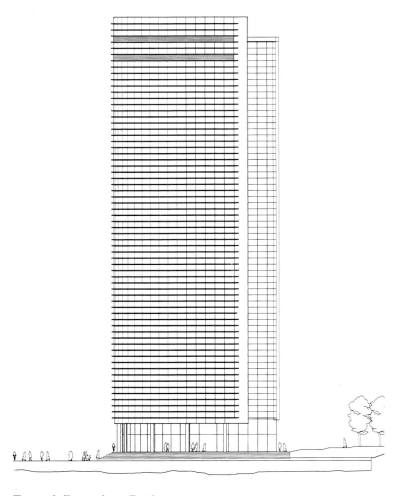

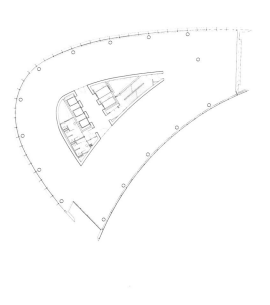

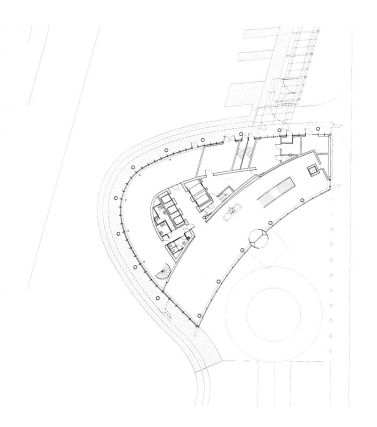

0   20 m

High-rise floor plan, Pharos

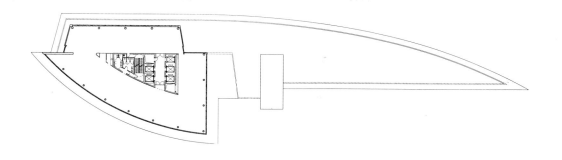

Low-rise floor plan, Pharos

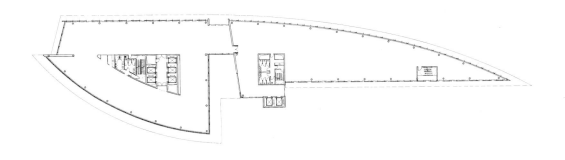

Ground floor plan, Pharos

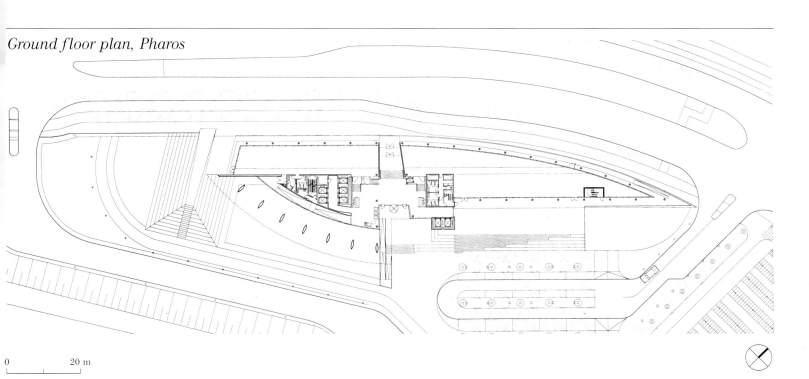

0   20 m

449

The design of this three-story Bloomingdale's anchor store recognizes the integral role of the car in the day-to-day life of metropolitan Orlando, Florida, and derives its geometry from the immediate physical and cultural context. Situated at the end of a suburban mall, the store is surrounded on three sides by parking lots, with parking on the east side at level one and parking on the west side rising up to the second level of the store.

Rather than creating a department store box, the design took advantage of the site conditions to create a building that emerges from the landscape of the parking lot. The ground surface warps and folds to create horizontal and vertical planes that define and enclose spaces. Painted metal exterior stairs float within the folds of the wall. The loading dock is concealed from view under a floor plane. Planes of transparent and translucent glass slip between the folding floor surfaces to complete the store enclosure.

The Bloomingdale's design also incorporates bold use of color and graphics to make the store legible at the fast speed of the automobile. The building is a billboard sitting within a network of interstate highways.

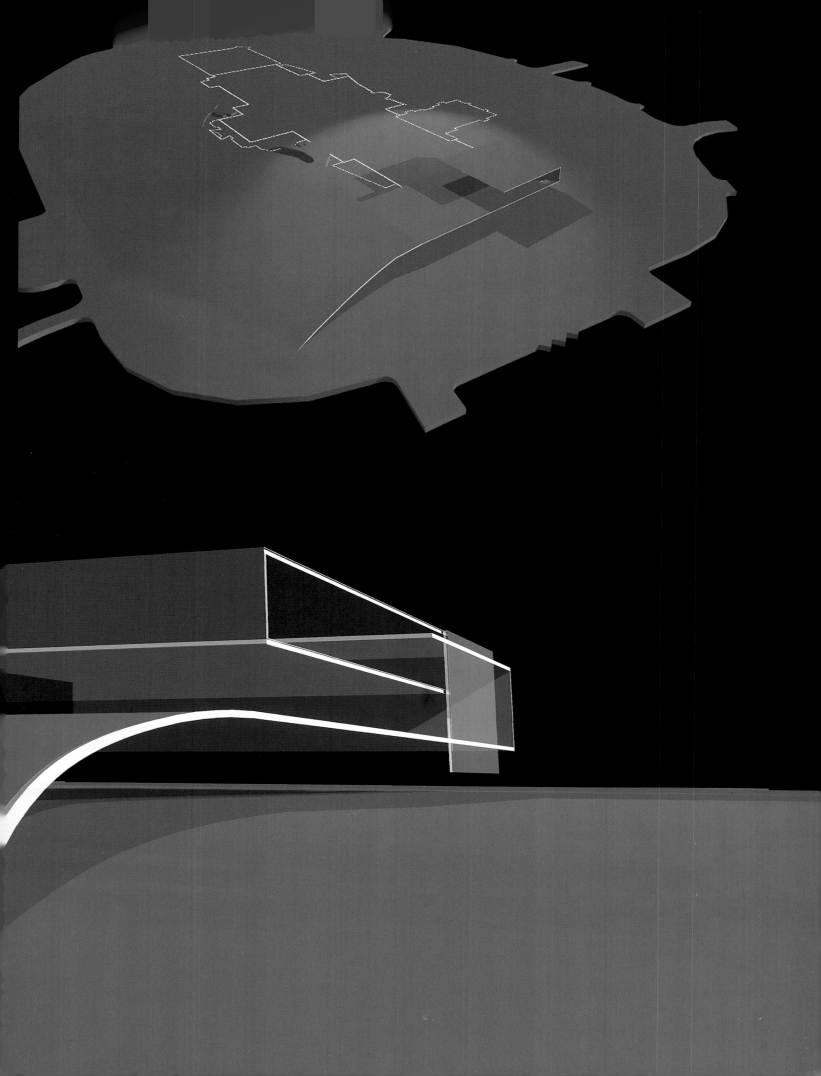

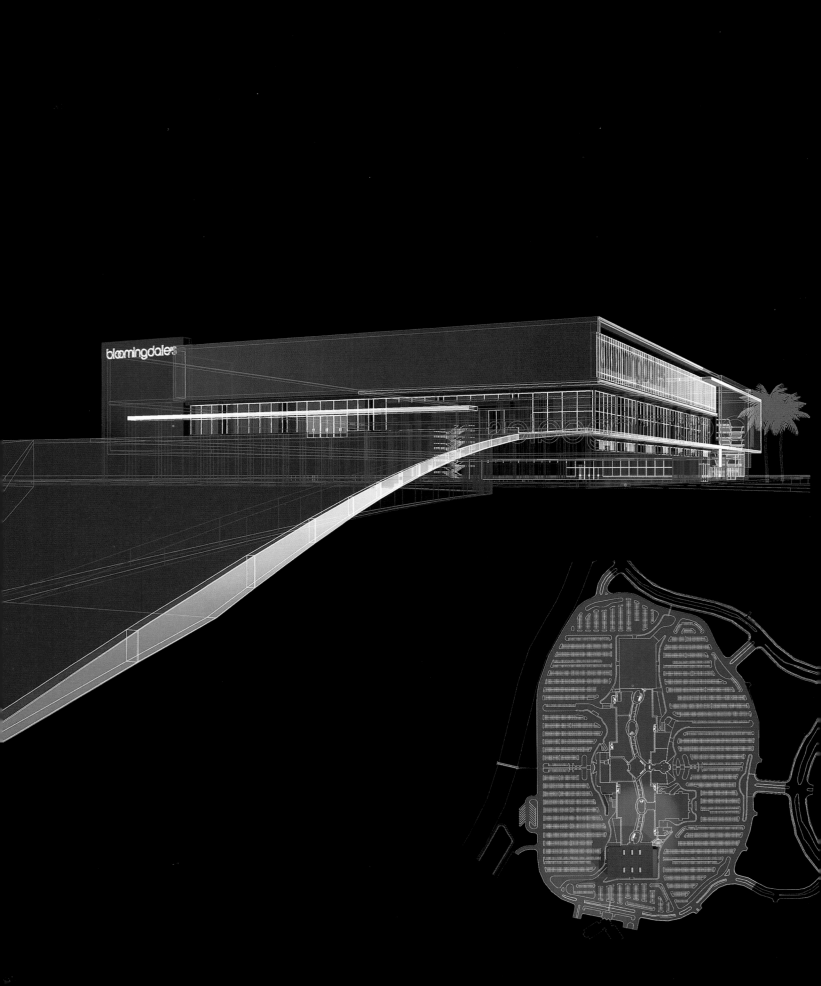

Nihonbashi-1 Project

Tokyo, Japan
2000-2004

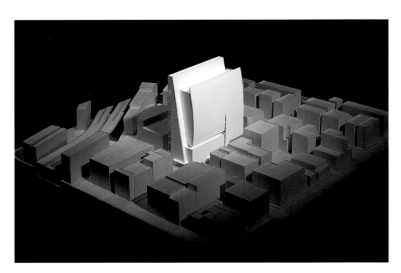

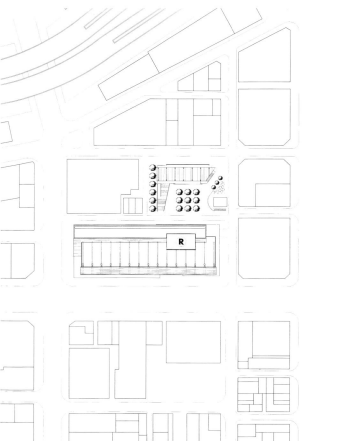

This twenty-story mixed-use development stands on two parcels formerly occupied by the Tokyo Department Store in the Nihonbashi district, and is adjacent to a number of historic sites in the city. Two important urban axes frame the western and southern sides of the site. One of these, Chuo-dori extends from the Ginza district to the south and is predominantly a retail avenue. The other, Etai-dori, connects to the financial district of Tokyo. The existing city fabric surrounding the building is relatively low. The design solution proposes a structure that connects to this scale as it rises substantially above it.

The predominant component is commercial office space designed to meet the requirements of international financial institutions. The design places all of the vertical service elements along the north side of the site, in order to accommodate the large depth desired for this type of office space within the confines of a relatively narrow site.

A pavilion of office space extends out from the core to the south along Etai-dori. The core and the office volume are expressed as distinct elements, and are clad in stone and glass respectively. The introduction of natural light into the office areas is carefully modulated by louvered shading devices along the south facing wall and high performance glass containment on the east and west exposures. A clear space of 66 feet (twenty meters) from core to wall structures the office volume; a 9.2-foot (2.8-meter) cantilever from the column line to the southern glass wall extends the space. This zone of extension provides the opportunity for internal circulation along the glass and gives to the curving south wall a sense of weightless suspension. This gently bowing surface is separated in its articulation from the mass it encloses by deep reveals at the east and west ends to enhance its role as an independent enclosing layer.

Below the office space is a five-story glass volume at the corner of Chuo-dori and Etai-dori. Extruded from the mass of the tower, it houses the retail space and is clad in an enclosure composed of closely spaced vertical glass fins projecting from a clear glass wall. Rising at a height of thirty meters, it establishes an urban connection with its neighbors.

Typical office floor plan

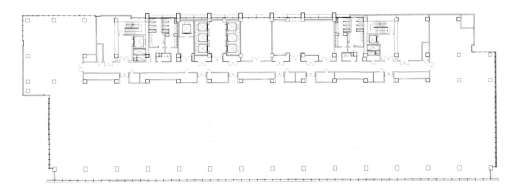

Trading floor plan

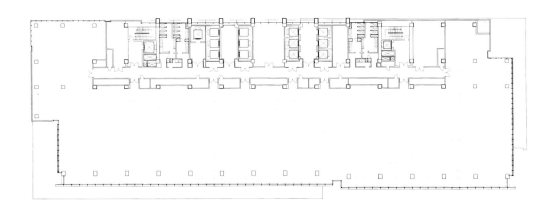

Skylobby floor plan

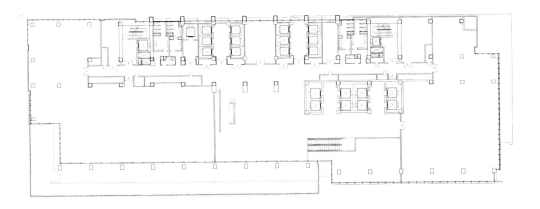

Ground floor plan

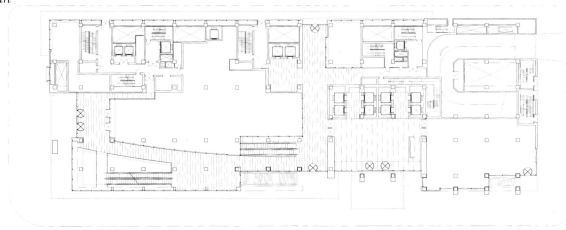

0   10 m

455

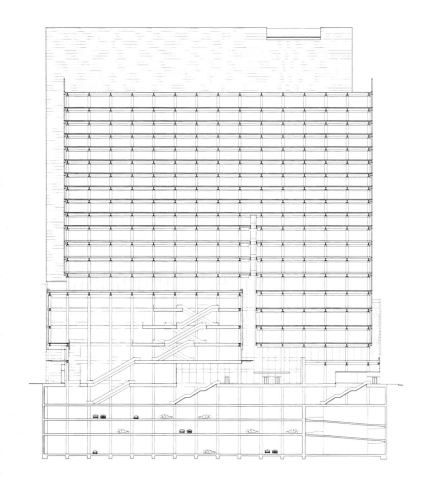

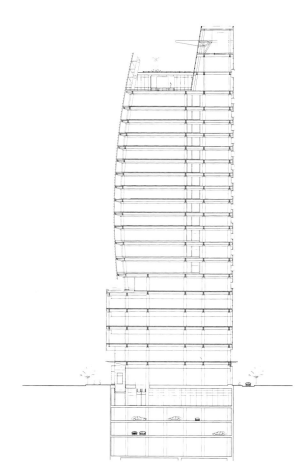

Section looking south

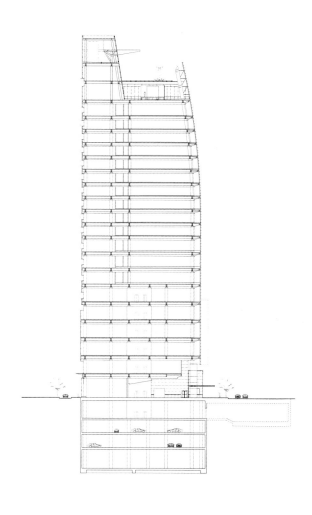

0   20 m

Kaiser Family Foundation Headquarters Competition

Washington, D.C.
2000

This design for the Washington D.C. headquarters of a non-profit organization devoted to public policy and health care issues is sited two blocks from the White House. The building consists of four floors of exhibition, conference, and broadcast studio functions, and four floors of office space. Each half of the building section has its own atrium, which provides a setting for group interaction. The two vertical spaces are connected by an intermediate transition floor, which serves as a link between lower public zones and the upper office zones.

The lower, north-facing atrium accommodates the building entry and provides views of balconies where conference pre-function activities occur. This space is finished with stone, wood, and metal and forms a hard surface "street garden."

The upper, south-facing atrium is designed as a "sky garden." It features tiers of hanging plants that screen the sun and provide a backdrop for office balconies. Both this space and the lower atrium create an upward convection airflow. The resulting negative pressure is used to facilitate the intake of fresh air at the extremities of the office floors, saving energy and improving the air quality of the work place.

The street facade on the north side opens the lower half of the building and its public functions to the street, thus supporting the foundation's aims of broadcasting its activities to a diverse constituency. The upper half of this facade is screened by operable wood slats sandwiched between layers of glass. Straddling the two zones is a rectangular frame that corresponds to the transition floor where public and internal office functions meet.

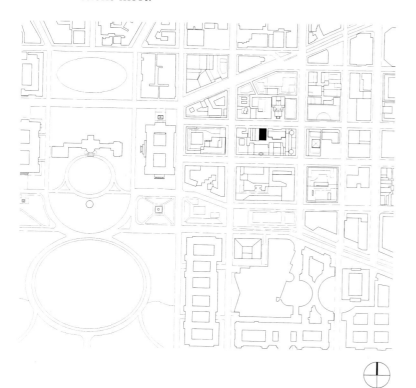

Fourth floor plan

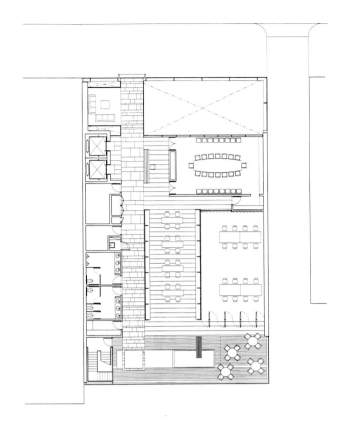

Typical floor plan

Ground floor plan

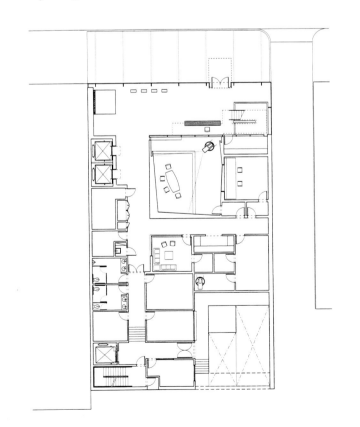

Second/Conference floor plan

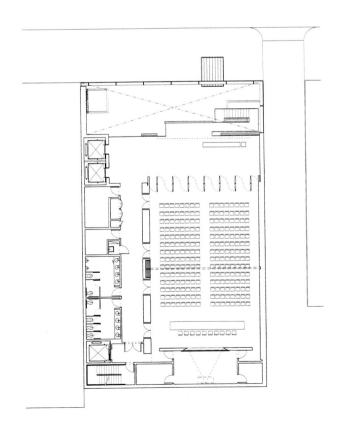

0   50 ft

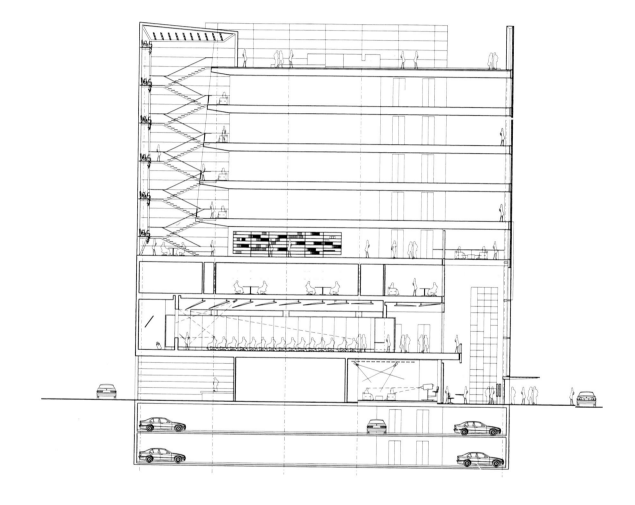

0   50 ft

KAISER FAMILY FOUNDATION

118 Gloucester Road

Hong Kong SAR
2000

The context for this 35-story tower—containing appoximately 100,000 square feet (9,300 square meters) of leaseable office space and 65,000 square feet (6,000 square meters) allocated for the use of the client, the Mormon Church—is a densely developed area of office buildings in Hong Kong's Wanchai district. The site adjoins a major thoroughfare.

The brief mandated a new chapel, classroom and offices for the Church, plus parking below grade. Distinct from office functions, the chapel is accessed from a separate entrance along Fleming Road. The building injects new life and dignity into the locality. While necessarily addressing the busy highway, it subtly introduces a degree of metaphor and sculptural drama into the existing street frontage. The form of the tower is that of a gently sloping, glazed northern facade facing the waterfront—the solid cladding of the south facade is an environmental response and reflects the placing of service cores along the southern edge of the office floors.

The lower floors of the building are faced in strongly modeled masonry. The masonry facade is continued as a theme in the walls of the chapel spaces, punctuated by series of narrow vertical windows. At the top of the tower, the glazed plane is continued upward as a symbolic feature, to be illuminated by night as a marker of the building's spiritual dimension.

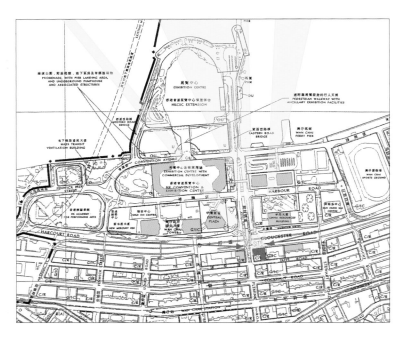

Fifth floor plan

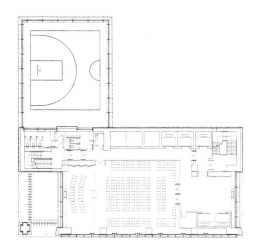

Typical office floor plan

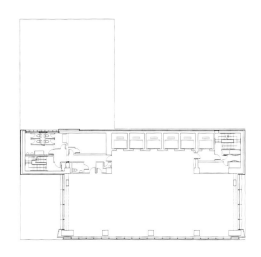

Ground floor plan

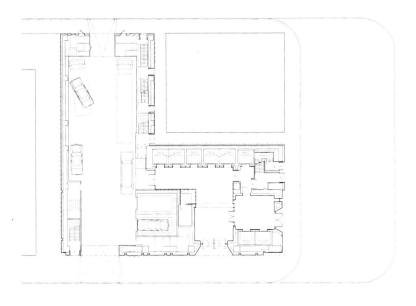

Second/Chapel floor plan

0   20 m

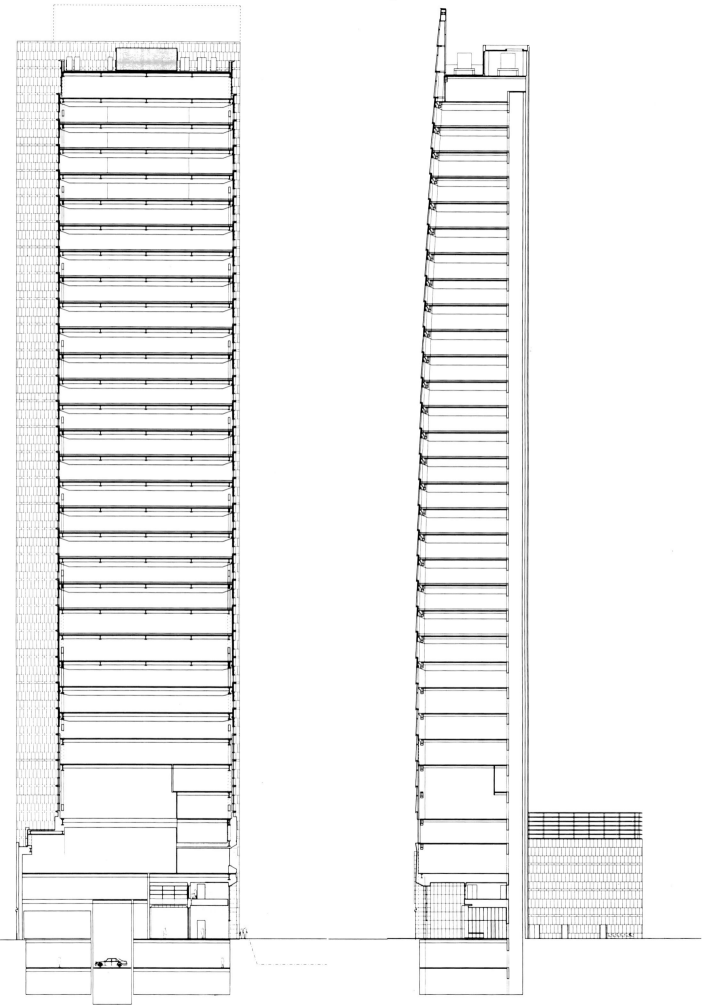

Section looking south

Section looking east

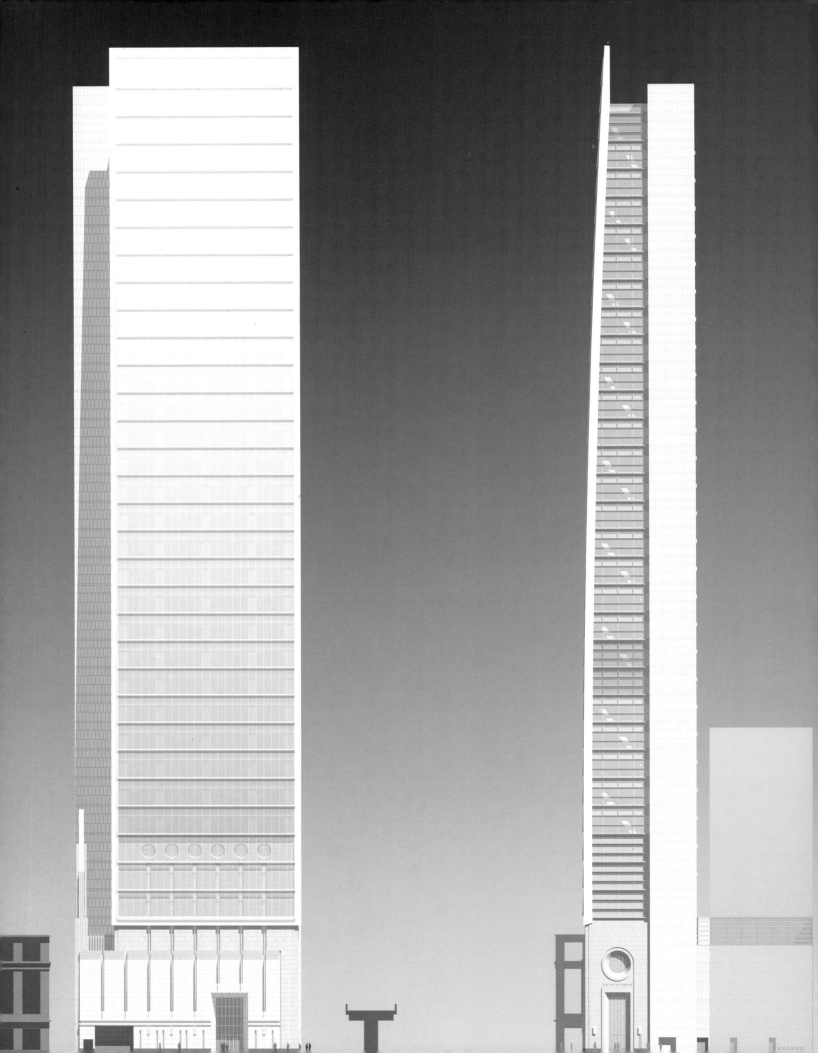

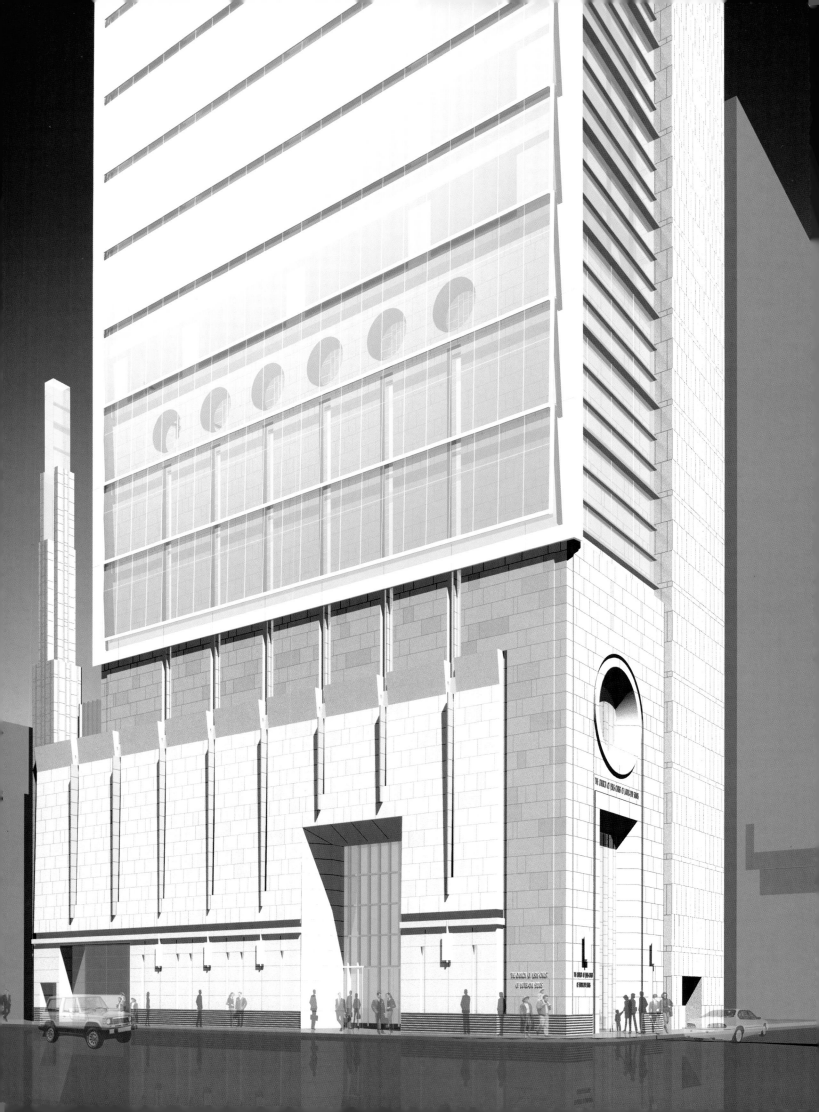

Kowloon Station Tower

Hong Kong SAR
2000-2008

This 108-story tower is the centerpiece of a master plan for a massive reclamation project in West Kowloon. Facing downtown Hong Kong across Victoria Harbor, the development was conceived as a transportation hub connecting Hong Kong to Chep Lap Kok airport, and a new urban center comprised of residential, office, retail, hotel and recreation uses.

The brief for the Kowloon Station Tower called for a 2.7 million square-foot (251,000 square meter) office provision, together with a 300-room boutique hotel, and an observation deck on the 90th floor. The office floors are generous in scale, with central cores. The hotel rooms occupy the upper levels of the tower, radiating from a cylindrical atrium topped by a restaurant. A vertical city all by itself, the tower will be one of the tallest structures in the world upon completion in 2008.

The winning entry in a design competition, the scheme suceeds in wedding the high-rise building form with a highly efficient structural and operational agenda. Square in plan, the tower's re-entrant corners taper to create a graceful profile against the sky. At its base, the tower splays out, creating an impression of a plant emerging from the ground. The walls of the tower peel away at the base, creating canopies on three sides, and a dramatic atrium on the north side. The atrium gestures towards the rest of the development and serves as a public linkage space to the retail and rail station functions. The concept of the building as a plant is further aticulated as its crown assumes flower-like qualities of transparency and delicacy. The four façade elements extend up beyond the roof and slope back to create the building's profile. During the day, the transparent crown dissolves against the sky; at night this volume will appear as a glowing beacon.

The overall simplicity of the tower's form belies a richly textured cladding system, made up of glass and metal shingles, each a story high. These shingles serve to further dematerialize the tower, breaking up its mass as it reflects the sky, giving its form an appearance of great lightness.

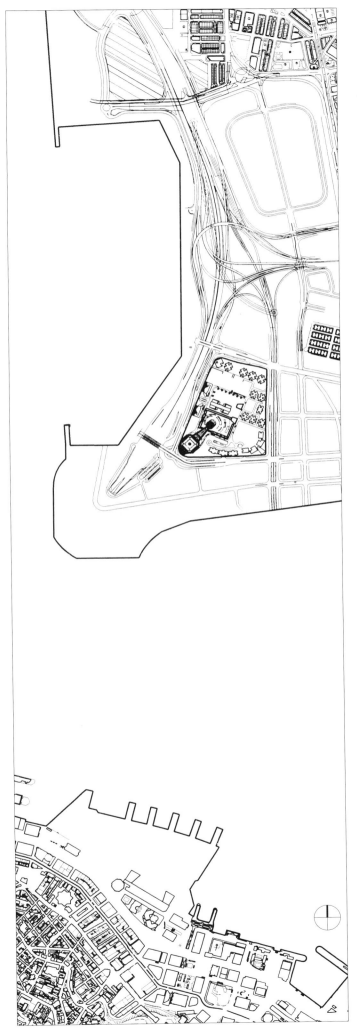

Ground floor plan

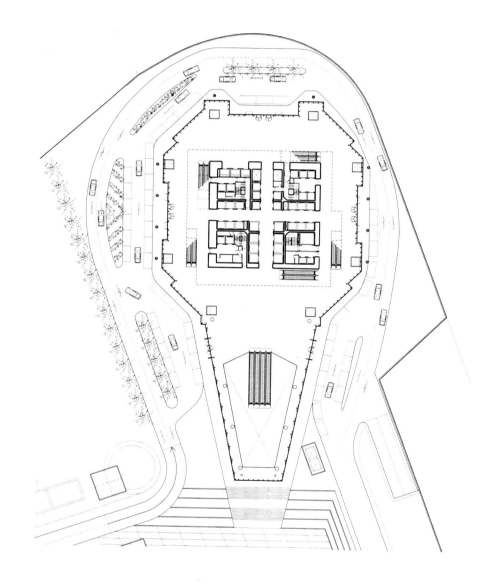

0   30 m

7th floor plan

Refuge floor plan

25th to 38th floor plan
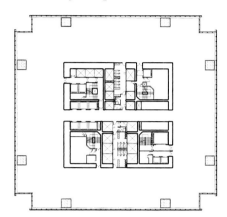

Skylobby/51st floor plan
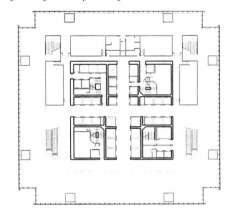

Observation level/90th floor plan
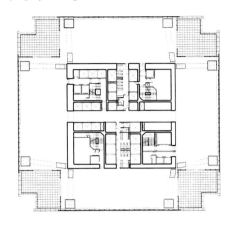

Hotel reception/93rd floor plan
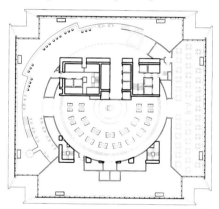

Typical hotel/107th floor plan
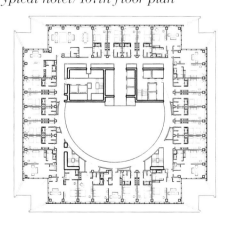

Hotel restaurant/108th floor plan
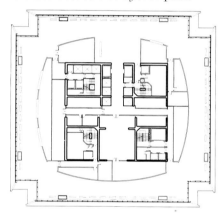

Roof plan
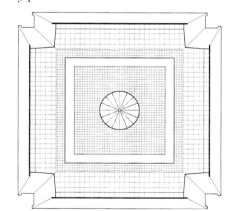

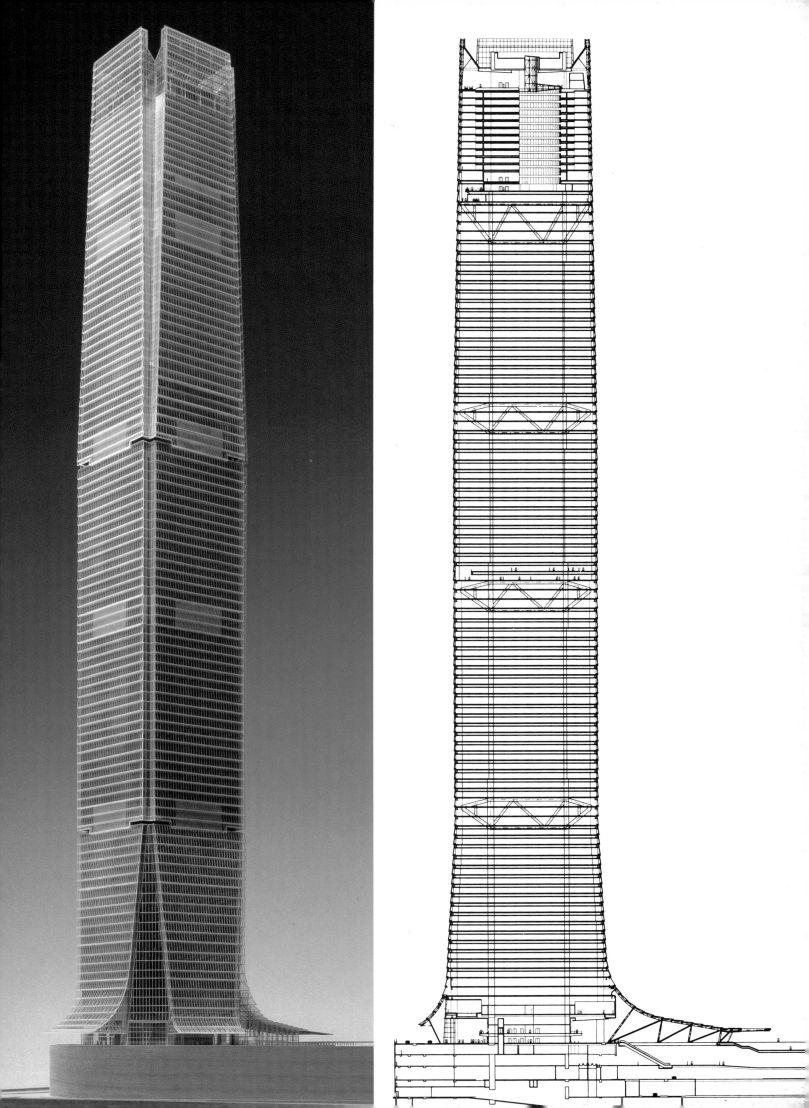

Tour Granite

Paris, France
2001

Tour Granite occupies a triangular site in the suburb of Nanterre, and borders the western limit of La Défense. Marking the transition from one neighborhood to another, the building is linked to the existing Société Générale twin tower complex at the edge of the La Défense *dalle*—the raised pedestrian platform that sets the district apart from the city proper. The program is comprised of 27 floors of office space stacked above a podium containing six levels of long-span trading floors, and five levels of service space. The tower is connected to the existing structures by a pedestrian bridge at the lobby level, and an enclosed sky-bridge located nine floors above.

The design reconciles a series of programmatic and environmental conditions within a simple geometric form, shaping the plan of the tower as an isosceles triangle that gradually transforms into an equilateral configuration at its crown. The three primary tower facades are articulated as distinct vertical planes. As a result, the tapering triangular form is not closed and complete, but rather gives way to centripetal forces, liberating these planes from one another toward the top. Larger floor plates at the base are accommodated by a series of canted layers that peel away from the main form of the tower. The *dalle* level walkway connects pedestrians to the tower lobby and extends through a landscaped outdoor space at the western apex of the triangle. This triple-height 'pocket-park' allows pedestrians to transition from the *dalle* to the street below while preserving exposure to natural light and air.

The triangular floor plates, punctuated by three-corner meeting rooms, lend a visual hierarchy to the plan, encouraging teamwork and communication. Community experience is further encouraged by two program-related perimeter atrium spaces that introduce landscape into the office interior. The executive atrium in the tower apex at the top creates a beacon that gestures outward to Nanterre while the liaison-level atrium maintains a direct dialogue with the existing complex and La Défense.

Typical high-rise plan

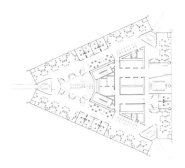

Atrium level plan

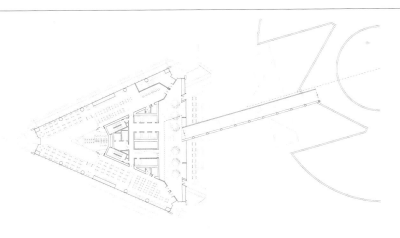

Trading floor plan

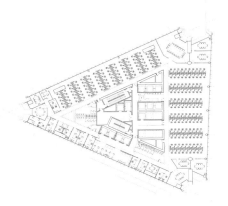

Lobby level plan

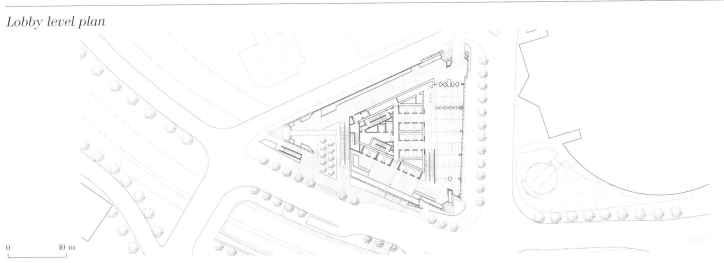

0   10 m

485

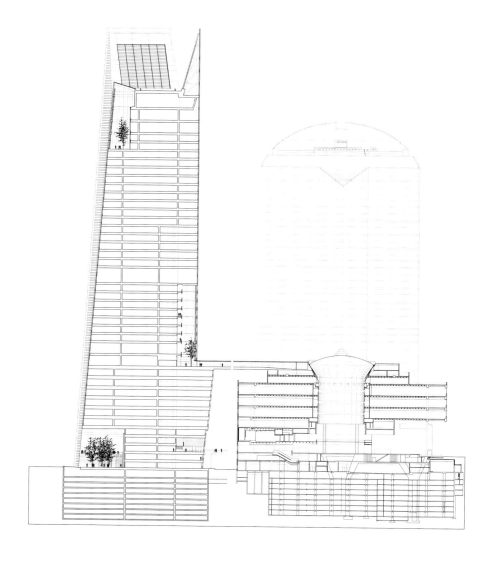

NY Jets Stadium

New York, New York
2001

The new home of the New York Jets football team is a 75,000-seat, open air stadium proposed for a site between 30th and 34th streets on Manhattan's west side. The focus of a redeveloped Hudson River waterfront, the stadium will be built on a deck above an existing rail yard, with an extensive public plaza and a multipurpose convention space on the 34th street side.

Aside from holding the ten National Football League games played per season, the stadium will also incorporate expanded convention facilities for the adjacent Jacob Javits Center. As New York City looks toward the possibility of hosting the 2012 Olympiad, the stadium is designed to expand to meet the requirements of the International Olympic Committee.

A principal consideration of the design is the integration of the development into the immediate context. On axis with the Empire State Building, the stadium continues the city grid, and with the addition of the public park, unites the neighborhoods of north Chelsea and Hell's Kitchen with the river. In plan and elevation, the scheme suggests an "inland pier," formally establishing a relationship with the artifacts of the city's maritime history. The design also preserves and extends the Highline, an elevated two-track freight train platform running 1.6 miles (2.57 kilometers) from Gansevoort Street in Greenwich Village to 34th street and Eleventh Avenue. Built in the 1930s as part of the West Side Improvement, the now-derelict platform is reconceived as an historic opportunity to create an elevated green space connected to the stadium's landscape program.

The scheme is a significant departure from conventional sports facilities-planning in North America. It promotes an unprecedented, environmentally sensitive agenda for a building of this type. Through the use of over 100,000 square feet (9,290 square meters) of solar panels, 36 wind turbines, rainwater collection and wastewater treatment, the stadium complex is conceived as entirely self-sustaining—able to generate energy for itself and the surrounding city grid.

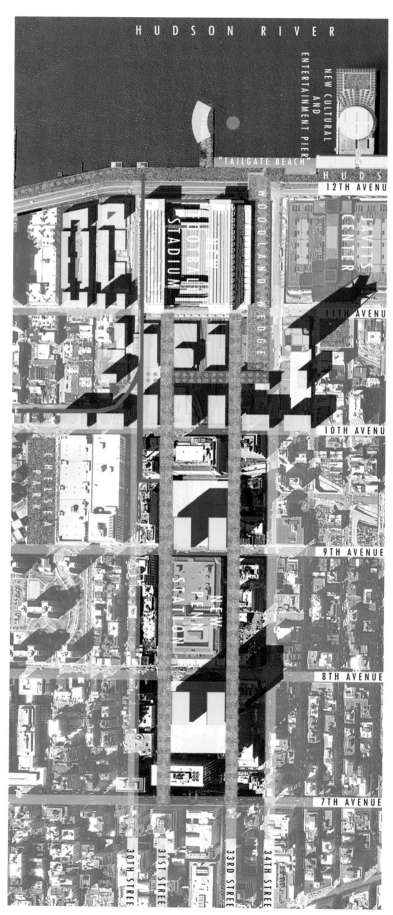

Stadium floor plan

0   300 ft

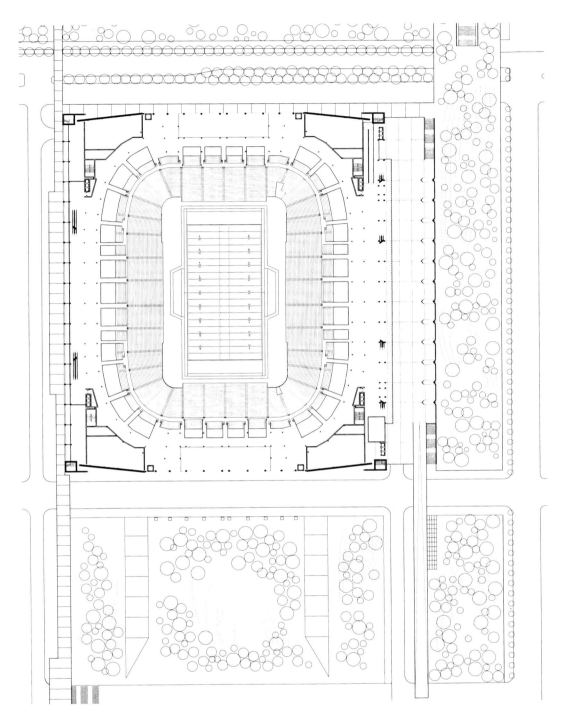

Stadium section looking west

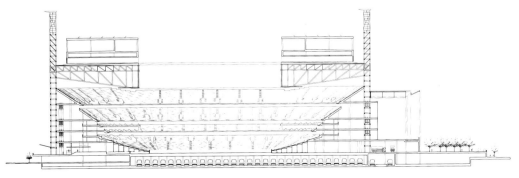

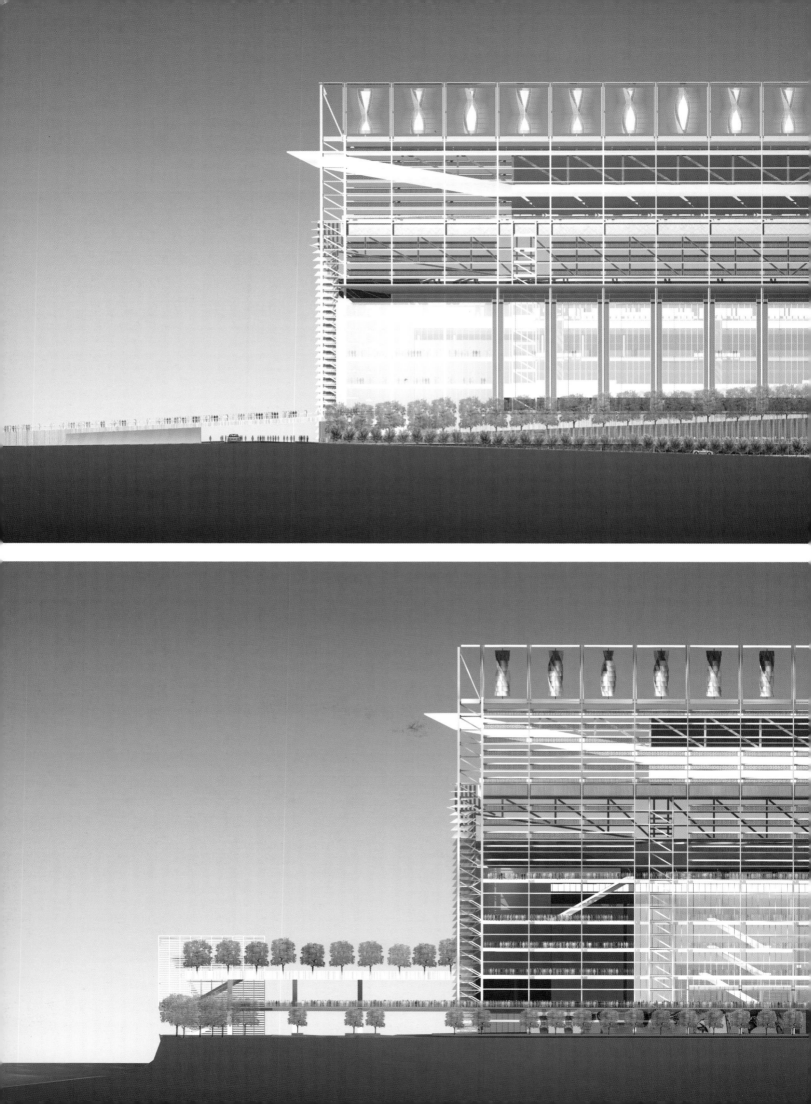

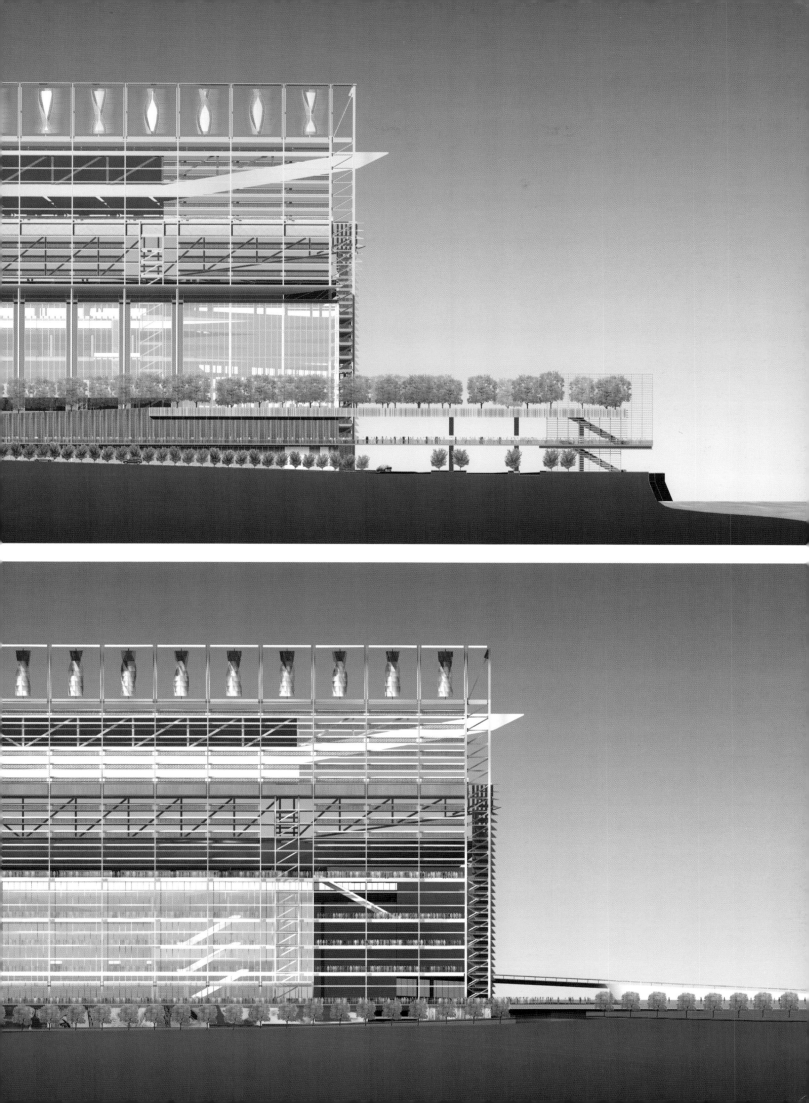

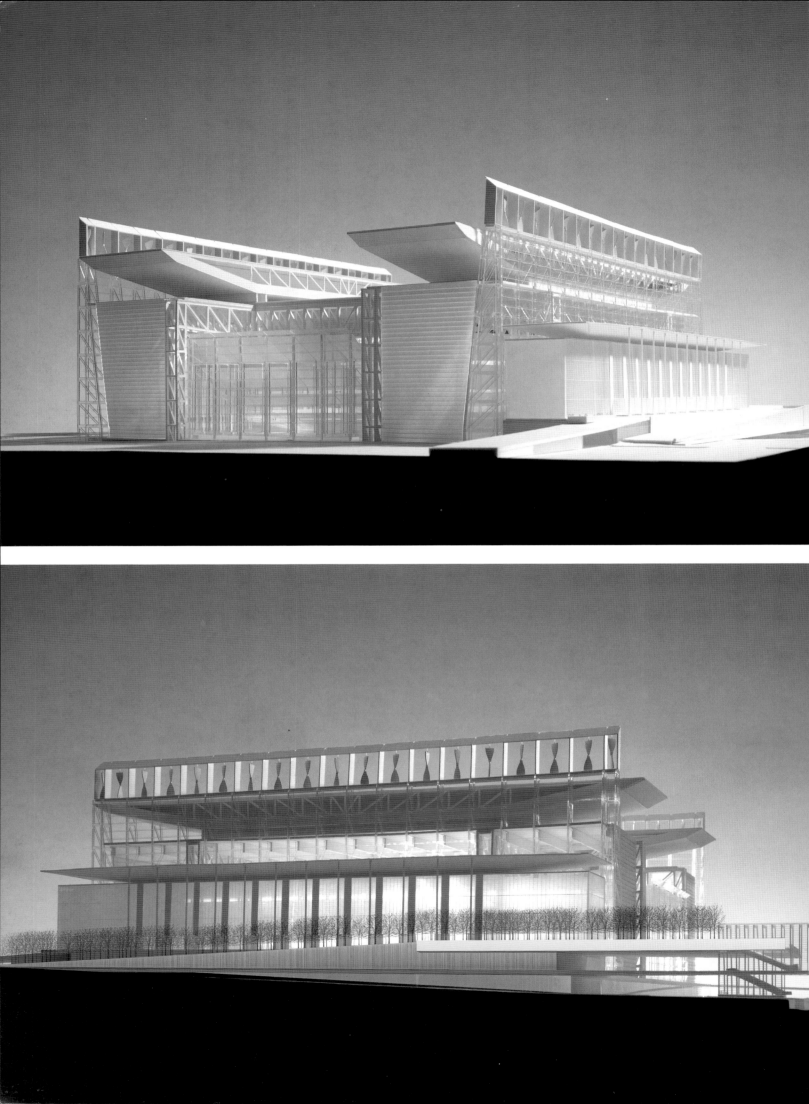

Energy planning: *Solar and thermal*
                        Wind harvesting
                        Rain collection & plantings

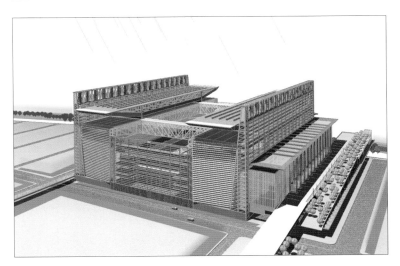

Principals

A. Eugene Kohn FAIA RIBA JIA

A. Eugene Kohn was born in Philadelphia, Pennsylvania, in 1930. He received a Bachelor of Architecture degree in 1953 and a Master of Architecture degree in 1957, both from the University of Pennsylvania, where he was a Theopolis Parsons Chandler Graduate Fellow. Mr. Kohn is a former lieutenant commander of the United States Navy, and was on active duty from 1953 to 1956.

Prior to founding Kohn Pedersen Fox in 1976, Mr. Kohn was President and Partner of John Carl Warnecke and Associates (1967-76); Design Director of Welton Becket Associates New York (1965-67); and Senior Designer at Vincent G. Kling Associates in Philadelphia (1960-65), where two of his designs received AIA National Honor Awards. Mr. Kohn has been the President of KPF since its inception. He is registered in twenty-six states, as well as the United Kingdom and Japan. He is a Fellow of the American Institute of Architects. In 1998, he held the position of president of the AIA New York City Chapter. He is also a member of the Royal Institute of British Architects, the Japan Institute of Architects, and Honorary Member of the Fellows of the Philippine Chapter of the American Institute of Architects. He has served as a Trustee for the University of Pennsylvania. In addition, he was a member of the board of the Museum for African Art of New York and the Silvermine Art Guild. Mr. Kohn currently serves on the Wharton Real Estate Center Advisory Board, the Board of Overseers at the University of Pennsylvania's Graduate School of Fine Arts, and is a trustee of the National Building Museum in Washington, D.C. He is also on the Board of Sheltering Arms Children Service as well as a Trustee for the Urban Land Institute. He was honored by the Sheltering Arms Children Service in 1995. In 1996, he received the Sidney L. Strauss Award from the New York Society of Architects, and in 1997, he was honored with the Lifetime Achievement Award by the Wharton Real Estate Center. He was also recognized, in 1998, with the Ellis Island Medal of Honor, and in 1999, with the President's Award from the New York Chapter of the AIA for KPF. Mr. Kohn has lectured extensively throughout North America, Asia and Europe. He was the keynote speaker at the 1992 Second Asian Congress of Architects in Kuala Lumpur and the 1997 National Philippine Institute of Architects Convention in Manila. Mr. Kohn also lectured on behalf of the US Information Agency in several cities of the former Soviet Union. He is currently a trustee of the Citizen's Budget Commission of New York City.

Mr. Kohn has chaired and served in a number of design award juries. His architectural articles have been published widely, and he has contributed to several architectural monographs. He has recently co-authored a book on the design of the office building with Paul Katz. As a visiting critic and lecturer, he has taught and lectured at numerous colleges and universities. Mr. Kohn has conducted courses at the Harvard Graduate School of Design for the last ten years, and he is Executive Fellow of the school's Executive Education Program.

William Pedersen FAIA FAAR

William Pedersen was born in St. Paul, Minnesota, in 1938. He received a Bachelor of Architecture degree from the University of Minnesota in 1961 and was a recipient of the school's Gargoyle Club Prize. In 1963 he received a Master of Architecture degree from the Massachusetts Institute of Technology, where he was a Whitney Fellow. In 1965 he won the Rome Prize in Architecture.

Prior to founding Kohn Pedersen Fox in 1976, Mr. Pedersen was Vice President of John Carl Warnecke and Associates (1971-76), an associate with I. M. Pei and Partners (1967-71), and a designer with Eduardo Catalano (1964-65) and Pietro Belluschi (1963).

Mr. Pedersen has received numerous design awards for his work at Kohn Pedersen Fox. These include the 1990 American Institute of Architects Architectural Firm Award, the New York Chapter of the AIA Gold Medal of Honor in 1989, the New York Chapter of the AIA 1999 President's Award, and four National AIA Honor Awards for The World Bank Headquarters, Washington, D.C. (1998); Westendstraße 1, Frankfurt, Germany (1994); Procter and Gamble World Headquarters, Cincinnati, Ohio (1987); and 333 Wacker Drive, Chicago, Illinois (1984). He also received several Progressive Architecture Design Awards from 1987 to 1996, and the Prix d'excellence from L'Ordre des Architectes du Québec for 1250 Boulevard René Levésque/IBM Canadian headquarters in Montréal, Canada in 1992. In 1994, the General Services Administration's Design Excellence Program bestowed his work with its highest honor, awarding the Mark O. Hatfield United States Courthouse in Portland, Oregon the Building Design Excellence Award, and in 1998, the courthouse won the GSA Honor Award. Mr. Pedersen has also received a Citation in Architecture for the United States Courthouse in Minneapolis (1996), and a number of awards from other building congresses and architectural associations. In 1998, he was awarded the Gold Medal for lifetime achievement in architecture from Tau Sigma Delta, National Architectural Honor Society. Additional honors include the Arnold W. Brunner Memorial Prize in Architecture for Contributions in Architecture as an Art (1985), awarded by the American Academy and the Institute of Arts and Letters and the 1990 University of Minnesota Alumni Achievement Award.

Mr. Pedersen has been a visiting critic at the Rhode Island School of Design, Columbia University, Harvard University, and held the Eero Saarinen Chair at Yale University in 1986. In addition, he has been honored as the Herbert S. Greenward Distinguished Professor in Architecture at the University of Illinois at Chicago. He is a member of the Architectural League, the New York State Association of Architects, and the Society of Architectural Historians. He is an Honorary Member of the St. Paul Chapter of the AIA; and a Fellow of the American Institute of Architects and of the American Academy in Rome.

Robert L. Cioppa FAIA

Robert L. Cioppa was born in Mount Vernon, New York, in 1942. Mr. Cioppa was a liberal arts honor student at Boston College before receiving his Bachelor of Architecture Degree from Pratt Institute in 1967. That same year, he was the recipient of the New York State Society of Architects Alpha Ro Chi Medal. He is also a graduate of the Stanford University Graduate School of Business Executive Program, which he attended in 1983.

Mr. Cioppa has more than 35 years of experience as an architect and administrator. Prior to Joining Kohn Pedersen Fox, Mr. Cioppa was an Associate at John Carl Warnecke and Associates (1973-76) in New York City. He also worked at Hobart Betts Associates (1968-73) and at Unimark Associates (1967-68). In 1979, three years after joining Kohn Pedersen Fox, Mr. Cioppa was asked to become a Principal of the firm and assumed primary responsibility for the management of major projects. In 1995, upon the retirement of Sheldon Fox, he undertook responsibility for the administration of financial operations for KPF, and has been the Managing Principal for the design and construction of government, corporate headquarters, and investment office buildings totaling more than $1 billion.

Many of the projects for which Mr. Cioppa has served as Managing Principal have received national awards for their design and execution. These awards include: the New York City and the New York State AIA Distinguished Design Award for the ABC Television Studios 23/24, and the New York City Bard Award for the ABC Armory, both in New York City; the New York Chapter AIA Distinguished Design Award for One Logan Square in Philadelphia, Pennsylvania; the Washington, D.C. Chapter AIA Excellence in Design Award for the Washington News Bureau; the Philadelphia Chapter AIA Design Award for Eight Penn Center in Philadelphia, Pennsylvania; a National AIA Design Award for the Procter & Gamble Headquarters in Cincinnati, Ohio; and three General Services Administration Design Awards for the United States courthouses in Portland, Oregon, Foley Square, New York, and Minneapolis, Minnesota. Mr. Cioppa is a member of BOCA International, the Construction Specifications Institute and is a Fellow of the American Institute of Architects.

William C. Louie FAIA

William C. Louie was born in New York City in 1942. Mr. Louie began
working as an architect in 1961, and he received a Bachelor of Science in
Architecture degree from the City College of New York in 1974. Prior to
joining Kohn Pedersen Fox in 1977, Mr. Louie was a Senior Associate at
John Carl Warnecke and Associates (1969-77). At KPF, he has served as a
Design Principal since 1984 on projects accounting for over $4 billion of
new construction, and has helped lead the firm's practice overseas with
projects in Australia, Indonesia, Singapore, Malaysia, Taiwan, Hong
Kong, China, Korea, and Lebanon.

Mr. Louie has received numerous design awards for his projects. Espirito
Santo Plaza, a mixed-use tower in downtown Miami, Florida, received a
2001 New York City AIA Design Award and a 2000 Aurora Award for
best commercial building. The Yuksamdong project, a mixed-use office
tower in Seoul, South Korea, received the Silver 1999 Seoul
Architectural Award. The U.S. Courthouse at Foley Square in New York
City was the recipient of the 1996 GSA Design Honors Award for
Building Design Excellence. In 1990, the New York State AIA Excellence
in Design Award was awarded to his 1325 Avenue of the Americas office
tower in New York City. His General Re Corporation Headquarters in
Stamford, Connecticut, received a New York State AIA Merit Award in
1986. Arbor Circle North & South (Prudential Business Campus) in
Parsippany, New Jersey, received the 1988 National Associates of
Industrial Office Parks' Grand Award. For his creative use of precast
concrete, he received three Pre-stressed Concrete Institute Professional
Awards in 1984, 1986, and 1990 for the Goldome Bank Headquarters in
Buffalo, New York, Arbor Circle North & South, and the Shearson
Lehman Hutton Plaza in New York City, respectively. For the integration
of engineering solutions, he received three New York Association of
Consulting Engineers Awards, two in 1991 and one in 1993, for the
Mellon Bank Center in Philadelphia, Pennsylvania, the Shearson
Lehman Hutton Plaza and the Chifley Tower in Sydney, Australia,
respectively.

Mr. Louie has been a guest lecturer to architects in various cities in Asia
and has served on design juries. He is a Fellow of the American Institute
of Architects.

Lee A. Polisano FAIA RIBA

Lee A. Polisano was born in Atlantic City, New Jersey, in 1952.
In 1974, he received a Bachelor of Arts degree from LaSalle College in
Philadelphia, Pennsylvania, and, in 1977, a Master of Architecture
degree from the Virginia Polytechnic Institute in Blacksburg, Virginia.
Prior to joining Kohn Pedersen Fox in 1981, Mr. Polisano worked at
Kevin Roche-John Dinkeloo & Associates (1977-80) in New Haven,
Connecticut. In 1989, he co-founded Kohn Pedersen Fox International
in London.

Mr. Polisano's work emphasizes the civic and ecological responsibility of
the built environment. Projects such as the innovative World Trade
Center in Amsterdam and the large-scale urban regeneration master
plan for the City of Glasgow have been widely recognized for achieving
these goals. His headquarters for Rabobank in the City of London—
Thames Court—was recently awarded The British Council for Offices'
National Award for Best Urban Workplace for 1999, the 1999 Structural
Steel Design Award (sponsored by British Steel) and a Civic Trust
Commendation.

Mr. Polisano has published several articles on a range of subjects in
Europe and North America, and is frequently invited to address
academic and professional symposia. He was the first recipient of
Virginia Polytechnic Institute's Outstanding Professional Accomplishment
Award and delivered the 125th Anniversary Distinguished Alumni
Address to the university. Mr. Polisano is a Member of the American
Institute of Architects, where he was recently elevated to The College of
Fellows because of his "notable contributions to the advancement of
the profession of architecture". He is also a member of the Royal
Institute of British Architects and the Architektenkammer Berlin.

David M. Leventhal AIA

David. M. Leventhal was born in Boston, Massachusetts, in 1949. He received his Bachelor of Arts degree in 1971 and a Master of Architecture degree in 1978, both from Harvard University. Prior to Joining Kohn Pedersen Fox in 1979, Mr. Leventhal worked at the Metropolitan Museum of Art (1972-73) in New York City, and at Cain Farrell & Bell (1978-1979), the successor firm to McKim, Mead and White, also in New York City. He was made a Principal of Kohn Pedersen Fox Associates and Partner in Charge of Design for KPF International in London in 1989. His design responsibilities include numerous office, mixed-use, institutional, residential and master planning schemes in Europe and Asia.

Mr. Leventhal was the design principal for the recently completed Provinciehuis, headquarters of the Province of South Holland, as well as for the Bismarckstraße office block in Berlin. He is also design partner for two institutional projects which the firm won in international competitions: the new Parliament House in Nicosia, Cyprus and the Rothermere Institute for American Studies at Oxford University. The Oxford project, which has been displayed at the Royal Academy, has recently been completed. He is currently working on designs for a building at the London School of Economics, and office and mixed-use schemes in The Netherlands and the Middle East.

In 1988, Mr. Leventhal received the New York AIA Chapter design award for 70 East 55th Street. The same building received the Tucker Award for Design Excellence in 1989. Mr. Leventhal has lectured at Harvard, the University of Delft, and the and at several international conferences of the A.I.A. He is a member of the collection committee at the Fogg Art Museum at Harvard University and the American Institute of Architects.

Gregory Clement AIA

Gregory Clement was born in Providence, Rhode Island in 1950. He received a Bachelor of Arts degree in 1973 and a Master of Architecture degree in 1975, both from the University of Pennsylvania in Philadelphia. He was the recipient of the Dales Traveling Fellowship in 1974 as well as other merit scholarships. Prior to joining Kohn Pedersen Fox in 1984, Mr. Clement was a Senior Designer at I.M. Pei & Partners (1982-84) in New York City and an Associate at Cathers, Lukens, Thompson (1980-82) in Philadelphia, where he was responsible for the Philadelphia College of Art expansion and restoration, which received an Honorable Mention from the Philadelphia chapter of the AIA in 1982. A Principal at Kohn Pedersen Fox since 1993, he has been responsible for the management of major commercial, corporate, institutional and cultural projects across the United States, Europe, South America and Asia.

Among a wide range of projects, he was the principal-in-charge for the IBM World Headquarters in Armonk, New York; a recently completed office tower for Morgan Stanley sold to Lehman Brothers in New York City; the Rodin Museum in Seoul, South Korea; a new academic facility for the Wharton School of the University of Pennsylvania; the Warsaw Financial Center in Warsaw, Poland; the William Gates Law School at the University of Washington and the Engineering Centers Building at the University of Wisconsin. He currently leads KPF in its role as the Executive Architect for the expansion of the Museum of Modern Art in New York City, and is in charge of a two-phase speculative office project in Rio de Janeiro, Brazil.

Mr. Clement has received prestigious design awards for his work at KPF. These include a Progressive Architecture Design Citation for Rockefeller Plaza West 1 (1989), the AIA/BIA Brick in Architecture Award for the Capital Cities/ABC Headquarters in New York City (1993), the Westchester, New York Chapter AIA Award (1997) for the IBM Corporate Headquarters in Armonk, New York, and a Chicago Athenaeum American Architecture Award (1998) for the same building. He has also received awards for the Rodin Museum and Samsung Headquarters Plaza in Seoul, South Korea, including a Progressive Architecture Design Award (1996), a Design Award from the New York City AIA (1996), the Design Award for Excellence from the New York State AIA and the ID Magazine Annual Design Review Award (Environment Category), both in 1999.

Mr. Clement's commitment to architectural education includes participating in reviews at several institutions, including Princeton University and the University of Hawaii, where he is currently an Adjunct Professor. In addition to his professional pursuits Mr. Clement has shown his collage art in New England art galleries in recent years. He is a member of the American Institute of Architects and the Large Firm Roundtable. He is a registered architect in Pennsylvania, Delaware, Connecticut and New York.

Michael Greene AIA

Michael Greene was born in Winston-Salem, North Carolina, in 1954. He received a Bachelor of Environmental Design degree in 1976, from North Carolina State University in Winston-Salem, and in 1978, a Master of Architecture degree from the Virginia Polytechnic Institute in Richmond, Virginia. Prior to joining Kohn Pedersen Fox in 1985, Mr. Greene was affiliated with Edwin E. Bouldin, Winston-Salem, North Carolina (1983-1984).

A Principal at Kohn Pedersen Fox since 1997, Mr. Greene has more than 24 years of experience as an architect. He has been responsible for the management of projects in North America, Europe and Asia, accounting for well over $2 billion dollars in construction, and has been instrumental in shaping the operational methodology of the firm. His past projects for KPF include the Hyatt Regency in Old Greenwich, Connecticut, Shearson Lehman Plaza in New York City, 20 Cabot Square in Canary Wharf, London, and the JR Central Towers and Station in Nagoya, Japan. More recently, he is Managing Principal for the Gannett/USA Today Headquarters complex outside Washington, DC; the Singapore Exchange Headquarters in downtown Singapore; and a high-rise and residential development for the Monarch Group in Toronto, Ontario.

Mr. Greene is a member of several professional associations, including the Architects Advisory Committee of the New York Building Congress. He has also served as guest critic and lecturer at universities and professional conferences. Mr. Greene is a registered architect in New York, Delaware, and North Carolina and is a member of the American Institute of Architects.

Paul Katz AIA

Paul Katz was born in 1957 in Cape Town, South Africa, where he began studying architecture at the University of Cape Town. He graduated with a Bachelor in Architecture and Town Planning from the Technion, Israel Institute of Technology in 1982, and received a Master in Architecture from Princeton University in 1984. Before joining KPF in 1984, Mr. Katz worked for Michael Graves in Princeton, New Jersey, and Karmi Associates in Israel.

At Kohn Pedersen Fox, Mr. Katz has senior responsibilities in all aspects of commercial architecture including business development, management and design, and is Principal-in-Charge of several projects in North America, Europe and Asia. Mr. Katz established KPF's office in Japan and has been responsible for developing the majority of the projects in the region. The projects include the JR Central Towers, the largest commercial building in Japan, and the World Financial Center in Shanghai.

A Principal at Kohn Pedersen Fox since 1998, Mr. Katz has directed projects in over 10 countries for international developers, including Canary Wharf, Hongkong Land, Mitsui Fudosan, the Mori Building Company, Sun Hung Kai, and many U.S. developers. He has recently been in charge of the Mohegan Sun Resort in Connecticut; an office tower at Canary Wharf, London; the Roppongi 6-Chome development, the largest mixed-use project in Tokyo; the Kowloon Station Tower, which will be the tallest building in Hong Kong; and the Chater House mixed-use development, also in Hong Kong.

Mr. Katz has served as a guest critic and lecturer at universities and international professional conferences. Together with Mr. A.E. Kohn, he has conducted a course on the design of office buildings at the Harvard Graduate School of Design for the last four years, and they are currently co-authoring a book on the subject to be published in 2001.
Mr. Katz is a member of the American Institute of Architects and the Urban Land Institute.

James von Klemperer AIA

James von Klemperer was born in Northampton, Massachusetts, in 1957. He graduated from Phillips Academy Andover in 1975 and went to Harvard University where he received a Bachelor of Arts in History and Literature in 1979. He studied architecture at Trinity College in Cambridge, England as a recipient of the Charles Henry Fiske Scholarship. He then received a Master in Architecture degree from Princeton University in 1983. Prior to joining Kohn Pedersen Fox Associates in 1984, Mr. von Klemperer worked as a designer at Booth Hanson in Chicago, Illinois (1981) and at Batey and Mack in San Francisco, California (1982).

A principal at Kohn Pedersen Fox Associates since 1998, Mr. von Klemperer has been responsible for the design and management of major commissions in North America and Asia; attending projects from conception to completion. In the United States, his work includes the Foley Square Courthouse in New York City, which was the recipient of the 1996 GSA Design Honors Award for Building Design Excellence In the United States. Other projects include: the headquarters for International Economics in Washington D.C.; the Mohegan Sun Resort hotel, casino and arena complex totaling 5 million square feet in northern Connecticut; and 119 North Wacker Drive, an office tower in Chicago, Illinois.

Mr. von Klemperer has also had significant experience designing projects abroad, beginning with the U.S. Ambassador residence in Nicosia, Cyprus, completed in 1993. In Shanghai, he designed Plaza 66 on Nanjing Road, a 900-foot high office tower. In Indonesia, he completed the Bank Niaga Headquarters. In Korea, he has worked for the Dongbu Corporation, first on the Yuksamdong building, which was awarded the silver medal from the city of Seoul, and on their recently completed headquarters tower on Teheran Road. In Singapore, he designed 30 Hill Street, an environmentally efficient office building on the site of the former U.S. Embassy, and in Paris, a courtyard office complex for EMGP.

Mr. von Klemperer has lectured at Cambridge University, Harvard University, Smith College and the École Spéciale d'Architecture (ESA) in Paris. He has served on design juries in various universities including Harvard, Princeton, Yale, and Cambridge. He is a member of the American Institute of Architects and the Urban Land Institute.

Peter Schubert AIA

Peter Schubert was born in Evanston, Illinois, in 1955. He received his Bachelor of Arts degree from Ohio State University in 1978, and a Master in Architecture degree from Columbia University in 1981. Prior to joining Kohn Pedersen Fox in 1984, Mr. Schubert was a staff architect at Jon Michael Schwarting and Associates (1981-82), where he was a member of the team that designed the Fashion Institute of Technology campus. The FIT project was a recipient of the Progressive Architecture Award for an Urban Design Master Plan. He was also a staff architect at Peterson/Littenberg Architects (1982-83), and at Skidmore, Owings & Merrill (1983), both in New York City.

A Principal at Kohn Pedersen Fox since 1998, Mr. Schubert has been Design Principal for a variety of projects in North America, Asia and Europe. His academic and institutional work includes a master plan for New York University Law School in Manhattan; a design entry for the Sloan School of Management at MIT, a master plan for Regis College in Weston, Massachusetts, and the renovation of the Children's Hospital of Philadelphia. He was also Principal-in-Charge on the First Hawaiian Bank Center in Honolulu, Hawaii, and his public sector work includes serving as Design Principal for the Atlanta Federal Center for the General Services Administration. Additional corporate work includes a mixed-use corporate headquarters for the Samyang Foods Company, and a headquarters building for Posteel, both in Seoul, South Korea. He has extensive master planning, residential and interiors experience.

For his work at Kohn Pedersen Fox Mr. Schubert has received the Certificate of Engineering Excellence from the New York Association of Consulting Engineers for the Mellon Bank Center (1991); a Design Citation from 38th Annual Progressive Architecture Awards for the World Bank Headquarters (1990); and both the Award of Merit in Design and Manufacturing Excellence from the Architectural Precast Association (1990), and Best High-Rise/Urban Building from the National Association of Industrial and Office Parks (1988) for 500 E Street. His work on the First Hawaiian Bank Center was featured in 12 Prophesies for the 21st Century by L'Arca Edizioni (1997). He has taught at Columbia University, and at the Catholic University, in Washington, D.C., and Rome. He is currently a member of the faculty at the Cooper Union for the Advancement of Science and Art in New York City

Mr. Schubert is a member of the New York State Association of Architects, the Society of Architectural Historians, the Society for Historic Preservation, and the American Institute of Architects.

Jill N. Lerner AIA

Jill N. Lerner was born in Metuchen, New Jersey in 1953. In 1976, Ms. Lerner received her Bachelor of Architecture degree from Cornell University where she was a recipient of the Alpha Rho Chi Medal awarded for Leadership, Service and Merit. Prior to joining Kohn Pedersen Fox in 1994, she was a Senior Vice President and Project Director with Ellerbe Becket (1987-1994).

Ms. Lerner, an architect with over 25 years of design and management experience, has been a leader in diversifying Kohn Pedersen Fox's body of work into new building types, particularly in academic and institutional design work. A Principal at the firm since 1999, she had led numerous award-winning projects and competitions. She is responsible for all aspects of the projects and is the primary client contact, from initial programming and conceptual design through completion. Her focus has been on complex institutional buildings. Current projects include the new NYU School of Law in New York City; a major expansion of the Children's Hospital of Philadelphia; and a new campus for Amgen in Puerto Rico. Other recent work at KPF includes major projects for the Wharton School at the University of Pennsylvania, in Philadelphia; the University of Maryland Medical Systems in Baltimore; and a new mixed-use academic complex for CUNY's Baruch College in New York City.

Ms. Lerner's projects at Ellerbe Becket have received national awards for their design and execution, including the New York State AIA Architecture Award in 1999; the New York City AIA Design Award 1990; the Progressive Architecture Design Award 1991; and the Modern Healthcare/AIA Design Award for the New York Psychiatric Institute in 1993.

Ms. Lerner has been an active member of the American Institute of Architects. She has served on the Board of Directors of the NYC AIA Chapter, and also chaired the NYC Finance Committee in 1997, after serving on the committee from 1995-1996. She has been a featured speaker for a variety of organizations including the Society of College and University Planners (SCUP), and Cornell University/AISC. Most recently, she was a contributor and co-editor of *Construction in Cities: Social, Environmental, Political, and Economic Concerns*, published by CRC press in 2001.

Following the World Trade Center disaster on September 11, 2001, M. Lerner has co chaired the New York New Visions Memorials Process team involved in reseach, outreach, temporary memorials, and advocacy issues. She is presently co-chair of the Memorial Committee for the Civic Alliance as well.

Anthony Mosellie AIA

Anthony Mosellie was born in Brooklyn, New York, in 1962. In 1984, he received his Bachelor of Science in Architecture degree from the University of Michigan in Ann Arbor, Michigan. Prior to joining Kohn Pedersen Fox in 1988, he worked for Welton Becket Associates (1984-85) and Murphy/Jahn Architects (1985-88).

Mr. Mosellie has over 18 years of experience as an architect and manager on a wide variety of projects. His projects include: 20 Cabot Square, Canary Wharf, London, England; Carwill House, Stratton, Vermont; Taichung Tower I, Taichung, Taiwan; Four First Union Tower, Charlotte, North Carolina; 555 Mission Street, San Francisco, California; and Baruch College in New York City.

Since 1993, Mr. Mosellie has been responsible for airport and transportation related projects for Kohn Pedersen Fox. He has managed four major aviation projects, which include: International Terminal One, Philadelphia International Airport; Terminal B South Addition, Logan International Airport; New Terminal, Buffalo Niagara International Airport; and Regional Commuter Terminal, Ronald Reagan Washington National Airport. A Principal at KPF since in 1999, he has assumed the role of Principal-in-Charge for Aviation Projects. He is currently the Managing Principal for the $ 1 billion Tier 2 Midfield Concourse project at Washington Dulles International Airport.

Mr. Mosellie is a member of the American Institute of Architects, the Airports Consultant Council and the American Association of Airport Executives. He has served on design juries at the University of Pennsylvania, and his articles have been published in architectural and aviation journals.

Ir Ron Bakker

Ron Bakker was born in Arnhem, The Netherlands, in 1962. In 1989 he received his degree from Delft University of Technology, Department of Architecture and Urban Planning. As a student, he studied under the tutorship of Aldo van Eyck, Herman Hertzberger, Niels Prak and Joop van Stigt. Prior to joining Kohn Pedersen Fox in 1992, Mr Bakker worked for Tecton Architects, Amsterdam, The Netherlands between 1983 and 1984 on the renovation of ten historic houses on local canals. In 1986 he worked for Kruger, van Duin en van Basten Architects in Rijswijk, The Netherlands where he worked on the restoration of the Queens Palace in The Hague. Mr Bakker has also worked for Wickham Van Eyck Architects, London (1987), Fitch Benoy, London (1989), and Verbeek & Bell Architects, London (1989-92).

A Director at Kohn Pedersen Fox since 1999, Mr. Bakker has extensive experience in a number of European countries and is primarily responsible for the firm's work in The Netherlands as a senior designer and project manager. In recent years he has been involved in a range of renovation and design projects including urban planning schemes, office and residential buildings, that include the Hoofddorp East and West Masterplan, the renovation and expansion of the World Trade Centre in Amsterdam and Provinciehuis, and the legislative headquarters for the Province of South Holland. Prior to working in The Netherlands for KPF, Ron Bakker was the project architect on the Bismarckstraße office building in Berlin. Currently he is senior designer on the Masterplan for the new town of Almere Poort in The Netherlands.

Ron Bakker is a registered architect in the United Kingdom, the Netherlands and Belgium. During his studies, he was a Dutch national representative involved in the organization of the European Architecture Students Assembly and taught at the Danish Summer School in 1984.

Karen Ann Cook AIA

Karen Cook was born in Los Angeles, California, in 1962. She received a Bachelor of Art in Art and Architecture (1984) and a Bachelor of Architecture (1986) from Rice University, Houston, Texas. She also studied architecture at the University of Virginia's program in Vicenza, Italy. Ms. Cook received her Master in Architecture from Harvard University Graduate School of Design in 1990. In 1998, she attended an executive course, "Women Leading Business" at Harvard University Business School.

Ms. Cook joined KPF in 1984, working on American and European projects, and in 1989 helped found KPF International in London. In 1999 she was made a Director. She has led design teams for projects in Great Britain, Germany, the Netherlands and the Czech Republic. She has worked on small and large office buildings, mixed-use developments, urban masterplan projects and airport design.

In January 2000 her article, "Influences on European Architectural Design," was published in the US journal *Urban Land*. She has lectured on European architectural practice and the influence of technology on design at several American Institute of Architects national conventions. She is licensed in New York State, and as a member of the AIA, she has served as a Board member and Treasurer of its UK Chapter. Ms. Cook has participated on student and professional juries for American and European universities.

Fred Pilbrow RIBA

Fred Pilbrow was born in London, England, in 1962. He received his Bachelor of Arts Degree at the University of Cambridge in 1984 and his Architectural Association Diploma in 1991. Prior to joining KPF in 1993, Mr. Pilbrow worked in private practice as a partner in AO Partnership (1987-1991).

Since joining Kohn Pedersen Fox, Mr. Pilbrow has been responsible for the design of prestigious projects for both public and private sector clients. Such projects include the new House of Representatives, Cyprus (1st Prize in an international open competition), the Rothermere Institute for American Studies, University of Oxford and 110 Bishopsgate, an innovative multi-tenant high-rise tower in the City of London. He was promoted to Director in December 1999.

Mr. Pilbrow's awards include: Professional First Prize in Open Competition for the Blanc de Bierges Street Furniture; the Royal Academy Summer Show Architect's Journal/Bovis Design Award 1991 for the Otemon Housing project in Fukuoka, Japan; and the 1989 Connolly Prize for furniture design. He has taught at the Bartlett School of Architecture, the University of North London and has also served as a visiting critic at the Liverpool Winter School, the Architectural Association, South Bank Polytechnic and East London Polytechnic.

Prior to his architectural career, Mr. Pilbrow worked in theatre as a set and lighting designer. Productions include: Apart from George, Royal Court 1987, The Strangeness of Others, National Theatre 1988, and Macbeth, 1988 National Theatre, US Tour. He is a member of the Royal Institute of British Architects.

James E. Outen

James E. Outen was born in Kannapolis, North Carolina in 1947. In 1966 he served in the U.S. Army and did a tour of duty in the 5th Special Forces Group in Vietnam between 1967-68. He was awarded Bachelor of Science in Architecture at the City University in New York in 1975. Prior to joining Kohn Pedersen Fox in 1980, Mr. Outen worked for I.M. Pei & Partners and Philip Johnson Architects in New York City.

Mr. Outen has over 25 years of experience in the design and management of a series of high-profile office, commercial and hospitality projects in North America, Europe (particularly in the United Kingdom and Spain), the Middle East and Asia. He has been responsible for the execution of some of the most technically complex projects. Promoted to Director in December 2001, he is currently responsible for contracts, fees, schedule, staffing, monitoring day-to-day progress, working with consultants, snd ensuring that projects are delivered on time and within agreed budgets at KPF's London office.

His built projects at KPF include the One Logan Square office tower and Four Seasons Hotel in Philadelphia, Pennsylvania; the executive offices and TV studios of the American Broadcasting Company in New York City; 225 Wacker Drive in Chicago, Illinois; Goldman Sachs' European Headquarters in London; the Atlanta Federal Center in Atlanta Georgia, the Bur Juman Centre in Dubai, the United Arab Emirates, the Corporate Headquarters for Endesa in Madrid, Spain; the Posteel Corporation's Headquarters tower in Seoul, South Korea; and the mixed-use Orchard Road project in Singapore.

Selected Building Credits
1993-2002

This list of credits for buildings and projects is arranged in chronological order within each given year, according to the date when first commissioned. It includes buildings and projects designed in the New York and London offices. Those featured in this monograph are indicated by their page number. First year indicates year of commission; followed by year of completion when the building was completed prior to 2001; estimated year of completion if the project is going ahead or under construction as of December 2001; or year design work was completed on an unbuilt project or competition. Area of construction, given in both square feet and square meters, is almost always approximate. Number of floors given may vary with the actual building due to mechanical floors, parking levels, above and below ground, etc. Note that distinctions between levels below and above grade are not always indicated.

Forum Frankfurt
Frankfurt am Main, Germany
1988-1997
Client: Oppenheim Immobilien-Kapitalanlage-gesellschaft mbH, and Despa Deutsche Sparkassen-Immobilien-Anlage-Gesellschaft mbH. Principal-in-Charge: Lee A. Polisano. Design Principal: William Pedersen. Associate Principal: Andreas Hausler. Project Architect: Gunter Dörr. Job Captain: David Long. Project Team: Simon Appelby, Craig Burns, J. William Davis, Katherine Dean, Astrid Fuhrmeister, Suzanne Geiger, Andreas Hausler, Lars Hesselgren, Annette Kachel, Paul King, Ursula Klein, Cecilia Kramer, Cindy Marshall, Wolfgang Neumüller, Michael Regan, Francisco Rencoret, Gerhard Rinkens, Marcus Springer, Brigit Zwankhuizen. Associate Architect: Nägele Hofmann Tiedemann + Partner, Frankfurt. Structure: Concrete frame. Major Exterior Materials: Glass, aluminum, stone. Area: 828,500 gross square feet, 77,000 gross square meters. Number of Floors: 25 and 35.

The World Bank Headquarters   *page 32*
Washington, D.C.
1989-1998
Client: The International Bank for Reconstruction & Development (The World Bank). Principal-in-Charge: A. Eugene Kohn. Managing Principal: Sheldon Fox. Design Principal: William Pedersen. Project Designer: Craig B. Nealy. Project Managers: William H. Cunningham, Thomas Holzmann. Job Captain: Joseph P. Ruocco. Project Team: Robin Andrade, Isabelle Autones, Dayo Babalola, Pavel Balla, Vladimir Balla, Joseph Barnes, Mark Barnhouse, Gabrielle Blackman, Nathan Clark Corser, Suzanne Cregan, Cynthia Crier, Glen DaCosta, Eric Daum, Anthony DiGrazia, Dominic Dunn, Valerie Edozien, Mark Fiedler, Robin Goldberg, Armando Gutierrez, Fia Hekmat, Angeline Ho, Koichiro Ishiguro, Sulan Kolatan, Judy Lee, Ming Leung, Jenny Ling, Michael Martin, Kristen Minor, Nicole Mronz, Beth Niemi, Hun Oh, James Papoutsis, Paul Regan, Duncan Reid, James Seger, Esmatollah Seraj, Audrey Shen, Frank Shenton, Emil Stojakovic, John Stoltze, Hisaya Sugiyama, David Thompson, Thomas Vandenbout. Competition Associate Architect: Kress Cox Associates, Washington, D.C. Structure: Poured-in slurry wall foundation, post-tensioned concrete superstructure. Major Exterior Materials: Glass, aluminum, painted, pre-cast concrete curtain wall. Area: 1,324,334 gross square feet, 123,163 gross square meters. Number of Floors: 18.

JR Central Towers and Station   *page 46*
Nagoya, Japan
1990-2000
Client: Central Japan Railway Co. Principals-in-Charge: A. Eugene Kohn, Paul Katz. Design Team Leader: John Koga. Project Manager: Michael Greene. Job Captain: Roger Cooner. Project Team: Christine Awad, Dawn Burcaw, Carey Chu, Jerry Conduff, Milton Curry, Thomas Demetrion, John Lucas, Lucinda Dip, Mary Sue Gaffney, Yukio Hasegawa, Tomas Hernandez, Douglas Hocking, Akiko Jacobson, Takatomo Kashiwabara, Kevin Kennon, Kristen Minor, James Moustafellos, Glenn Rescalvo, Erika Schmitt, Lloyd Sigal, Emil Stojakovic, Hisaya Sugiyama, Edward Tachibana, Shinichiro Yorita. Master Architect: Seizo Sakata, Sakakura Associates, Tokyo. Associate Architect: Taisei Corporation: Nagoya, Sakakura Associated, Tokyo. Structure: Steel, reinforced concrete. Major Exterior Materials: Pre-cast concrete panels with glass and tile, glass and aluminum curtain wall. Area: 4,483,871 gross square feet, 417,000 gross square meters. Number of Floors: 86 floors total: 36 floors (hotel), 34 floors (office), 14 floors (department store), 2 floors (entertainment).

Roppongi Hills Tower   *page 302*
Tokyo, Japan
1990, 1997-2003
Client: Mori Building Development Co., Ltd. Principals-in-Charge: A. Eugene Kohn, Paul Katz. Design Principal: William Pedersen. Senior Designers: Craig B. Nealy, Douglas Hocking, Joshua Chaiken. Coordination Leaders: John Lucas, Hisaya Sugiyama, Rashmi Vasavada. Project Team: Darlington Brown, Philip Brown, Anna Crittenden, Hogan Chun, Johannes Knoops, Plato Marinakos, Hiroshi Nakajima, Kenichi

Noguchi, Wat Puntoumpoti, Gabriel Wick, Shinichiro Yorita, Jason Zerafa. Associate Architect: Mori Biru Architects & Engineers, Tokyo. Structure: Concrete, steel. Major Exterior Materials: Glass, pre-cast concrete. Area: 3,530,000 gross square feet, 328,290 gross square meters. Number of Floors: 58.

Warsaw Financial Center
Warsaw, Poland
1991-1999
Client: EP Partners, Ltd., Golub & Company. Principals-in-Charge: Gregory Clement. Senior Designer: Richard Clarke. Project Manager: Ming Leung. Project Team: Vladimir Balla, Valerie Edozian, Trish Flemming, Ming Leung, Jenny Ling, Kristen Minor, Beth Neimi, Erika Schmitt. Associate Architect: Biuro Projekty Architektury J&J, Warsaw, A. Epstein and Sons International, Chicago. Structure: Reinforced concrete. Major Exterior Materials: Granite, aluminum, insulated glass. Area: 709,677 gross square feet, 66,000 gross square meters. Number of Floors: 32.

First Hawaiian Center   *page 52*
Honolulu, Hawaii
1991-1996
Client: First Hawaiian Bank. Principals-in-Charge: William Pedersen, Peter Schubert. Managing Principals: Sheldon Fox, Robert Cioppa. Project Manager: Charles Alexander. Job Captains: Deborah Booher, Kristen Minor, Bun-Wah Nip. Interior Project Architect: Barbara Lewandoska. Project Team: Juan Alavo, Michelle Biancardo, Barbara Bures, Celia Chiang, Carey Chu, Irvin Glassman, Robert Goodwin, Armando Gutierrez, Tomas Hernandez, Merrie Hevredeis, Takatomo Kashiwabara, Malvina Lampietti, Molly McGowan, Elaine Newman, Marcie Moss, Elaine Newman, Ichiro Oda, Dex Ott, Glenn Rescalvo, Erika Schmitt, Audrey Shen, Joseph Spada, Yutaka Takiura, Paul Tarantino. Associate Architect: Luersen Lowrey Tsushima. Structure: Steel, concrete. Major Exterior Materials: Granite, limestone, low-energy glass. Area: 699,920 gross square feet, 65,092 gross square meters. Number of Floors: 30.

Bismarckstraße 101   *page 62*
Berlin, Germany
1992-1994
Client: Ferinel Deutschland GmbH. Principal-in-Charge: Lee. A Polisano. Design Principal: David Leventhal. Project Architect: Karen Cook. Job Captain: Ron Bakker. Project Team: Astrid Fuhrmeister, Lars Hesselgren, Sorina Kopp, Eliseo Rabbi, Yasmin Al-Ani Spence. Associate Architects: Patschke Klotz & Partner, Berlin and IPB, Berlin. Structure: Concrete frame. Major Exterior Materials: Glass, aluminium. Area: 80,700 gross square feet, 7,505 gross square meters. Number of Floors: 6.

Mark O. Hatfield United States Courthouse   *page 66*
Portland, Oregon
1992-1997
Client: General Services Administration. Principal: William Pedersen. Design Team Leaders: Jerri Smith, Gabrielle Blackman, Douglas Hocking. Project Manager: Sudhir Jambhekar. Project Team: Juan Alavo, Isabelle Autones, Vladimir Balla, Nathan Clark Corser, Trent Tesch. Associate Architect: BOORA Architects, Inc. Structure: Steel. Major Exterior Materials: Low-energy glass at public lobbies and circulation, reflective glass at office and chambers, painted aluminum mullions, limestone, granite, standing seam metal roof. Area: 563,000 gross square feet, 52,359 gross square meters. Number of Floors: 16.

Taichung Tower   *page 74*
Taichung, Taiwan
1992-2001
Client: Tzung Tang Development Group. Principal-in-Charge: A. Eugene Kohn. Design Principal: William Louie. Project Manager: Peter Gross. Senior Designer: Robert Goodwin. Coordination Leader: Bun-Wah Nip. Project Team: Alexander Apetkar, Vladimir Balla, Monika Brugger, Luben Dimcheff, Nazila Schabestari Duran, Christopher Ernst, Patrick

Hwang, Carrie Johnson, Michael Levy, Yan Meng, Aida Saleh, Eva Tiedemann, David Weinberg, Ehrmei Yuan. Associate Architect: Chang & Jan Architects & Planners. Structure: Steel superstructure, concrete subgrade. Major Exterior Materials: Aluminum and glass curtain wall, low-energy high performance glass, stainless steel, marble, granite. Area: 634,408 gross square feet, 59,000 gross square meters. Number of Floors: 47.

Telecom Headquarters
Buenos Aires, Argentina
1993-1998
Client: Benito Roggio e Hijos SA. Principal-in-Charge: A. Eugene Kohn. Managing Principal: Gregory Clement. Senior Designer: Tómas Alvarez. Coordination Team: Andrés Lorenzo (Roggio), Patricia Manghi (Roggio), Claudio Tabanera (Roggio). Project Manager: Walter Chabla. Job Captain: Glen DaCosta. Interior Designer: Carey Chu. Interior Project Manager: Miguel Perez (Hampton Rivoira y Asociador). Project Team: Elina Cardet, Celia Chiang, Larry Cohen, Kurt Dannwolf, Angeline Ho, Pablo Seggiaro. Associate Architect: Hampton-Rivoira y Asociados. Structure: Concrete core, steel floor. Major Exterior Materials: Glass, metal, architectural concrete. Area: 344,086 gross square feet, 32,000 gross square meters. Number of Floors: 13.

Minneapolis United States Courthouse
Minneapolis, Minnesota
1993-1996
Client: BPT Properties, General Services Administration. Design Principal: William Pedersen. Managing Principal: Robert Cioppa. Senior Designer: Richard Clark. Project Manager: Laurie Butler. Job Captain: Roger Cooner. Project Team: Walter Chobla, John Lucas, Elaine Newman, James Seger, Lloyd Sigal, Christopher Stoddard. Associate Architect: The Alliance (Minneapolis). Structure: Post-tensioned concrete. Major Exterior Materials: Pre-cast concrete, low-energy glass, aluminum, granite. Area: 740,000 gross square feet, 68,820 gross square meters. Number of Floors: 15.

Dongbu Kangnam Tower   *page 80*
Seoul, South Korea
1993-2001
Client: Dongbu Corporation. Design Principals: William Pedersen, James von Klemperer. Project Managers: Gregory Clement, Peter Gross. Senior Designer: Jisop Han. Job Captain: Isabelle Autones. Project Team: Hao Ko, Halim Lee, Jinseuk Lee, Methanee Massirarat, Jaeyoung Shin. Associate Architects: Do Si Architecture, Samarac Architects & Consultants. Structure: Concrete, steel. Major Exterior Materials: Glass curtain wall with stainless steel mullion caps. Area: 636,000 gross square feet, 59,148 gross square meters. Number of Floors: 35 (above grade), 7 (below grade).

Buffalo Niagara International Airport   *page 90*
Cheektowaga, New York
1993-1997
Client: Niagara Frontier Transportation Authority. Principals-in-Charge: A. Eugene Kohn, Anthony Mosellie. Design Principal: William Pedersen. Design Team Leader: Duncan Reid, Richard Clarke. Coordination Leader: Lucinda Dip, Peter Gross, Bun-Wah Nip. Project Manager: Anthony Mosellie. Project Team: Philip Brown, Carey Chu, Christopher Ernst, Kar-Hwa Ho, Brian Kaufman, I-Ann Lin, Elaine Newman, Lucinda Veikos, William Vinyard. Associate Architects: William Nicholas Bodouva and Associates, Cannon Design Inc. Structure: Steel. Major Exterior Materials: Metal cladding, glass. Area: 285,000 gross square feet, 26,505 gross square meters. Number of Floors: 3.

Atlanta Federal Center
Atlanta, Georgia
1993-1996
Clients: Prentiss Properties, Atlanta Economic Development Corp., General Services Administration. Principal-in-Charge: A. Eugene Kohn. Design Principal: Peter Schubert. Senior Designer: Tómas Alvarez.

Project Manager: Jim Outen. Job Captain: Dayo Babalola. Associate Architects: Turner Associates Architects and Planners, Inc., Stevens & Wilkinson, Inc., Cheeks/Hornbein & Associates. Structure: Concrete. Major Exterior Materials: Stone, aluminum, pre-cast concrete. Area: 1,800,000 gross square feet, 167,400 gross square meters. Number of Floors: 30.

William H. Gates Hall
University of Washington Law School   *page 100*
Seattle, Washington
1993-2002
Client: University of Washington. Principal-in-Charge: Gregory Clement. Design Principal: William Pedersen. Senior Designer: Jerri Smith. Project Managers/Job Captains: Nathan Clark Corser, Victor Pechaty. Director of Computer Services: Tomas Hernandez. Project Team: Luigi Ciaccia, Eunsook Choi, Miranti Gumayana, Susana Su, Trent Tesch. Structure: Steel columns/beams, concrete sheer walls. Major Exterior Materials: Brick masonry, stone base, fritted glass, and pitted aluminum wall. Area: 204,000 gross square feet, 18,972 gross square meters. Number of Floors: 6.

Provinciehuis   *page 108*
The Hague, Netherlands
1994-1998
Client: Mabon BV (Owner Commerz Grundbesitz Inv. CGI). Principal-in-Charge: Lee A. Polisano. Design Principal: David Leventhal. Senior Designer: Kevin P. Flanagan. Project Architect: Ron Bakker. Project Manager: Bernard Tulkens. Job Captains: Craig Burn, Sarah Susman. Interior Project Designer: Eve Waldron. Project Team: Hanny Aichman, Vanessa Bartulovic, Niamh Billings, Brenda Bowman, Florence Coleman, Lynda Dossey, Lindsay Gwilliam, Willemina Hagenauw, Claudia Hasselbach, Herman Hotze, Craig Kiner, Ursula Klein, Robert Mathewson, Gareth McLachlen, Neil Merryweather, Kevin O,Leary, Ross Page, Kia Pedersen, Howard Rosenberg, Katherine Soulas, Andrew Waugh, Dean Weeden, Anna Williamson. Associate Architect: LIAG Architekten en bouwadviseurs. Structure: Concrete frame. Major Exterior Materials: Brick, clear glass, white aluminum, stainless steel. Area: (New Building) 251,000 gross square feet, 23,343 gross square meters. (Renovation) 215,200 gross square feet, 20,013 gross square meters. Number of Floors: 5 and 7.

Plaza 66   *page 118*
Shanghai, China
1994-2001
Client: Hang Lung Development Co., Ltd. Managing Principals: A. Eugene Kohn, Paul Katz. Design Principals: William Louie, James von Klemperer. Coordination Leader: Dominic Dunn. Project Manager: William Schweber. Project Coordinator: John Lucas. Project Team: Donna Barry, Andrew Bernheimer, Carol Chang, Joy Chen, Larry Cohen, Angelo Directo, Nazila Shabestari Duran, Steven Frankel, Armando Gutierrez, Rena Gyftopoulos, Daniel Heuberger, Francisca Insulza, John Lucas, Qingyun Ma, Tracy Malfetano, Beth Niemi, Roy Pachecano, Marie Richter, Joseph Spada, Kees Van Der Sande, William Vinyard, Nicola Walter. Associate Architect: Frank C. Y. Feng Architects and Associates, (HK) Ltd. Structure: Concrete. Major Exterior Materials: Aluminum, glass, stainless steel storefronts. Area: 3,225,806 gross square feet, 300,000 gross square meters. Number of Floors: 60 (Tower 1), 44 (Tower 2), 5 (Retail), 3 (Below grade parking).

Singapore Exchange Centre   *page 130*
Singapore
1994-2001
Client: United Overseas Bank Limited. Principal-in-Charge: Robert Cioppa. Design Principal: William Louie. Managing Principal: Michael Greene. Senior Designer: Robert Whitlock. Project Manager: Paul Pichardo. Job Captains: Bun-Wah Nip, Ming Leung. Project Team: Christine Awad, Christopher Gebhart, Douglas Hocking, Eric Höweler, Eun Kim, Richard Lee, David Lukes, Michael Marcolini, Widia Ranti, Michael Sewell, Tony Song, Andrea Tedesche, Mark Edward Townsend,

Hugh Trumbull, Helen Wang. Associate Architect: Architects 61. Structure: Concrete, steel. Major Exterior Materials: Granite, marble, slate, stainless steel, aluminum panels, painted aluminum, glass. Area: 872, 600 gross square feet, 81,152 gross square meters. Number of Floors: 29.

The Rothermere American Institute,
Oxford University   *page 138*
Oxford, England
1994-2001
Client: Oxford University Surveyors Office. Principal-in-Charge: David Leventhal. Design Principal: Fred Pilbrow. Project Architect: Jim Dunster. Project Manager: Jon Neville-Jones. Project Team: Geoff Cartwright, Ben Elsdon, Melissa Doughty, Simon Hall, Clare Mason, Neil Merryweather, Rick Milliship, Masahiro Nakatani, Graham Newell, Ross Page, Dean Weeden, Paul Yuen. Structure: Concrete, steel. Major Exterior Materials: Stone, concrete, glass, cast steel, lead. Area: 26,900 gross square feet, 2,502 gross square meters. Number of Floors: 4.

Cyprus House of Representatives   *page 150*
Nicosia, Cyprus
1994
Client: Ministry of Communication & Works, Republic of Cyprus. Principal-in-Charge: Lee Polisano. Design Principal: David Leventhal. Senior Designer: Fred Pilbrow. Project Architect: Jim Dunster. Project Manager: Jon Neville-Jones. Project Team: Vanessa Bartulovic, Scott Berry, Nikki Blustin, Pat Bryan, Nicola Devine, Mark Gausepohl, Willemina Hagenauw, Lars Hesselgren, Karen Hilton, Herman Hotze, Katherine Kennedy, Steve King, James Langford, Neil Merryweather, Ian Milne, Luc Monsigny, John Morgan, Lucy O' Brien, Ross Page, Kia Pedersen, Peter Provost, Marcus Springer, Sarah Susman, Nick Swannell, Teal Usher, Dean Weeden. Associate Architect: D. Kythreotis & Associates. Structure: Reinforced concrete frame. Major Exterior Materials: Sandstone, marble, clear glass. Area: 215,280 gross square feet, 20,000 gross square meters. Number of Floors: 4.

Bloomingdale's Beverly Hills
Beverly Hills, California
1994
Client: Bloomingdale's/Federated Department Stores, Inc. Principal-in-Charge/Design Principal: Kevin Kennon. Project Team: Angelo Directo, Charles Ippolito, Chulhong Min, Joseph Spada, Trent Tesch. Structure: Steel. Major Exterior Materials: Clear and translucent glass, limestone, fabric and aluminum canopy. Area: 265,000 gross square feet, 24,645 gross square meters. Number of Floors: 4.

Seocho Fashion Center
Seoul, South Korea
1994-1998
Client: Samsung. Principal-in-Charge/Design Principal: William C. Louie. Design Team Leader: Robert Goodwin. Coordination Leader: Christine Bruckner. Project Manager: Peter Gross. Project Team: Carey Chu, Jason DePierre, Jen-Suh Hou, Dohee Lee, Richard Lee, Sae-Young Lee, Jill Lerner, Chulhong Min, Joshua Penn Ruderman, Scott Schiamberg, Raquel Sendra, Nelson Tom, Gary Turton, Thomas Turturro, Marguerite Wiltshire. Associate Architect: Samwoo Architects, Seoul, South Korea. Structure: Steel, concrete. Major Exterior Materials: Low-energy glass, stainless steel, marble, granite, aluminum, limestone. Area: 120,000 gross square feet, 11,160 gross square meters. Number of Floors: 40.

Shanghai World Financial Center   *page 156*
Shanghai, China
1994-2005
Client: Mori Building Co. Ltd. Principals-in-Charge: A. Eugene Kohn, Paul Katz. Design Principal: William Pedersen. Senior Designer: Joshua Chaiken. Coordination Leaders: John Lucas, Hisaya Sugiyama, Mabel Tse. Project Team: Hannelore Barnes, Christine Bruckner, Larry Burkes, Vicky Cameron, Cathleen Chua, Mark Gausepohl, Rena Gyftopoulos,

Tomas Hernandez, Doug Hocking, Jen-Suh Hou, Rico Kanthatham, Vivian Kuan, Barbara Lewandowska, John Lucas, Methanee Massirarat, William McNamara, Elaine Newman, Yayoi Ogo, Harutaka Oribe, Cordula Roser, Susana Su, Trent Tesch, Robert Thome, Nelson Tom, Gregory Waugh, David Weinberg, Suzan Wines, Shinichiro Yorita, Jason Zerafa. Associate Architect: Mori Building Architects & Engineers, East China Architectural Design and Research Institute. Structure: Composite concrete and steel frame. Major Exterior Material: Smooth and rough granite (tower base), horizontally banded stainless steel, lightly reflective glass (tower shaft). Area: 3,408,602 gross square feet, 317,000 gross square meters. Number of Floors: 95.

Thames Court   *page 166*
London, England
1995-1998
Client: Markborough Properties Ltd. Principal: Lee A. Polisano. Senior Designer: John Bushell. Project Team: Dennis Austin, Nikki Blustin, Simon Close, J. William Davis, Karin Feddersen, Keb Garavito, Carl Gulland, Karen Hilton, Mark Kelly, Ursula Klein, Neil Merryweather, Ross Page, Rob Peebles, Tony Pryor, John Silva de Sousa, Nick Swannell, Ian Walker, Andrew Waugh, Dean Weeden. Structure: Steel. Major Exterior Materials: Steel, aluminum, glass, limestone. Area: 322,800 gross square feet, 30,000 gross square meters. Number of Floors: 6.

IBM World Headquarters   *page 180*
Armonk, New York
1995-1997
Client: IBM. Principal-in-Charge: Gregory Clement. Design Principal: William Pedersen. Design Team Leader: Jerri Smith, Douglas Hocking. Coordination Leader: Gregory Waugh, Simona Budeiri. Project Manager: Christopher Keeny. Project Team: Christine Awad, Vladimir Balla, Darlington Brown, Christine Bruckner, Elina Cardet, Winston Anthony Edwards, Armando Gutierrez, Rena Gyftopoulos, Markus Hahn, Charles Ippolito, David Kaplan, Ming Leung, John Locke, Harutaka Oribe, Yin Teh, Trent Tesch, Suzan Wines. Structure: Steel. Major Exterior Materials: Painted aluminum mullions, reflective glass, glass bead-blasted stainless steel panels, granite, metal standing seam roof. Area: 280,000 gross square feet, 26,040 gross square meters. Number of Floors: 3 main floors plus cafeteria terrace.

ICEC/LKG Tower   *page 192*
Manila, Philippines
1995-2000
Client: International Copra Export Corporation. Principals-in-Charge: A. Eugene Kohn, Paul Katz. Project Designer: Craig B. Nealy. Project Manager: Thomas Holzmann. Job Captain: Russell Patterson. Project Team: Isabelle Autones, Monica Brugger, Yayoi Ogo. Associate Architect: Recio & Casas, Manila. Structure: Concrete. Major Exterior Materials: Aluminum, granite, stainless steel vision glass. Area: 500,000 gross square feet, 46,500 gross square meters. Number of Floors: 43.

Rodin Museum, Samsung Headquarters Plaza   *page 198*
Seoul, South Korea
1995-1997
Client: Samsung. Principal-in-Charge/Design Principal: Kevin Kennon. Managing Principal: Gregory Clement. Project Manager: Andreas Hausler. Design Team Leaders: Marianne Kwok, Luke Fox. Coordination Leader: Francis Freire. Project Team: Vladimir Balla, Christopher Ernst, Andrew Kawahara, John Locke, Michael Marcolini, Chulhong Min, Cordula Roser, Aida Saleh, Trent Tesch. Associate Architect: Samoo Architects & Engineers. Structure: Glass, steel. Major Exterior Materials: Glass, steel. Area: Museum—20,000 gross square feet, 1,860 gross square meters; Pavilion—5,000 gross square feet, 465 gross square meters; Plaza—120,000 gross square feet, 11,160 gross square meters. Number of Floors: 1.

World Trade Center Amsterdam
Renovation and Extension   *page 210*
Amsterdam, The Netherlands
1995-2002
Client: ING Vastgoed, Kantoren Fonds Nederland Management. Developer: Trimp & van Tartwijk. Principal: Lee A. Polisano. Senior Designer: Ian Milne. Project Manager: Andre Van Oudheusden, Bernard Tulkens. Job Captain: Dirk Vroegindeweig. Project Team: Jacqueline Daniels, Neil Merryweather, Ross Page, Cosmo de Piro, Mark Richard, Ramiro Salceda, Amy Schmieding, Chris Schoonover, Dean Weeden. Associate Architect: Van den Oever, Zaaijer, Roodbeen & Partners. Structure: Concrete frame, steel roof. Major Exterior Materials: Concrete, wood, aluminum, glass, steel. Area: 968,400 gross square feet, 90,061 gross square meters. Number of Floors: 25 (Extension), 7 (Renovation).

Baruch College Academic Complex
The City University of New York   *page 218*
New York, NY
1995-2001
Client: Baruch College, Dormitory Authority, State of New York, City University of New York. Principal-in-Charge: A. Eugene Kohn. Design Principal: William Pedersen. Managing Principals: Jill Lerner, Anthony Moselle. Senior Designer: Gabrielle Blackman. Project Manager: Lloyd Sigal. Job Captain: Christopher Stoddard. Interior Project Designer: Mavis Wiggins. Interior Project Manager: Robert Hartwig. Project Team: Paul Baird, Gary Brown, Christine Bruckner, Angela Davis, Christopher Ernst, Terri Figliuzzi, Tomas Hernandez, Jen-Suh Hou, Charles Ippolito, Johannes Knoops, I-Ann Lin, Michael Marcolini, Methanee Massirarat, Yan Meng, Lynne Miyamoto, David Ottavio, Duncan Reid, Marie Richter, Cordula Roser, Gerald Sullivan, Yutaka Takiura, Paul Tarantino, Juliet Whelan, Thomas Yo, Julie Young. Associate Architect: Castro-Blanco Piscioneri. Structure: Steel with staggered truss system. Major Exterior Materials: Brick masonry, profile aluminum siding, punched windows in curtain walls. Area: 750,000 gross square feet, 69,750 gross square meters. Number of Floors: 17.

Bloomingdale's Aventura   *page 234*
Aventura, Florida
1995-1997
Client: Bloomingdale's/Federated Department Stores, Inc. Principal-in-Charge/Design Principal: Kevin Kennon. Project Managers: Andreas Hausler, David Weinberg, Nathan Clark Corser. Design Team Leaders: Marianne Kwok, Nicola Walter. Coordination Leaders: Angeline Ho, David Kaplan. Project Team: Gregorio Brugnoli, Elina Cardet, Luke Fox, Rena Gyftopoulos, Tomas Hernandez, Michael Marcolini, Widia Ranti, Corula Roser, Lisa Ross, Aida Saleh. Structure: Steel. Major Exterior Materials: Four-sided silicone-glazed curtain wall with perforated metal aluminum screen, precast concrete panels, stucco. Area: 251,000 gross square feet, 23,343 gross square meters. Number of Floors: 3.

Dacom Headquarters Building   *page 240*
Seoul, South Korea
1995-1999
Client: Dacom Corporation. Design Principal: William Pedersen. Design Team Leader: John Koga. Coordination Leader: Glen DaCosta. Project Team: Vicky Cameron, Angela Davis, Kurt Dannwolf, Nazila Shabestari, Garrett Finney, Tomas Hernandez, Jen-Suh Hou, Katherine Kennedy, Eun Kyong Kim, Chulhong Min, Roy Pachecano. Associate Architect: Chang-Jo Corporation. Structure: Steel, reinforced concrete. Major Exterior Materials: Glass and aluminum curtain wall. Area: 539,600 gross square feet, 50,189 gross square meters. Number of Floors: 26.

G.T. International Tower
Manila, Philippines
1995-2002
Client: Philippine Securities Corporation. Principal-in-Charge: Paul Katz. Project Designer: Craig B. Nealy. Coordination Leader: Russell Patterson. Project Manager: Thomas Holzmann. Project Team: Paul Baird,

Armando Gutierrez, Eric Höweler, Michael Levy. Associate Architect: GF & Partners. Structure: Reinforced concrete. Major Exterior Materials: Painted aluminum, three types of glass, stainless steel. Area: 712,500 gross square feet, 66,263 gross square meters. Number of Floors: 38.

SBS Broadcast Center   *page 244*
Seoul, South Korea
1995
Client: Seoul Broadcasting System. Principal-in-Charge/Design Principal: William Pedersen. Senior Designer: Duncan Reid. Project Manager: Paul Pichardo. Project Team: Philip Brown, Nazila Shabestari, Sae-Young Lee, Chulhong Min, Christopher Stoddard, Thomas Turturro. Associate Architect: Chang-Jo Corporation, Seoul, Korea. Structure: Steel. Major Exterior Material: Stainless steel roof, glass curtain wall, aluminum panels. Area: 904,516 gross square feet, 84,120 gross square meters. Number of Floors: 21.

Niaga Tower II
Jakarta, Indonesia
1996-1999
Client: PT Grahaniaga Tatautama. Design Principal: James von Klemperer. Managing Principal: Michael Greene. Senior Designer: Tómas Alvarez. Project Manager: Michael Greene. Job Captain: Isabelle Autones. Project Team: Jisop Han, Andrew Bernheimer, Celia Chiang, Widia Ranti. Associate Architect: Atelier 6. Structure: Concrete. Major Exterior Materials: Aluminum, blue-green glass, granite. Area: 731,183 gross square feet, 68,000 gross square meters. Number of Floors: 44.

Samyang Mixed-use Building   *page 248*
Seoul, South Korea
1996-1999
Client: Samyang Foods Co., Ltd. Design Principals: William Pedersen, Peter Schubert. Project Managers: Laurie Butler, Chulhong Min. Job Captain: Glen DaCosta. Design Team: Andrew Kawahara, Roger Klein, David Lukes. Project Team: Isabelle Algor, Luke Fox, Francis Freire, Jen-Suh Hou, Eun Kyong Kim, David Lukes, Lisa Ross, Scott Teman. Associate Architect: Chang-Jo Architects, Inc., Seoul, South Korea. Structure: Composite concrete and steel. Major Exterior Materials: Polished and flamed granite, glass with horizontally banded aluminum spandrel. Area: 1,002,914 gross square feet, 93,271 gross square meters. Number of Floors: 25.

Bloomingdale's Sherman Oaks
Century City, California
1995-1997
Client: Bloomingdale's/Federated Department Stores, Inc. Principal-in-Charge/Design Principal: Kevin Kennon. Project Managers: Laurie Butler, David Weinberg. Design Team Leader: Marianne Kwok. Project Team: Michael Levy, Dex Ott, Widia Ranti, Lisa Ross, Christopher Stoddard. Associate Architect: Associated Architects & Planners. Structure: Steel. Major Exterior Materials: Glass, perforated metal screens. Area: 231,525 gross square feet, 21,532 gross square meters. Number of Floors: 3.

Rue Foch Building
Beirut, Lebanon
1996-2000
Client: Fochville. Managing Principal: William C. Louie. Senior Designer/Project Manger: Robert Whitlock. Project Team: Michael Arad, Isabelle Autones, Monica Brugger, Patrick Hwang, Mohamed Ziad Jameleddine, Hao Ko, Jennifer Taylor. Associate Architect: Nabil Gholam Architecture & Planning. Structure: Concrete. Major Exterior Materials: Limestone, marble panels, curtain wall system, clad in stainless steel with clear low-energy glass. Area: 102,323 gross square feet, 9,516 gross square meters. Number of Floors: 10.

Suyoung Bay Landmark Tower, Daewoo Marina City   *page 254*
Pusan, South Korea
1996-1999
Client: Daewoo Corporation. Managing Principal: Robert Cioppa. Design Principal: William Pedersen. Senior Designers: Robert Whitlock, Tómas Alvarez. Project Manager: Chulhong Min. Project Team: Joshua Chaiken, Luke Fox, Brian Girard, Lisa Huang, Eric Höweler, Marianne Kwok, John Lucas, Yujiro Yorita, Jason Zerafa. Associate Architect: Namsan Architects & Engineers. Structure: Perimeter tube system, steel construction with concrete slab, cut metal deck. Major Exterior Materials: Pewter-colored glass, painted aluminum mullions, stainless steel canopies, granite base. Area: 2,714,000 gross square feet, 252,402 gross square meters. Number of Floors: 102.

Hong Kong Electric Company Head Office   *page 266*
Hong Kong SAR
1996-2001
Client: Hong Kong Electric Company. Principal-in-Charge/Design Principal: William C. Louie. Managing Principal: Paul Katz. Design Team Leader: Hugh Trumbull. Interior Project Manager: Peter Gross. Project Team: Hannelore Barnes, Monika Brugger, J. Gregorio Brugnoli, Nazila Shabestari, Christopher Ernst, Widia Ranti, Terence Koh, Richard Lee, Methanee Massirarat, Cordula Roser, Yutaka Takiura, Thomas Turturro. Associate Architect: Hsin Yieh Architects and Associates, Ltd. Structure: Post-tensioned concrete. Major Exterior Materials: Limestone, glass, stainless steel. Area: 310,000 gross square feet, 28,830 gross square meters. Number of Floors: 13.

University of Maryland, Medical System Redevelopment
Baltimore, Maryland
1996-2001
Client: University of Maryland Medical System. Principal-in-Charge: A. Eugene Kohn. Design Principal: William Pedersen. Senior Designer: Robert Goodwin. Deputy Director: Jill Lerner. Project Manager: Gregory Waugh. Job Captain: Bun-Wah Nip. Project Team: Trudy Brens, Larry Cohen, Carl Chapman, Philip White, Onah Chung, Jennifer Taylor, Eva Tiedemann, Jonathan Zane, Jason Zerafa. Associate Architect: Perkins & Will. Structure: Reinforced concrete, steel. Major Exterior Material: Insulated, clear, low-energy glass, precast concrete, aluminum, Impala black granite, limestone. Area: 375,000 gross square feet, 34,875 gross square meters. Number of Floors: 8.

One Raffles Link   *page 276*
Singapore
1996-2000
Client: Hong Kong Land Ltd. Principal-in-Charge: Paul Katz. Design Principal: William Pedersen. Senior Designer: Duncan Reid. Project Manager: Paul Pichardo. Job Captain: Scott Teman. Project Team: Philip Brown, Brian Cuff, Michael Flath, Jenny Francis, Cedra Ginsberg, Rena Gyftopoulos, Soichiro Suzuki, Trent Tesch, Jason Zerafa. Associate Architect: Liang Peddle Thorp Architects and Planners Ltd. Structure: Steel. Major Exterior Materials: Aluminum and glass curtain wall, zinc roof, granite base, stainless steel and stone storefront. Area: 365,000 gross square feet, 33,945 gross square meters. Number of Floors: 7.

745 Seventh Avenue   *page 284*
New York, New York
1996-2001
Client: Morgan Stanley Dean Witter, Rockefeller Center Development Corp. (Sold to Lehman Brothers). Principal-in-Charge: Gregory Clement. Design Principal: Kevin Kennon. Project Manager: Dominic Dunn. Job Captains: Glen DaCosta, Guy Ewald. Senior Designer: Steven Frankel. Project Team: Bernard Chang, Eunsook Choi, Andrew Cleary, Robert Clement, Brian Cuff, Mark Gausepohl, Jason Gomez, Lourdes Gavilanes, Yuuki Kitada, Marianne Kwok, Hui Min Liaw, Inkai Mu, Victor Pechaty, Jeromy Powers, Matthew Rudert, Michael Sewell, Peter Tripp, Stacie Wong. Structure: Steel. Major Exterior Materials: Granite, stainless steel, painted aluminum, clear low-energy glass, granite. Area: 1,200,000 gross square feet, 111, 600 gross square meters. Number of Floors: 32.

Posteel Headquarters Tower   *page 290*
Seoul, South Korea
1996-2003
Client: POSCO. Design Principals: William Pedersen, Peter Schubert. Senior Designer: Kar-Hwa Ho. Project Manager: Chulhong Min. Job Captain: Glen DaCosta. Project Team: Bernardo Gogna, Andrew Kawahara, Dohee Lee, Susana Su. Associate Architect: POSCO. Structure: Steel. Major Exterior Materials: Reflective and clear glass, stainless steel. Area: 477,000 gross square feet, 44,361 gross square meters. Number of Floors: 25 (above grade), 6 (below grade).

ADIA Headquarters   *page 296*
Abu Dhabi, The United Arab Emirates
1997-2004
Client: Abu Dhabi Investment Authority (ADIA). Principal-in-Charge: David Leventhal. Senior Designer: Kevin Flanagan. Project Manager: Kieran Breen. Job Captain: David Doody. Project Team: James Amos, Jacquie Bignell, Chris Challonner, Jacqueline Daniels, Pedro Font-Alba, Ute Heinlein, Karen Hilton, Elke Kielman, Lee Marsden, Neil Merryweather, Ross Page, Fernando Palacios, Paul Simovic, Blair Stewart, Nick Swannell, Julian Townson, Andreas Trisveis, Dean Weeden, Owen Williams. Structure: Concrete. Major Exterior Materials: Aluminum, glass. Area: 828,520 gross square feet, 77,000 gross square meters. Number of floors: 42.

Jon M. Huntsman Hall, The Wharton School of the University of Pennsylvania
Philadelphia, Pennsylvania
1997-2002
Client: University of Pennsylvania. Principal-in-Charge: A. Eugene Kohn. Design Principal: William Pedersen. Managing Principal: Gregory Clement. Senior Designer: Gabrielle Blackman. Planning Principal: Jill Lerner. Project Manager: Christopher Keeny. Project Planner: Robert Hartwig. Interiors: Terri Figliuzzi. Project Team: Angela Amoia, Angela Davis, Betty Fisher, Chris Gebhart, Sarah Gerber, Kristy Graham, Ming Leung, David Ottavio, Lauren Rubin, Margaret Sedyka, Seher Shah, Eva Tiedemann, Peter Tripp, Helen Wang, Philip White. Structure: Steel. Major Exterior Material: Brick, stone, aluminum, glass. Area: 320,000 gross square feet, 29,760 gross square meters. Number of Floors: 9.

Sotheby's Worldwide Headquarters Expansion   *page 306*
New York, New York
1997-2001
Client: Sotheby's. Principal-in-Charge: A. Eugene Kohn. Design Principal: Kevin Kennon. Project Manager: Andreas Hausler. Project Architects: Christine Mahoney, Ernesto Trindade. Design Team Leader: Lisa Ross. Project Team: Alexander Aptekar, Isabelle Autones, Vladimir Balla, Alison Binks, Bernard Chang, Nicholas Chin, Lily Chiu, Kristen Danzig, Terri Figliuzzi, Mark Gausepohl, Robert Hartwig, Eric Höweler, Hazel Joseph, Connie Lee, Sam Wible, Stacie Wong. Interior Architects: Swanke Hayden Connell Ltd., Gluckman Mayner Architects (Galleries). Structure: Steel, concrete. Major Exterior Materials: Clear and translucent glass, granite, pre-cast concrete panels, painted aluminum, stucco, limestone. Area: 450,000 gross square feet, 41,850 gross square meters. Number of Floors: 10.

Center For Creative Studies
Master Plan and Walter B. Ford II Design Arts Building
Detroit, Michigan
1997-2001
Client: Center for Creative Studies. Principal-in-Charge: A. Eugene Kohn. Design Principal: William Pedersen. Managing Principal: Jill Lerner. Senior Designer: Jerri Smith. Design Team Leader: Roger Klein. Coordination Leader: Lisa Ross. Project Manager: Gregory Waugh. Project Team: Andreas Buettner, Mirante Guyamana. Associate Architect: Ghafari Associates. Structure: Steel. Major Exterior Materials: Insulated clear vision low-energy glass, painted aluminum mullions, stainless steel, brick. Area: 101,720 gross square feet, 9,460 gross square meters. Number of Floors: 5.

Chagrin Highlands Building One
Beachwood, Ohio
1997-2000
Client: The Richard E. Jacobs Group. Principal-in-Charge: A. Eugene Kohn. Senior Designer: Tómas Alvarez. Project Manager: Gregory T. Waugh. Job Captain: Michael Levenduskey. Project Team: Mariesha Blazik, Kurt Dannwolf, Jason Zerafa. Structure: Steel frame. Major Exterior Materials: Glass, stone. Area: 100,000 gross square feet, 9,300 gross square meters. Number of Floors: 5.

Gannett/USA Today Corporate Headquarters   *page 314*
McLean, Virginia
1997-2001
Client: Gannett Co., Inc., USA Today, Hines. Principals-in-Charge: A. Eugene Kohn, Robert Cioppa. Design Principal: William Pedersen. Managing Principal: Michael Greene. Planning Principal: Jill Lerner. Design Team Leaders: Jerri Smith, David Lukes. Project Manager/Job Captains: Roger Robison, Takatomo Kashiwabara. Project Team: Vlad Balla, Trudy Brens, Andrew Cleary, Jason Gomez, Adolfo Guerrero, Miranti Gumayana, Eric Höweler, Ming Leung, Nicholas Martone, Lynne Miyamoto, Victor Pechaty, Audrey Torina, Mark Townsend, Jason Wright. Interior Planners and Designers: Lehman-Smith & McLeish. Structure: Reinforced concrete, steel. Major Exterior Materials: Glass, aluminum. Area: 700,000 gross square feet, 65,100 gross square meters. Number of Floors: 11(Gannett Tower), 9 (USA Today Tower).

835 Market Street
San Francisco, California
1997-2002
Client: Bloomingdale's/Federated Department Stores, Inc. Principal-in-Charge: A. Eugene Kohn. Design Principal: Kevin Kennon. Project Manager: Gregory Waugh. Design Team Leader: Stacie Wong. Coordination Leaders: Lily Chiu, Ernesto Trindade. Project Team: Hannelore Barnes, Kevin Cannon, Connie Lee, Anthony Mrkic. Associate Architect: KA RTKL Inc. Structure: Steel. Major Exterior Materials: Low-energy clear glass and translucent glass curtain wall, painted aluminum metal panel, painted EFIS, granite, limestone. Area: Department Store: 360,000 gross square feet, 33,480 gross square meters; Hotel: 350,000 gross square feet, 32,550 gross square meters. Number of Floors: 5 (Department Store), 24 (Hotel).

30 Hill Street   *page 332*
Singapore
1997-2000
Client: Sembawang Properties Pte. Ltd. Managing Principal: Paul Katz. Design Principal: James von Klemperer. Senior Designer: Kar-Hwa Ho. Project Manager: Paul Pichardo. Project Team: Nicholas Chin, Yayoi Ogo, Michael Tunkey. Associate Architect: LPT Architects Pte. Ltd., Singapore. Structure: Concrete. Major Exterior Materials: Clear glass, stainless steel, limestone. Area: 120,000 gross square feet, 11,160 gross square meters. Number of Floors: 4 (above grade), 1 (below grade).

Trinity Bridge
London, England
1997
Client: Markborough Properties Ltd. Principal-in-Charge: Lee Polisano. Design Principal: Karen Cook. Project Manager: Mark Kelly. Senior Designer: Edgar Gonzalez. Project Architect: Robert Holder. Structure: Steel frame. Major Exterior Materials: Structural steel, glass and aluminium. Area: 95,000 gross square feet, 10,000 gross square meters. Number of Floors: 6.

US Airways International Terminal One
Philadelphia International Airport   *page 340*
Philadelphia, Pennsylvania
1997-2002
Client: US Airways, Philadelphia International Airport. Principals-in-Charge: A. Eugene Kohn, Anthony Mosellie. Design Principal: William Pedersen. Senior Designer: Trent Tesch. Project Team: Liatt Avigdor,

Alison Binks, Li Min Ching, Michael Flath, Hidehisa Furuta, Bernardo Gogna, Zohed Jilal, Scott Loikits, George Murillo, Elaine Newman, Basak Yuksul. Associate Architect: Pierce Goodwin Alexander & Linville. Structure: Steel, concrete. Major Exterior Materials: Metal cladding, concrete. Area: 750,000 gross square feet, 69,750 gross square meters. Number of Floors: 3 with a mezzanine level.

Engineering Centers Building, University of Wisconsin   page 354
Madison, Wisconsin
1997-2002
Client: University of Wisconsin at Madison. Principal-in-Charge: Gregory Clement. Design Principal: William Pedersen. Senior Designer: Robert Goodwin. Project Team: Michael Gallin, Matt Rudert, Thomas Turturro, Phillip White, Helen Wang. Associate Architect: Flad & Associates. Structure: Concrete, steel frame. Major Exterior Materials: Brick and precast panels, metal roof, glass curtain wall, translucent polycarbonate, screen wall. Area: 200,000 gross square feet, 18,600 gross square meters. Number of Floors: 4.

Espirito Santo Plaza   page 360
Miami, Florida
1997-2002
Client: Estoril Inc. Principal-in-Charge: A. Eugene Kohn. Design Principal: William C. Louie. Senior Designer: Robert Whitlock. Project Manager: Peter Gross. Job Captain: Jorge Gomez. Project Team: Christopher Ernst, Kavitha Matthew, Jeffrey McKean, Daniel Treinen, Michael Arad, Steve Carlin, Jae Chang, Domenico Lio. Associate Architect: Plunkett & Associates. Structure: Concrete. Major Exterior Materials: Low-energy glass, Aluminum mullions. Area: 1,261,533 gross square feet, 117,200 gross square meters. Number of Floors: 37.

5 Times Square   page 366
New York, New York
1997-2001
Client: Boston Properties. Principal-in-Charge: Robert Cioppa. Design Principal: William Pedersen. Managing Principal: Robert Cioppa. Senior Designer: Douglas Hocking. Project Manager: Laurie Butler. Job Captain: Charles Lamy. Project Team: James Suh, Devin Ratiff, Edward Robinson, Jonathan Zane, Trudy Brens, Luigi Ciaccia, Avishay Manoach, Jose Sanchez-Reyes. Structure: Steel. Major Exterior Materials: Glass curtain wall, metal panels. Area: 957,820 gross square feet, 89,077 gross square meters. Number of Floors: 41.

The Sloan School of Management
Massachusetts Institute of Technology   page 372
Boston, Massachusetts
1997
Client: Massachusetts Institute of Technology. Principals-in-Charge: Peter Schubert, Jill Lerner. Senior Designer: Brian Girard. Project Team: Lisa Huang, Andrew Kawahara, Cynthia Toyoda. Structure: Steel, concrete. Major Exterior Materials: Glass, limestone, aluminum. Area: 127,000 gross square feet, 11,800 gross square meters. Number of Floors: 5

Children's Hospital of Philadelphia
Facade Remediation and Expansion   page 376
Philadelphia, Pennsylvania
1997-2002
Client: Children's Hospital of Philadelphia. Principal-in-Charge: A. Eugene Kohn. Managing Principal: Jill Lerner. Design Principal: Peter Schubert. Senior Designer: Jerri Smith. Project Manager: Gregory Waugh. Senior Technical Coordinator: Ming Leung. Project Team: Mariesha Blazik, Andreas Buettner, Carl Chapman, Lily Chiu, Brian Gerard, Miranti Gumayana, Ryan Hullinger, Eun Kim, Min Kim, Anne Lewison, Sean O'Brien, Carlos Rodriguez, Jennifer Taylor, Cynthia Toyoda, Nancy Yin. Associate Architect: Robert D. Lynn Associates. Structure: Steel. Major Exterior Materials: Glass, metal, stone. Area: 300,000 gross square feet, 27,900 gross square meters. Number of Floors: 10.

Capital Place, Fort Bonifacio
Manila, Philippines
1997-2002
Client: Capital Consortium, Inc. Principal-in-Charge: Paul Katz. Senior Designer: John Koga. Managing Principal: Paul Katz. Associate Principal: Tom Holzmann. Project Manager: Russell Patterson. Job Captain: Glen DaCosta. Project Team: Mariesha Blazik, Hogan Chun, Michael Flath, Luke Fox, Hidehisa Furuta, Lisa Huang, Hisanori Mitsui, Jennifer Park, Edward Robinson, Cordula Roser, Yin Teh, Mason White. Associate Architect: GF & Partners Architect, Co. Structure: Reinforced concrete, steel. Major Exterior Materials: Aluminum and glass curtain wall. Area: 4,735,000 gross square feet, 440,355 gross square meters. Number of Floors: Phase I: 45 & 36.

Four First Union   page 382
Charlotte, North Carolina
1998-2000
Client: First Union Bank. Principals-in-Charge: A. Eugene Kohn. Design Principal: William Pedersen. Managing Principal: Robert Cioppa. Senior Designer: Douglas Hocking. Project Manager: Anthony Mosellie. Job Captain: George Murillo. Project Team: Soren Fischer, Luis Fornez, Ko Makabe, Avishay Manoach, Methanee Massirarat. Associate Architect: Kendall/Heaton Associates, Inc., William D. Kendall, Rex Wooldridge, Pat Ankey. Structure: Hybrid steel shell, concrete and steel core. Major Exterior Materials: Glass, aluminum. Area: 1,300,000 gross square feet, 120,900 gross square meters. Number of Floors: 85.

Mid City Place   page 386
London, England
1998-2002
Client: MID (UK) Ltd. Principal: Lee A. Polisano. Senior Designer: John Bushell. Project Manager: Steve King. Project Team: Jacquie Bignell, Sasha Birksted-Breen, Joanne Carpenter, Geoff Cartwright, Chris Challonner, Julian Cross, Karin Feddersen, Pedro Font-Alba, John Gordon, Simon Hall, Jim Keen, Jae-Wook Kim, Paul Lynch, Christa Masbruch, Neil Merryweather, Graham Newell, Ross Page, Jorge Seabrooke, Paul Simovic, Blair Stewart, Simon Stubbs, Andreas Trisveis, Ian Walker, Dean Weeden, Alex Yule, Alanna Zie. Developer: Stanhope Plc. Structure: Steel. Major Exterior Materials: Glass, colored glass, aluminum, steel. Area: 473,400 gross square feet, 44,026 gross square meters. Number of Floors: 10.

Mohegan Sun Casino and Resort Phase II
Uncasville, Connecticut
1998-2002
Client: Mohegan Tribal Gaming Authority. Developer: Trading Cove Associates. Principal-in-Charge: Paul Katz. Design Principal: James von Klemperer. Senior Designer: Joshua Chaiken. Project Manager: Lloyd Sigal. Job Captain: Russell Patterson. Project Coordinators: Richard Berdan, Pablo Jendretzki, Richard Nemeth, Shig Ogyu, Thomas Schlesser. Project Team: Marcus Acheson, Isabelle Autones, Vladmir Balla, Elizabeth Biedler, Darlington Brown, Nicholas Chin, Jamil Coppin, Anna Crittenden, David Cunningham, Kenneth Darbeau, Adelaide Degezelle, Shawn Duffy, Amanda Faye, Manny Garcia, Jisop Han, Darren Hoppa, Eric Höweler, Vivian Huang, Fritz Johnson, Hideki Kakimoto, Matthew Krissel, Johannes Knoops, Bonnie Leung, Gaetane Michaux, Peter Niles, Margaret Sedyka, Yin The, Audrey Torina, Rashmi Vasavada, Gabriel Wick, Shinichiro Yokote, Jonathan Zane, Xiaofeng Zhu. Interior Architect: The Rockwell Group. Hotel Convention Interior Designer: Hirsch Bedner Associates. Arena Consultant: Heinlein + Schrock Architecture. Gaming Consultant: Friedmutter Group. Structure: Podium: Reinforced concrete basement with filigree deck, steel frame above grade; Hotel Tower: Post-tensioned flat plate concrete system, concrete mat foundation. Major Exterior Materials: Podium: Metal panels, granite, limestone, glazed aluminum storefront, standing seam metal roofs, pvc roof system; Hotel Tower: Glass and painted aluminum curtain wall system, protected membrane roof system. Area: 4,500,000 gross square feet, 418,500 gross square meters. Number of Floors: 36.

Chater House *page 390*
Hong Kong SAR
1998-2002
Client: Hong Kong Land Ltd. Principal-in-Charge: Paul Katz. Design Principal: William Pedersen. Senior Designer: Eric Höweler. Project Manager Thomas Holzmann. Job Captain: Paul Pichardo. Project Team: Bruno Caballe, Mark Gausephol, Lisa Huang, David Malott, Gene Miao, Jennifer Park, Daisuke Tanaka, Yin Teh. Associate Architect: Liang Peddle Thorp Architects & Planners Ltd. Structure: Concrete. Major Exterior Materials: Reflective glass curtain wall, stone base, painted aluminum mullions. Area: 900,000 gross square feet, 83,700 gross square meters. Number of Floors: 30.

110 Bishopsgate *page 394*
London, England
1998-2005
Client: Heron Property Corporation Ltd. Principal-in-Charge: Lee A. Polisano. Design Principal: Fred Pilbrow. Senior Designer: Robert Peebles. Project Coordinator: Danielle Tinero. Project Team: Geoff Cartwright, Turgay Hakverdi, Lars Hesselgren, Josh Ma, Clare Mason, Neil Merryweather, Ted Neilan, Graham Newell, Ross Page, Shiboleth Schecter, Marcus Springer, Alec Stewart, Dean Weeden, Tim Yu. Structure: Steel. Major Exterior Materials: Glass, bead blasted stainless steel. Area: 699,400 gross square feet, 65,044 gross square meters. Number of Floors: 42.

Heron Quay Site 5, Canary Wharf *page 400*
London, England
1999-2003
Client: Canary Wharf Limited. Principal: Paul Katz. Senior Designers: Marianne Kwok, Duncan Reid, Kar-Hwa Ho. Job Captain: Richark Nemeth Project Team: Marcus Acheson, Trudy Brens, Sebastian Cifuentes, Bonnie Leung, Juan Lladser, Jaskran Kalirai, Edward Robinson, Gaetane Michaux, Daisuke Tanaka, Gabriel Wick. Associate Architect: Adamson Associates. Structure: Steel frame. Major Exterior Materials: Stainless steel and glass curtain wall. Area: 1,000,000 gross square feet, 93,000 gross square meters. Number of Floors: 30.

Institute for International Economics *page 406*
Washington, D.C.
1999-2002
Client: Institute for International Economics. Principal-in-Charge: A. Eugene Kohn. Design Principal: James von Klemperer. Senior Designer: Kar-Hwa Ho. Project Manager: Gregory Waugh. Project Architect/Job Captain: Scott Springer. Project Team: Lauren Rubin, Adam Woltag, Michael Tunkey, Jason Zerafa. Structure: Post-tensioned concrete frame, stainless steel. Major Exterior Materials: Low-energy clear glass curtain wall with fritted surfaces, stainless steel-capped mullions, translucent stone, limestone. Area: 40,000 gross square feet, 3,720 gross square meters. Number of Floors: 4.

River City Prague *page 414*
Prague, The Czech Republic
1999-2004
Client: River City Prague (RCP) ALFA, RCP BETA, RCP GAMMA, RCP DELTA, and RCP ISC. Principal-in-Charge: Karen Cook. Project Managers: Phase II: Steve King, David Doody. Phase III: Andre van Oudheusden. Job Captain: Phase II: Andrea Jung. Project Team: Hanne Barnes, Rebecca Carpenter, Geoff Cartwright, Malcolm Cormack, John Gordon, Tony Harris, Jae Wook-Kim, Laurey Lucree, Paul Lynch, Alan Marten, Clare Medford, Neil Merryweather, Jamie Moston, Graham Newell, Ross Page, Fernando Palacios, Stepan Toman, Dean Weeden, Denisa Whiteson, Alex Yule. Associate Architect: ADNS Architekti, Prague. Structure: Concrete frame. Major Exterior Materials: Building One: Red sandstone; Buildings Two and Three: coloured plaster; Building Four: sandstone and pre-cast concrete. Area: 807,000 gross square feet, 75,051 gross square meters. Number of Floors: 11 (Building 1), 7 (Buildings 2, 3 and 4).

MetLife Headquarters Building Lobby Renovation
New York, New York
1999-2002
Client: Metropolitan Life Insurance Company. Principal-in-Charge: Robert Cioppa. Design Principal: Peter Schubert. Senior Designer: Roger Goodhill. Project Manager: Robert Hartwig. Job Captain: Marta Enebuske. Project Team: Andreas Buettner, Kristy Graham. Structure: Steel, concrete. Major Materials (Interior): Bronze, marble, terrazzo, glass. Area: 80,000 gross square feet, 7,440 gross square meters. Number of Floors: 2.

Tour CBX *page 420*
Paris, France
1999-2003
Client: Tishman Speyer Properties. Principal-in-Charge: A. Eugene Kohn. Design Principal: William Pedersen. Managing Principal: Robert Cioppa. Senior Designer: Tómas Alvarez. Project Manager: Paul Pichardo. Job Captain: Ernesto Trindade. Project Team: Li Min Ching, Patrick Daniels, Luis Fernandez, Dean Kim, Ka-Kuen Lai, Allison McKenzie, Seher Shah. Associate Architect: Saubot-Rouit & Associes. Structure: Concrete. Major Exterior Materials: Glass curtain wall, metal. Area: 482,741 gross square feet, 44,895 gross square meters. Number of Floors: 32.

Tour CB16 *page 424*
Paris, France
1999-2002
Client: Hines France. Principal-in-Charge: A. Eugene Kohn. Design Principal: Peter Schubert. Senior Designer: Thomas Schlesser. Project Manager: Paul Pichardo. Project Team: Liatt Avigdor, Pedro Font-Alba, Lourdes Gavilanes, Chris Gebhart, Joey Wong. Associate Architect: Saubot-Rouit & Associates. Structure: Concrete. Major Exterior Materials: Glass curtain wall, metal. Area: 320,000 gross square feet, 29,729 gross square meters. Number of Floors: 33.

Endesa Headquarters *page 430*
Madrid, Spain
1999-2002
Client: Grupo ENDESA SA. Principal: Lee A. Polisano. Senior Designer: Cristina Garcia. Project Manager: James E.Outen. Project Coordinator: Eliseo Rabbi. Interior Project Designer: Silvia Busato. Project Team: Yanko Apostolov, Geoff Cartwright, Chris Challonner, Jean Cedric de Foy, John Gordon, Simon Hall, Tony Lett, Paul Lynch, Neil Merryweather, Graham Newell, Ross Page, Fernando Palacios, Cosmo De Piro, Robert Peebles, Susana de la Rosa, Jorge Seabrooke, Simon Stubbs, Neus Viu, Andrew Watts, Dean Weeden, Alex Yule. Associate Architect: Rafael de La-Hoz Arquitectos S.L., Madrid. Project Manager: Gerens Hill International SA. Structure: Concrete, steel roof. Major Exterior Materials: Concrete, stone, glass, aluminum, steel, Photovoltaic panels. Area: 968,400 gross square feet, 90,061 gross square meters. Number of Floors: 6.

Museum of Modern Art Renovation and Expansion
New York, New York
1999-2005
Client: Museum of Modern Art. Principal-in-Charge: Gregory Clement. Senior Associate Principals: Tom Holzmann, Stephen Rustow. Job Captain: George Hauner. Team Leaders: Robert Hartwig, Bun-Wah Nip, Brian Girard, Greg Weithman, Steven Frankel, Jeffrey McKean. Project Team: Vladmir Balla, Trudy Brens, Judd Chapman, Eunsook Choi, Robert Cody, Claudia Cusamano, Craig England, Guy Ewald, Betty Fisher, Kara Jankelowitz, Onah Jung, Yuuki Kitada, Ethan Kushner, Anne Lewison, Han Kuang Li, Hui-Min Liaw, Dan Lenander, Scott Loikits, Rebecca Seamens, Dan Treinen, Kristen Wogen, Nathan Wong, Dirk Zschunke.

Design Architect: Taniguchi Associates, Tokyo, Japan.

Structural System: Steel and concrete superstructure. Major Exterior

515

Materials: Glass, stone and metal panel curtain wall system. Area: 630,000 square feet (58,000 square meters) of renovation and new construction. Floors: 6 floors of gallery and public space; 8 floors of curatorial, office and support; total equivalent of 16 floors of new construction & restoration of sculpture garden.

Columbus Learning Center   page 436
Columbus, Indiana
1999-2003
Client: Community Education Coalition. Principal-in-Charge/Design Principal: Kevin Kennon. Managing Principal: Jill Lerner. Senior Associate Managing Principal: Gregory Waugh. Project Manager: Mark Townsend. Senior Designer: Stacie Wong. Project Team: Hui Min Liaw, Anthony Mrkic, Flavio Stigliano, Peter Tripp. Structure: Composite concrete and steel. Major Exterior Materials: Clear and translucent glass, brick, brick pavers, painted aluminum, polished concrete. Area: 123,300 gross square feet, 11,470 gross square meters. Number of Floors: 2.

Beukenhorst Zuid (East Development)   page 442
Hoofddorp, The Netherlands
1999-2002
Client: Van den Bruele & Kaufman. Principal-in-Charge: Ron Bakker. Design Principal: David Leventhal. Senior Designer: Eva Brümmendorf. Job Captain: Matthew Crawford. Project Team: Cindy Banzhaf, Dianna Beaufort, Rebekah Berry, Geoff Cartwright, Michelle Chalkley, Iris Debremaeker, Cristina Garcia, Stefan Jentsch, Leif Lomo, Neil Merryweather, Ross Page, Simone Plekkepoel, Stephan Silver, Jessica Strauss, Dean Weeden, Lambert Zandt. Structure: Concrete frame. Major Exterior Materials: Stone, glass, aluminum. Area: 548,750 gross square feet, 51,030 gross square meters. Number of Floors: 5 (Buildings A, B and C), 7 (Buildings D, E and F), 1(Avenue Building), 21 (Tower).

Beukenhorst Zuid (West Development)   page 442
Hoofddorp, The Netherlands
1999-2002
Client: NS Vastgoed. Principal-in-Charge: Ron Bakker. Design Principal: David Leventhal. Senior Designer: Cristina Garcia. Job Captain: Arjan Mulder. Project Team: Yanko Apostolov, Dianna Beaufort, Geoff Cartwright, Malcolm Cormack, Iris Debremaeker, Tony Kauppila, Neil Merryweather, Ross Page, Simone Plekkepoel, Ramiro Salceda, Dean Weeden. Structure: Concrete frame. Major Exterior Materials: Steel, glass, aluminum Area: 269,000 gross square feet, 25,017 gross square meters. Number of Floors: 23.

Tysons II Development, Building F (1800 Tysons Blvd.)
McLean, Virginia
2001-2004
Client: Lerner Enterprises (TYF Development Company L.L.C.). Managing Principal: Gregory Clement. Design Principal: William Louie. Project Manager: Peter Gross. Senior Designer: Hugh Trumbull. Job Captain: Manny Garcia. Project Team: Daniel Fisher, Robert Jamieson, Daniel Killinger, Joanna Kuo, Peter Lauer, Esther Park, Jonathan Wall, Xiaofeng Zhu. Structure: Post-tension concrete and steel superstructure. Major Exterior Materials: Precast concrete with textured natural and tile finishes, glass, painted aluminum. Area: 300,000 square feet, 27,870 square meters. Number of Floors: 13.

Tysons II Development, Building G (1725 Tysons Blvd.)
McLean, Virginia
2000
Client: Lerner Enterprises (TYF Development Company L.L.C.). Managing Principal: Gregory Clement. Design Principal: William Louie. Project Manager: Peter Gross. Senior Designer: Hugh Trumbull. Job Captains: Daniel Trienen, Inkai Mu. Project Team: Robert Jamieson, Daniel Killinger, Junsuk Lee, Richard Nugent, Esther Park, Seher Shah, Jonathan Wall, Kristen Wogen. Structure: Post-tension concrete and steel superstructure. Major Exterior Materials: Precast concrete with textured natural and tile finishes, glass, painted aluminum. Area: 300,000 square feet, 27,870 square meters.

Tysons II Development Master Plan
McLean, Virginia
2000
Client: Lerner Enterprises (Tysons II Land Company L.L.C.). Managing Principal: Gregory Clement. Design Principal: William Louie. Project Manager: Peter Gross. Senior Designer: Hugh Trumbull. Project Team: Robert Jamieson, Daniel Killinger, Warren Kim, Peter Lauer, Courtney Marshall, Richard Nugent, Esther Park, Daniel Trienen. Major Exterior Materials: Glass and painted aluminum. Area: 4,000,000 square feet of new construction), 371,600 square meters. Number of Buildings: 9. Numver of Floors: 13 to 30.

New York University Law School, New Academic Building
New York, New York
2000-2003
Client: New York University School of Law. Principal-in-Charge: A. Eugene Kohn. Managing Principal: Jill Lerner. Design Principals: William Pedersen, Peter Schubert. Design Team Leader: Roger Klein. Project Manager: Christopher Keeny. Job Captain: Angelyn Chandler. Interior Architecture: Susan Lowance. Senior Technical Coordinator: Ming Leung. Project Team: Angela Amoia, Liatt Avigdor, Andreas Buettner, Luigi Ciaccia, Angela Davis, Brian Domini, Dawne Eng, Kristy Graham, Nurhan Gokturk, Alexis Kim, Dean Kim, Eun Kim, Michelle Kwok, Anne Lewison, Jennifer Taylor, Charles Thomson, Lubos Trcka, Andy Tsao, Helen Wang, Kevin Wegner. Structure: Steel. Major Exterior Materials: Glass, brick, stone, aluminum mullions & roof. Area: 171,295 gross square feet, 15,930 gross square meters. Number of Floors: 9 (above grade), 2 (below grade).

Bloomingdale's, Orlando   page 450
Orlando, Florida
2000-2002
Client: Bloomingdale's/Federated Department Stores, Inc. Principal: Kevin Kennon. Senior Associate: Gregory Waugh. Project Manager: Mark Townsend. Senior Designer: Eul-Ho Suh. Project Team: Kevin Cannon, Lily Chiu, Stacie Wong. Structure: Steel. Major Exterior Materials: Glass, EFIS stucco, painted concrete, painted metal. Area: 235,000 gross square feet, 21,855 gross square meters. Number of Floors: 3.

Nihonbashi-1 Project   page 454
Tokyo, Japan
2000-2004
Client: Mitsui Fudosan Co. Ltd, Corporation, Tokyo Land Corporation. Principal-in-Charge: Paul Katz. Design Principal: William Pedersen. Senior Designer: Tómas Alvarez. Design Team Leader: Ko Makabe. Coordination Leader: Ernesto Trindade. Coordination Tokyo: Shinichiro Yorita. Project Team: Li Ming Ching, Luis Fernandez, Lourdes Gavilanes, Ka Kuen Lai, Allison McKenzie, Jose Polidura. Associate Architect: Nihon Sekkei. Structure: Steel. Major Exterior Materials: Glass curtain wall, stone. Area: 935,376 gross square feet, 86,990 gross square meters. Number of Floors:19.

Kaiser Family Foundation Headquarters Competition   page 474
Washington, D.C.
2000
Client: Henry J. Kaiser Family Foundation. Principal: James von Klemperer. Senior Designer: Jason Zerafa. Project Manager: Gregory Waugh. Job Captain: Scott Springer. Project Team: Roger Goodhill, Hughy Dharmayoga, Methanee Massirarat, Luis Carmona. Structure: Steel. Major Exterior Materials: Glass and stainless steel curtain wall with wood louvers. Area: 68,000 gross square feet, 6,342 gross square meters. Number of Floors: 6.

118 Gloucester Road   page 466
Hong Kong, China
2000
Client: The Church of Jesus Christ of Latter-Day-Saints. Principal-in-Charge: A. Eugene Kohn. Design Principal: William C. Louie. Senior Designer: Robert Whitlock. Project Manager: Peter Gross. Project Team:

James Suh, Kristen Wogen, Dan Killinger, Xiaofeng Zhu, Daniel Fisher, Mark Debrauske. Associate Architect: LPT Architects. Structure: Concrete. Major Exterior Materials: Low-energy glass curtain wall with painted aluminum mullions, Granite panels, and Marble. Area: 145,875 gross square feet, 13,552 gross square meters. Number of Floors: 33.

Kowloon Station Tower   *page 474*
Hong Kong SAR
2000-2008
Client: Sun Hung Kai Properties Ltd. Principal-in-Charge: Paul Katz. Design Principal: William Pedersen. Senior Designers: Trent Tesch, Eric Höweler. Project Manager: Andreas Hausler. Associate Principal: John Lucas. Technical Coordinator: Glen DaCosta. Project Team: Michael Arad, Bruno Caballe, Hogan Chun, Gene Miao, Hisanori Mitsui, Jennifer Park, Yin Teh. Associate Architect: Wong & Ouygang. Structure: Steel, reinforced concrete. Major Exterior Materials: Aluminum mullions, glass curtain wall. Area: 3,200,000 gross square feet, 300,000 gross square meters. Number of Floors: 95.

Parc du Millenaire Buildings 3 & 4
Paris, France
2000-2003
Client: EMGP. Principal: James von Klemperer. Senior Designer: Jason Zerafa. Job Captain: Adam Woltag. Project Team: Methanee Massirarat. Charles Lamy. Structure: precast concrete plank and steel frame. Major Exterior Materials: Glass curtain wall with stainless steel, clay tile. Area: 700,000 gross square feet, 65,000 gross square meters. Number of Floors: 4-7 (above grade), 2 (below grade).

Tour Granite   *page 484*
Paris, France
2001
Client: Société Générale. Principal: James von Klemperer. Senior Designer: Jason Zerafa. Project Manager: Paul Pichardo. Job Captain: Charles Lamy. Project Team: Patrick Daniels, Hughy Dharmayoga, Ignacio Iratchet, Jinseuk Lee, Manon Pare, James Suh, Takeshi Yoshida. Structure: Concrete Frame with precast concrete plank. Major Exterior Materials: Double-skin air ventilated glass curtain wall with stainless steel mullions. Area: 700,000 gross square feet, 65,000 gross square meters. Number of Floors: 47.

New York Jets Stadium   *page 490*
New York, New York
2001
Client: New York Jets. Design Principal: William Pedersen. Managing Principal: Paul Katz. Senior Designer: Trent Tesch. Project Team: Andrew Klare, Kenichi Noguchi. Structure: Steel, reinforced concrete. Major Exterior Materials: Aluminum and glass. Area: 2,609,000 gross square feet, 242,384 gross square meters. Number of Floors: Multilevel.

Selected Bibliography
1993-2001

Projects are arranged in alphabetical order. For a selected bibliography covering the years 1986 through 1992, refer to the monograph on the firm edited by Warren A. James, published by Rizzoli in 1993; for the years 1976 through 1986, refer to the monograph on the firm edited by Sonia R. Chào and Trevor D. Abramson, published by Rizzoli in 1987.

Monographs

Dixon, John Morris. *The World Bank*. Mulgrave, Australia: Images Publishing Group, 2001.

Murray, Peter. *One Raffles Link, Singapore*. London: Wordsearch, 2001.

Kennon, Kevin. *The Rodin Museum*. New York: Princeton Architectural Press, 2000.

Kohn, A. Eugene, et al. *KPF: The First 22 Years. Featuring William Pedersen's Selected Building Designs 1976-1988*. Milan: L'Arca Edizioni, 1999.

Introduction by Clement, Gregory. *Kohn Pedersen Fox: Master Architect Series II*. Mulgrave, Australia: Images Publishing Group, 1998.

Edited by James, Warren. *Kohn Pedersen Fox: Architecture and Urbanism 1986-1992*. New York: Rizzoli, 1993.

Edited by Klotz, Heinrich and Sabau, Luminita. *DG Bank-Frankfurt Am Main*. Munich: Oktagon Verlag, 1993.

General

"Asia Bound." *Progressive Architecture*, March 1995, pp. 43-51.

"Atlantic Divide." *Building Design*, May 12, 2000, p. 8.

"Building in Glass." *Architecture*, December 1996, pp. 107-115.

"Civic Architecture: Government Buildings." *Architecture Magazine*, February 1993, p. 37.

"Computers: News Media." *Progressive Architecture*, October 1993, p. 80.

"Courthouses: Federal Buildings & Campuses." *Architecture*, January 1996, p. 64.

"Customizing Hardware." *Architecture*, July 1994, pp. 93-95.

"European Architecture." *Architecture*, September 1993, p. 134.

"Federal Architecture." *Architecture*, January 1996, pp. 76-77.

"Inside New York." *Interiors*, January 1995, p. 136.

"Is Asia's Boom Over?" *Architecture*, January 1998, pp. 65-70.

"KPF International." *World Architecture*, 1995, issue no. 34, pp. 26-65.

"KPF's Return to Modernism." *Dialogue: Architecture + Design + Culture* (Taiwan), April 1998, pp. 12-23.

"Multinational Corporate America: Risk/Reward Awards." *Interiors*, May 1993, pp. 111, 122.

"Profile: Kohn Pedersen Fox Associates, PC." *New York Construction News*, July 3, 1995, n.p.

"Projects." *Progressive Architecture*, October 1993, pp. 84-91.

"Projects from Around the Region." *Architectural Record, Pacific Rim Supplement*, July 1996, n.p.

"Redesigning Its House." *Crain's New York Business*, February 15, 1993, pp. 3, 23.

"Review of International Architecture." *Architecture*, September 1994, n.p.

"Some Boats, an Architect and New Furniture [by William Pedersen]." *Architectural Record*, September 1994, pp. 36-37.

"Sun Rising in Far East for City's Architects." *Crain's New York Business*, vol. 11, no. 14, April 3, 1995, pp. 19, 22.

"Synopsis Addresses Architect's Role in a Design-Build Contract." *New York Construction News*, July 2000, vol. 48, no. 12, p. 8.

"The Top 100 Architectural Practices." *World Architecture: Special Report*, March 1994, n.p.

"The Top 200 International Design Firms." *Engineering News-Record*, July 17, 2000, pp. 73-78.

"U.S. Designers Building a Towering Presence in Asia." *Building Design and Construction*, June 1996, p. 11.

Barreneche, Raul A. "Customizing Hardware." *Architecture*, July 1994, pp. 93-99.

Collyer, Stanley. "Bill Pedersen." *Competitions*, Winter 1996/97, pp. 52-61.

Coyle, Eddie. "Winner Shows Plenty of Heart." *Daily News*, July 4, 2000, Sports Section, p. 65. Cramer, Ned. "On the Boards: Four by Kohn Pedersen Fox." *Architecture*, April 1996, pp. 44-45.

Dean, Andrea Oppenheimer. "Breaking into New Markets." *Architecture*, August, 1999, pp. 91-94.

Dean, Andrea Oppenheimer. "The Nation's Biggest Landlord Just Found Style." *Architectural Record*, February 2000, pp. 62-68.

Dunlap, David. "Castles, and Planetariums, in the Air: With Floating Spheres and Curved Skyscrapers, Computers Add to the Wow Factor in Design." *New York Times*, March 11, 1999, sec. G, pp. 1, 7.

Dunlap, David. "The Delicate Matter of Passing the Torch." *New York Times*, November 17, 1999, sec. 11, p. 1.

Dunlap, David. "For Architects, It's a Boomtown." *New York Times*, August 8, 1999, sec. 11, p. 1.

Gault, Ylonda. "Redesigning Its House, Architect Star of 80's Pares, Seeks Partners." *Crain's New York Business*, February 15, 1993, p. 3.

Harrington, K. "Reflection on Chicago." *Inland Architect*, May-June 1993, p. 42.

Kamin, Blair. "Barrier Free; Outsiders, by Design, Should be Adding to Chicago's Building Legacy." *Chicago Tribune*, Arts & Entertainment Section, p. 7.

Kohn, A. Eugene. "Japan: Key to KPF's Global View." *Architecture + Urbanism* (Japan), June 1996, pp. 81-89.

Levinson, Nancy. "The New Client: Selecting the Architect." *Architectural Record*, November, 1993, pp. 26-30.

Lewis, Roger K. "Shaping the City; An Inspiring Development: Hines Honored for Four Decades of Contributions to Architecture." *The Washington Post*, July 1, 2000, Real Estate Section, p. G03.

Lieber, Ronald B. "Birth of the Groundscraper." *Fortune*, March 17, 1997, p. 154.

Maynard, Michael. "In Progress: Campus Buildings, Buildings in Korea, Buildings in China and Singapore." *Architecture*, November 1997, pp. 130-135.

McKee, Bradford. "Towering Ambitions." *Architecture*, November 1997, pp. 94-99.

Parcelle, Mitchell. "Architects Fret as Computers Supplant Pencils." *Wall Street Journal*, April 28, 1996, n.p.

Pedersen, William. "Strategies for the Design of Tall Buildings." *Architecture + Urbanism* (Japan), June 1996, pp. 81-89.

Reis, Michael. "Interview with William Pedersen, FAIA." *Stone Design*, vol. 4, no. 1, Winter 1998, pp. 56-71.

Sanchez, Jesse. "In the U.S., Skyscrapers Are Being Downsized by History." *Los Angeles Times*, November 12, 1996, n.p.

Slatin, P. and Cohn, D. "International Practice: Succeeding in a Volatile World." *Architectural Record*, July 1996, p. 41.

Solomon, N. "Practice: Large Firm Realities." *Architecture*, January 1993, pp. 101-105.

Thomas, Ralph. "Building Mega-glamourous Cities in the Sky." *South China Morning Post*, April 13, 2000, p. 18.

Tulacz, Gary J. "Hot Markets Shift into Higher Gear.", *Engineering News-Record*, April 10, 2000, vol. 244, no. 14, p. 56.

Tulacz, Gary J. "A Look at a $3.4 Trillion Market." *Engineering News-Record*, December 4, 2000, vol. 245, no. 22, p. 30.

Usuda, Tetsuo and Taikura, Yutaka et al. "Kohn Pedersen Fox: 3 High Rise Building Projects." *Architecture + Urbanism* (Japan), June 1996, pp. 54-89.

Woods, Lebbeus. "All That is Solid." *Architecture + Urbanism* (Japan), May 1998, n.p.

5 Times Square

"Ernst & Young Signs for New Big Apple HQ." *Real Estate Forum*, September 1999, n.p.

"Image and Message Key to Ernst & Young Fit Out." *New York Construction News*, October 2000, vol. 49, no. 3, p. 67.

Braine, Theresa. "Ernst & Young Does the Deuce." *Grid Magazine*, March & April 2000, pp. 58-62.

Goldberger, Paul. "Busy Buildings; Post-Iconic Towers Invade Times Square." *The New Yorker*, September 4, 2000, p. 90.

Merkel, Jayne. "Times Square on the Record." *Oculus*, vol. 62, no. 10, Summer 2000, p. 6-9.

110 Bishopsgate

"Canada High Life." *Estates Gazette*, May 27, 2000, p. 63.

"Heron in Talks on Bishopsgate Sale." *Estates Gazette*, May 2000, p. 40.

"High Rise Shadow Over St. Paul's." *The London Times*, January 25, 2001, p. 24.

"Radical Building Leads to Prosperous City." *The London Times*, January 29, 2001, p. 32.

"Stony Ground." *The London Times*, January 16, 2001, p. 19.

Aalund, Dagmar. "Towering Imbroglio: A Tale of Two Cities." *Wall Street Journal Europe*, January 26-27, 2001, p. 5.

Bevan, Robert. "Planning Shouldn't Be a Tall Order." *Building Design*, January 19, 2001. p. 13.

Binney, Marcus. "Manhattan-on-Thames or the Heights of Folly." *The London Times*, September 5, 2000, p. 1.

Booth, Robert. "Towering Plan for City." *Architects' Journal*, September 14, 2000, p. 18.

Coffer, Adam. "Ronson Project Gets All Clear-But Opposition Mounts." *Estates Gazette*, January 20, 2001, p. 37.

Cohen, Norma. "Heron Set to Build City's Tallest Building." *Financial Times*, January 17, 2001, p. 6.

Cronin, Sean. "Ken Presses Heron to Increase Bishopsgate Tower Height." *Estates Gazette*, July 8, 2000, p. 39.

Gelb, Norman. "The Unstoppable March of the Skyscrapers." *Financial Times Weekend*, January 27-28, 2001, p. 111.

Hamson, Liz. "The Sky's the Limit." *Property Week*, September 8, 2000, p. 12.

Jenkins, Simon. "Ken Falls Victim to Big Apple Envy." *The Evening Standard*, January 18, 2001, p. 13.

Melvin, Jeremy. "Castles in the Air." *Estates Gazette*, June 17, 2000, pp. 82-85.

Taylor, David. "KPF's City Skyscraper." *Architects' Journal*, December 16-23, 1999, n.p.

Waples, John. "Ronson to Build £300M Office Tower." *The London Sunday Times*, May 21, 2000, n.p.

Welsh, John. "Ahead for Heights." *Property Week*, June 11, 2000 p. 27.

Baruch College, New Academic Complex
The City University of New York

"Baruch Builds an Urban Quadrangle," *New York Times*, November 29, 1998, sec. 11, pp. 1,6.

"CUNY Capital Construction Plan is $1.8B." *New York Construction News*, April 15, 1996, pp. 8-10.

"An Urban Campus Begun for Baruch." *New York Times*, June 22, 1997, n.p.

Brozan, Nadine. "On CUNY's Campuses, The Subject is Change." *New York Times*, September 17, 2000, sec. 11, p. 14.

Byles, Jeff. "The Bilbao Effect." *The Village Voice*: Education Supplement, August 8, 2000, p. 84.

Chartock, David S. "Vertical Campus: Four Buildings in One." *New York Construction News*, November 1997, pp. 42-45.

Giovannini, Joseph. "Open Admissions." *New York Magazine*, December 2001, p. 42.

Maynard, Michael. "Campus Buildings." *Architecture*, November 1997, pp. 130-131.

Merkel, Jayne. Ed. "Campus by Design." *Oculus*, vol. 62, no. 10, Summer 2000, p. 22.

Rayman, Graham. "Baruch Beginning Expansion Project." *New York Newsday*, June 25, 1997, n.p.

Sandler, Linda. "Architects Worry That News Is Too Good." *Wall Street Journal*, September 23, 1998, n.p.

Bismarckstraße 101

"Actualité Internationale: Spécial Berlin." ["International News: Berlin Special."] *Bâtiment* (France), December 1995-January 1996. p. 9.

"Best Foot Forwards for MIPIM Design Prize." *Estates Gazette*, February 18, 1995, Issue no. 9507, p. 44.

"Bismarckstraße 101." *Habitat Ufficio* (Italy), September 1995, no. 75, pp. 50-55.

"Bürohaus/Office Building Bismarckstraße 101." *Neue Architektur* (Germany), 1990-2000, n.d., p. 155.

"The Intelligent Exterior-Assessing Integrated Design." *Architectural Record*, October 1995, p. 84-85.

"Investors Rekindle Interest." *European-International Property*, March 14-20, 1996, p. 29.

"KPF International." *World Architecture*, March 1995, Issue no. 34, pp. 56-59.

"Mit Schwung um die Ecke." ["With Momentum Around the Corner."] *Bauwelt* [Germany], August 23, 1996, pp. 1784-1787.

Speaker, Scott. "An American Architect in Europe." *Urban Land: Europe Supplement*. vol. 2, no. 1, January 2000, pp. 32-35.

Bloomingdale's Aventura
Amelar, Sarah. "Box Cut." *Architecture*, May 1998, pp. 112-117.

Cantinella, Rita F. "Trendsetter." *Contract Design*, August 1998, pp. 44-47.

Heimlich, Cheryl Kane. "Survey Reveals: Who's the Fairest of the Malls?" *South Florida Business News*, August 8, 1997.

McKee, Bradford. "Towering Ambitions." *Architecture*, November 1997, pp. 93-99.

Buffalo Niagara International Airport
McKee, Bradford. "Towering Ambitions." *Architecture*, November 1997, pp. 93-135.

Mellins, Thomas. "The Sky's the Limit." *Architectural Record*, July 2000, vol. 188, no. 7, p. 147.

"Airport's Future Takes Off." *The Buffalo News*, May 17, 1993, Lifestyles Section, n.p.

"Infrastructure Architecture." Dialogue: *Architecture + Design + Culture* (Taiwan), May 2000, pp. 70-77.

Chater House
"Swire House to Be Razed." *Building Journal* (Hong Kong, China), September 1997, pp. 20-21.

Daswani, Kavita. "Building Shrines for Shoppers; Rodeo Drive, Madison Avenue and Provence in Hong Kong?" *South China Morning Post*, September 3, 2000, p. 3.

Tan, Michelle. "Swire House Looks to Major Transformation." *Building and Construction News: Asia's Weekly Industry Paper* (Hong Kong, China), September 24-30, 1997, p. 1.

Columbus Learning Center
"Architects Chosen for Learning Center." *The Republic* (Columbus, Indiana), February 27, 2000, n.p.

"In the Streetscape." *Oculus*, vol. 62, no. 6, February 2000, p. 7.

Meredith, Robyn. "A Town Aspires to Landmark Status." *New York Times*, January 5, 2000, sec. 1, p. 16.

Wissing, Douglas. "Tracking Down Architectural Treasures, from Pei to Pelli, Tucked Away in an Artful Indiana Town." *Little Columbus Builds a Reputation*, May 28, 2000, n.p.

Cyprus House of Representatives
"An Idealistic House for Government." *Progressive Architecture*, June 1995, p. 53.

Cramer, Ned. "On the Boards: Four by Kohn Pedersen Fox." *Architecture*, April 1996, pp. 44-45.

Dacom Headquarters
Maynard, Michael. "Buildings in Korea." *Architecture*, November 1997, pp. 132-133.

Endesa Headquarters
"Construction Begins" designarchitecture.com (http://www.designarchitecture.com), October 16, 2000.

"KPF Wins in Madrid." *Architects' Journal*, July 8, 1999, p. 6.

Bainbridge, Duncan. "Digging Trenches" archpedia.com (http://www.archpedia.com.) October 11, 2000.

Booth, Robert. "KPF Gains in Spain." *Architects' Journal*, October 5, 2000. p. 15.

Carrera, M. A. "Endesa ubicará su sede Central en el Campo de las Naciones." ["Endesa Will Locate Its Headquarters in Campo de las Naciones."] *Expansión*, October 20, 1998, n.p.

Cohn, David. "KPF's First Project in Spain is Energy-Savvy." *Architectural Record*, December 2000, p. 44.

Espirito Santo Plaza
"Banco Espirito Santo Rehubicará Sede." ["Banco Espirito Santo Relocates Its Headquarters."] *El Nuevo Herald*, November 24, 1998, sec. B, p. 3.

"Espirito Santo Bank to Move to Planned Brickell Tower." *Daily Business Review*, November 30, 1998, n.p.

"Espirito Santo Plaza." *Space* (Korea), June 1999, pp. 58-60.

"Hotel Boom Adds More than 4,500 Rooms." *South Florida Business Journal*, July 14, 2000, vol. 20, no. 48, p. 1, sec. A.

"Projects Awarded; Architectural and Construction Firms Projects." *Building Design & Construction*, September 1, 2000, vol. 41, no. 9, p. 13.

"Se Traslada a Nuevo Edificio El Banco Espirito Santo." ["Banco Espirito Santo is Moving to a New Building."] *Noticias*, December 22, 1998, sec. B, n.p.

"Two Projects From KPF Underway." *Space* (Hong Kong, China), February 2000, p. 38.

De Lollis, Barbara. "Espirito Santo Entra a Competir en Construcción." ["Espirito Santo Enters to Compete in Construction."] *El Nuevo Herald*, November 14, 1998, n.p.

De Lollis, Barbara. "Espirito Santo Family Tree Grows into Major Network." *Miami Herald*, November 23, 1998, n.p.

De Lollis, Barbara. "Glassy, Curvy and 34 Stories." *Miami Herald*, November 13, 1998, sec. C, pp. 1, 5.

Faschan, William J. and Sesil, Daniel A. "Rising High," *Urban Land Issue*, November/December 2000, pp. 62-67.

Garr, Rick. "Gateway to Latin America." *Weekly Sun*, November 27-December 3, 1998, n.p.

Hay, David. "The Scene Heats Up Under the Miami Sun." *New York Times*, February 27, 2000, sec. 2, p. 51.

Jones, Edgar. "Espirito Santo Plaza Could Fare Well, Office Market Analysts Say." *Miami Today*, November 19, 1998, p. 16.

First Hawaiian Center
"430 Foot Tower will be Hawaii's Tallest." *Building Design and Construction*, December 1994, p.14.

Kroloff, Reed. "Going Hawaiian." *Architecture*, November 1997, pp. 108-113.

Gannett/USA Today Corporate Headquarters
Forgey, Benjamin. "Having It Both Ways at USA Today's New Home." *Washington Post*, September 18, 1999, sec. C, pp. 1, 5.

Giovannini, Joseph. "USA Tomorrow." *Architecture*, March 2002, pp. 68-75.

Keri, Jonah. "Gannett Breaks Ground on Tysons Corner Building." *Washington Business Journal*. April 29, 1999, n.p.

Lockwood, Charles. "Behind the Scenes: Planning, Designing Gannett." *Corporate Real Estate Executive*, October 2000, pp. 24-28.

Heron Quay Site 5, Canary Wharf
"Canary Could Really Sing." *London Times*, September 18, 1999, n.p.

IBM Corporate Headquarters
"Architecture as Corporate Identity." *Architectural Record*, November 1997, n.p.

"Down-sized, Re-tooled and Re-styled." *World Architecture*, March 1998, pp. 88-91.

"IBM Planning a Scaled-Down New Headquarters." *New York Times*, August 20, 1995, sec. 9, p. 7.

Giovanni, Joseph. "Corporate Metamorphosis." *Architecture*, November 1997, pp. 114-121.

Henninger, Paul. "IBM Headquarters by Kohn Pedersen Fox in New York," *De Architect* (Netherlands), September 1999, pp.56-61.

Jacobs, Karrie. "Small Blue Things." *New York Magazine*, November 3, 1997, p. 24.

Zuckerman, Laurence. "At IBM, Few Offices, But Room for Boss to Roam." *International Herald Tribune*, September 18, 1997, p. 13.

Zuckerman, Laurence. "House that Lou Built Reflects a New IBM." *New York Times*, September 17, 1997, pp. 1, 10.

ICEC/LKG Tower
"Up! Up!" Ambassador: *Trans World Airlines*, May 1994, p. 18.

JR Central Towers and Station
Teo, Karen, et al. "Conceptualising Asian's Urban Landscape: Projects by Kohn Pedersen Fox." *Southeast Asian Building* (Singapore), November 2000, pp. 43-48.
Usuda, Tetsuo and Taikura, Yutaka et al. "Kohn Pedersen Fox: 3 High Rise Building Projects." *Architecture + Urbanism* (Japan), June 1996, pp. 54-89.
Wilson, Fiona. "Regeneration/Japan: Red-Light Reformation." *Wallpaper*, June 2000, p. 45

Mark O. Hatfield United States Courthouse
"GSA Design Awards Focus on Historic Preservation." *Architecture*, May 1995, p. 25.
"Monuments to a Crime-Fearing Age." *New York Times Magazine*, May 28, 1995, sec. 6, pp. 36-39.
"News: Malaysia, Oregon, and Los Angeles." *Architectural Record*, October 1993, p. 27.
"News Report: New Courthouse for Portland." *Progressive Architecture*, October 1993, p. 29.
"Portland Projects." *Progressive Architecture*, October 1993, p. 29.
Betsky, Aaron. "Search for Justice." *Architecture*, November 1997, pp. 122-129.
Edited by Dixon, John Morris. *Urban Spaces*. New York: Visual Reference Publications, Inc., 1999, pp. 174-175.

Mid City Place
"Building Research—New Buildings Show Their True Colour." *British Council for Offices*, September 1999, Issue no. 38.
Atkinson, James. "The Groundbreaking Ceremony for Mid City Place, *Contract Journal*, June 7, 2000, p. 3.
Bainbridge, Duncan. *London Architect*, August 2000, p. 3.
Climanace, Andrew. "Making Better Buildings." *Site*, December 1999, n.p.
Coffer, Adam. "Midtown Down to Its Last Big Three." *Estates Gazette*, January 20, 2001, p. 43.
Coffer, Adam. "So Hot That It Could Go Cold." *Estates Gazette*, January 20, 2001, p. 55.
Pearson, Andy. *Building*, June 9, 2000, p. 10.
Pearson, Andy. "Model Behavior." *Building*, February 2, 2001, p. 48.
Tiworth, Adam. "Geared Up For A Quick Change." *Estates Gazette*, November 27, 1999, n.p.

One Raffles Link
"Retail Design: CityLink." *Asian Architect & Contractor*, vol. 29, issue 9, p. 12.
"Shopping Goes Subterranean." *Business Times*, July 2000, n.p.
"Static, Yet Dynamic: One Raffles Link." *Building Journal* (Hong Kong, China), February 1998, pp. 22-23.
Lay Hoon, Thio. Ed. "More Mall, Less Memory?" *d. Magazine* (Singapore), April 2000, pp. 88-91.
Lim, Joseph. "Making Connections: One Raffles Link." *Space* (Hong Kong, China), August 2000, p. 36-41.
Lin, Teo Pau. "Shopping Down Under." *The Straits Times* (Singapore),
Lin, Teo Pau. "Singapore's First Underground Shopping Mall Opens on July 1." *The Straits Times* (Singapore), June 16, 2000, n.p.
Maynard, Michael. "Buildings in China and Singapore." *Architecture*, November 1997, pp. 134-135.
Teo, Karen, et al. "Connecting Singapore's Civic District." *Southeast Asian Building* (Singapore), November 2000, pp. 40-42.

Plaza 66
"Asia Bound." *Progressive Architecture*, October 1993, p. 29.
Campi, Mario. *Skyscrapers: An Architectural Type of Modern Urbanism*.

Birkhäuser, 2000, pp. 184-85.
Sudjic, Deyan. "Shanghai: La Citta Che Esplose." ["Shanghai: The City that Exploded."] *Domus* (Italy), no. 829, September 2000, pp.40-57.
Teo, Karen, et al. "Conceptualising Asian's Urban Landscape: Projects by Kohn Pedersen Fox." *Southeast Asian Building* (Singapore), November 2000, pp. 43-48.

Provinciehuis
Architects' Journal, August 25, 1994, p. 8.
"Het Nieuwe Provinciehuis van Zuid-Holland." ["The New Province House of South-Holland."] *NRC Handelsblad* (The Netherlands), n.d., p. 14.
"Het Nieuwe Provinciehuis van Zuid-Holland in Den Haag Begint al Duidelijke Vormen Aan Te Nemen." ["The New Province House of South Holland in The Hague is Beginning to Take Shape."] *Haagsche Courant* (The Netherlands), September 10, 1997, n.p.
"News: Hague Competition Winner." *Progressive Architecture*, October 1994, p. 28.
"Nieuw Provinciehuis Krijgt Vorm." ["The New Province House Gets into Shape."] *Haagsche Courant* (The Netherlands), September 10, 1997, p. 1.
"Openheid als Norm-Dorpsplein Vormt Centrum Provincie." ["Openness is the Standard—Village Square Forms the Centre of the Province."] *Stedenbouw* (The Netherlands), May 1998, pp. 21-26.
"Power and Ambition." *World Architecture*, September 1998, Issue no. 69, pp. 72-77.
"KPF International." *World Architecture*, March 1995, Issue no. 34, pp. 26-65.
"Provinciehuis Details." *Building*, September 12, 1998, n.p.
"Provinciehuis Golvend Langs Het Malieveld." ["Provinciehuis Situated Along the Malieveld Like a Wave."] *De Binnenstadskrant* (The Netherlands), n.d, p. 1.
"Provinciehuis Krijgt Vorm." ["Provinciehuis Takes Shape"] *Algemeen Dagblad*, September 10, 1997, n.p.
"Rond Provinciehuis." ["Around Province House."] *Algemeen Dagblad* (The Netherlands), September 25, 1997, n.p.

River City Prague
Construction News, April 27, 2000, n.p.
FX Magazine, April 2000, n.p.
"The New Image of Rohansky Ostrov." *Mlada Fronta* (Czech Republic), February 2, 2000, n.p.
"News." *Architect's Journal*, March 16, 2000, n.p.
PSM3 Construction News, April 2000, n.p.
"Waterside Site." *News Review MIPIM 2000*, May 2000, p. 4.
McLean, Robert. "Prague Sets Sail." *Construction Journal*, March 2000, n.p.
Ondrasek, Susan. "Knight Frank Takes Over at Ryden." *The Prague Post*, January 31, 2001, Spaces and Places Section.
Wazuka, Margaret. *Design Architecture Web News*, April 24, 2000, n.p.

Rodin Museum, Samsung Headquarters Plaza
"Announcing the Winners of the First annual Saflex Safe and Sound Award." *Architecture*, May 1999, pp. 180-182.
"Asia Bound." *Progressive Architecture*, March 1995, pp. 43-51.
"Projects From Around the Region." *Architectural Record*, July 1996. n.p.
"Rodin Museum at Samsung Plaza." *Architectural Record*, July 1996, n.p.
"The Rodin Pavilion." *C3 Magazine* (Korea), no. 178, June 1999, pp. 36-68.
"Samsung Plaza and Rodin Museum." *I.D. Magazine*, Annual Design Review 1999, July/August 1999, pp. 164-165.
"Winners of the First Annual Saflex Safe and Sound Awards Contest." *Glass Magazine*, August 1999, p. 56.
Barreneche, Raul A. "Gallery of Glass: Kohn Pedersen Fox Creates a Luminous Sanctuary for a Pair of Rodin Bronzes." *Architecture*, November 1998, pp. 148-155.
Butler, Ruth. "Rodin in Seoul: A Triumph of Multicultural Exchange." *Boston Globe*, August 1, 1999, sec. N, p. 2.
DiComo, April. "AIA/NY Awards Celebrate Design Excellence." *New York Construction News*, January 6, 1997, pp. 3, 9.

Jodidio, Philip. *Building a New Millennium*. Cologne: Taschen Verlag. 1999. pp. 286-291.
Mercedes Planelles Herero, Ed. "Proyectos y Obras: Museo Rodin." *Via Arquitectura* (Spain), vol. 7, March 2000, pp. 56-59.
Perlman, Chee. "Best of Category: Environment, I.D. Magazine Design Review 1999." *I.D. Magazine*, July/August 1999, pp. 164-65.
Rieks, Craig. "Through the Looking Glass." *Commercial Buildings*, June/July 1999, p. 53.

The Rothermere American Institute, Oxford University
Building Design, July 16, 1999.
"List of Works." Royal Academy of Art Summer Exhibition 2000, Summer 2000, p. 112.
"On the Boards." *Architecture*, April 1996, p. 44.
Baillieu, Amanda. "Study Aims to Restore 'Missing Link' in London Transport." *Architects' Journal*, February 1995, p. 7.
Cramer, Ned. "On the Boards: Four by Kohn Pedersen Fox." *Architecture*, April 1996, pp. 44-45.
O'Mahony, Eamonn. "America in Oxford." *Oxford Today: Trinity Issue*, 1995, p. 57.
Tyack, Geoffrey. "New Model Oxford." *Oxford Today: Trinity Issue*, 2000, p. 6.

Samyang Mixed-Use Building
Maynard, Michael. "Buildings in Korea." *Architecture*, November 1997, pp. 132-133.

Shanghai World Financial Center
"Are Tall Buildings a Measure Of Society's Well-Being?" *Metropolis*, October 1996, n.p.
"Asia Bound." *Progressive Architecture*, March 1995, pp. 43-51.
"Exporting Experience: Asia's Tallest Towers." *Architecture*, September 1996, pp. 155-163.
"Future Shock." *Conde Nast Traveler*, March 1999, p. 79.
"News: Shanghai's Financial Center." *Interiors*, May 1996, p. 62.
"Shanghai World Financial Center." *Architecture + Urbanism* (Japan), June 1996, pp. 56-84.
"Shanghai World Financial Center." *Dialogue: Architecture + Design + Culture* (Hong Kong), April 1998, p. 42-48.
"Shanghai's Financial Center Continues to Grow—Upwards." *Interiors*, May 1996, n.p.
"Tall Buildings." *Blueprint Review*, no. 124, January 1996, n.p.
"U.S. Designers Building a Towering Presence in Asia." *Building Design and Construction*, June 1996, pp. 11-12.
"Vertically Challenged." *Fortune Magazine*, n.d., p.144.
Anzillotti, Adriana B. "En Shanghai: El Más Alto Del Mundo." ["In Shanghai: The Tallest in the World."] *Nación* (Spain), May 24, 1999, p. 6.
Bey, Lee. "Chicago Architects Turn To Scraping Asia's Sky." *Chicago Sun Times*, April 1, 1996, n.p.
Cohn, David. "La Carrera Hacia El Cielo." ["The Race to the Sky."] *Gentleman's Quarters* (Spain), December 1996, pp. 100-105.
Conway, McKinley. "The Great Cities of the Future." *The Futurist*, June-July 1999, pp. 28-32.
Dunlap, David. "Castles, and Planetariums, in the Air: with Floating Spheres and Curved Skyscrapers, Computers Add to the Wow Factor in Design." *New York Times*, March 11, 1999, sec. G, pp. 1, 7.
Farley, Maggie. "World's Tallest Status Symbols." *Los Angeles Times*, November 11, 1996, sec. A, pp. 1, 12.
Goldberger, Paul. "Why Cities Set Their Sights So High." *New York Times*, August 4, 1996, n.p.
Harvey, Doug. "Remix: Utopian Vision Vs. American Dream." *LA Weekly*, June 2, 2000, Art Section, n.p.
Maynard, Michael. "Buildings in China and Singapore." *Architecture*, November 1997, pp. 134-135.
Pacelle, Mitchell. "American Architects Ride Boom In Asia: U.S. Companies Find the Only Way to Go Is Up." *Wall Street Journal* (Europe Edition), March 23, 1996, n.p.
Pacelle, Mitchell. "U.S. Architects in Asia: Only Way to Go Is Up." *Wall Street Journal*, March 21, 1996, sec. B, pp. 1-2.
Rampe, David. "Going Up: A New Look For Chinese Capitalism." *New York Times*, August 18, 1996, n.p.
Rouyer, Rémi. "Tours: Des Gratte-Ciel Aux Tours Habitables." ["Towers: Skyscrapers that are Livable Towers."] *CREE*. October/November 2000, pp. 28-37.
Smith, Craig S. "Circular Thinking: Dispute Brings the World's Tallest Compromise." *Wall Street Journal*, July 20, 1998, n.p.
Smith, Craig S. "Race for the Sky: Shanghai and Taipei Play 'Can You Top This?'" *Wall Street Journal*, June 2, 1999, sec. B, pp. 1, 12.
Steedman, Dr. Scott. "Block on Block." *BBC On Air*, August 1999, p. 5.
Sudjic, Deyan. "Shanghai: La Citta Che Esplose." ["Shanghai: The City that Exploded."] *Domus* (Italy), no. 829, September 2000, pp.40-57.
Tuchman, Janice L. "New Concepts Aired." *Engineering News-Record*, May 6, 1996, p. 20.
Usuda, Tetsuo and Taikura, Yutaka et al. "Kohn Pedersen Fox: 3 High Rise Building Projects." *Architecture + Urbanism* (Japan), June 1996, pp. 54-89.
Walker, Tony. "Shanghai's High Hopes." *Financial Times*, March 10, 1996, n.p.
Weiss, Lois. "New Challengers to Tallest Building Crown?" *Real Estate Weekly*, August 18, 1999, pp. 1, 15.

Singapore Exchange Center
"Pillars of Finance: Singapore Exchange Center." *Building Journal* (Hong Kong, China), August 1998, p. 18.

Sotheby's Worldwide Headquarters Expansion
"New York Construction News Selects Top Projects." *New York Construction News*, June 2000, vol. 48, no. 11, p. 11.
"Sotheby's World Headquarters Expansion." *New York Construction News*, March 1999, p. 50.
Geran, Monica. "Upping the Bid; Swank Hayden Connell Architects." *Interior Design*, August 1, 2000, vol. 71, no. 10, p. 58.
Vogel, Carol. "Sotheby's, Expanding, Plans a Showplace." *New York Times*, July 21, 1998, pp. 1, 7.

Steelcase
"Steelcase Worklife Gets an Entirely New Kind of Lighting." *Architectural Record*, February 1997, pp. 150-153.
"Steelcase Worklife New York." *Interiors*, February 1997, pp. 38-45.
Linn, Charles D. "Furniture Showroom." *Architectural Record*, February 1997, pp 150-153.

Suyong Bay Landmark Tower, Daewoo Marina City
Maynard, Michael. "Buildings in Korea." *Architecture*, November 1997, pp. 132-133.
Teo, Karen, et al. "Conceptualising Asian's Urban Landscape: Projects by Kohn Pedersen Fox." *Southeast Asian Building* (Singapore), November 2000, pp. 43-48.

Taichung Tower
"Dual System." *Modern Steel Construction*, July 1995, pp. 26-28.
Maynard, Michael. "Buildings in China and Singapore." *Architecture*, November 1997, pp. 134-135.

Thames Court
Aluminum Awards. *Architects' Journal*, June 17, 1999, n.p.
"BCO Best Urban Work Place Award." *Building*, June 18, 1999, n.p.
"BCO Best Urban Work Place Award." *Architects' Journal*, June 17, 1999, n.p.
"City Fights to Retain Top Status." *Financial Times*, December 1995, pp. 1, 20.
"City Lettings Soar—Tenant Anchors Thames Court." *Estates Gazette*, September 27, 1997, p. 49.
"Commendation Civic Trust Awards 2000." *Building*, March 24, 2000, p. 45.
"Court Room Drama." *NCE Progress In Steel*, September 1997, pp. 20-22.
"Crossing the Pond." *Architectural Record*, July 1999, n.p.
"European Manners." *Building Design*, February 28, 1997, pp. 24-25.
"Not for the Faint of Heart." *Architectural Record*, July 1996, pp. 40-41.

"OAS Awards Short List." *Property Week*, October 12, 1999, n.p.
"Palazzi for the Nineties." *Building Design*, September 13, 1996. pp. 22-23.
"Putting Art to Work." *The Independent Saturday Magazine*, May 9, 1998, p. 33.
"Rotating Paddles Following the Sun." *Design Lines Levolux Newsletter*, Summer 2000, p. 3.
"Structural Steel Awards." *Architects' Journal*, November 4, 1999, n.p.
"Structural Steel Awards." *Building Design*, November 5, 1999, n.p.
"Thames Court, London, UK." *BCO News*, Sept. 30, 1998, p. 18.
"Trading Spaces." *RIBA Journal*, October 1998, n.p.
Cadji, Miriam. "Office Glamour." *RIBA Journal*, October 1999, n.p.
Heathcote, Edwin. *Bank Buildings*, 1999, n.p.
Jones, Nick. "Glazing Systems" *ABCD*, May 2000, n.p.
Mastroberte, Tammy. "Bank Headquarters Provides a Display of British Stone." *Stone World*, October 2000, p. 96.
Millington, Rod. "A Winning Solution." *Construction Magazine*, October 1999, n.p.
O'Looney, Benedict. "New Thames Survey." *AA Files 40*, June 2000, p. 30.
Osman, Kemal. "Thames Court." *Tasarim* (Turkey), December 2000, p. 88.
Richards, Kirsten. "Thames Court Recollects the Opulence of Historic Banking Halls with a Contemporary Flair." *designarchitecture.com* (http://www.designarchitecture.com), June 14, 2000.
Santry, Claire. "The Right To Be Specified." *Natural Stone Specialist*, July 1999.
Wernick, Jane. "Structuring a Business." *Architect's Journal: Steel Design*, September 30, 1999, n.p.

Tour CBX

Sandler, Linda. "Building Abroad: Hines Hits Fees, Fuss in France." *Wall Street Journal*, September 13, 2000, sec. B, p. 14.

US Airways International Terminal One
Philadelphia International Airport

"International Terminal One, Philadelphia Airport." *Space* (Korea), pp. 60-63.

William H Gates Hall, University of Washington Law School

Maynard, Michael. "Campus Buildings." *Architecture*, November 1997, pp. 130-131.

The World Bank Headquarters

"AIA Honor Awards: Architecture." *Architecture*, May 1995, p. 121.
"At the World Bank, Architecture as Diplomacy." *New York Times*, March 9, 1997, n.p.
"Design Awards: Architecture Award." *Oculus*, Summer 1998, p. 6.
"World Bank Is Upgrading." *New York Times*, November 22, 1992, n.p.
"World Bank's Capital Gains." *Washington Post*, February 8, 1997, n.p.
Barreneche, Raul A. "Modern Development." *Architecture*, November 1997, pp. 100-107.
Dean, Andrea Oppenheimer. "Our Critic Goes Behind the Scenes at This Years' AIA Honor Awards." *Architectural Record*, May 1999, pp. 156-162.
Dibar, Carlos L. "Bancos al Estilo KPF." ["Banks in the KPF Style."] *El Cronista Buenos Aires: Arquitectura & Diseño*, (Argentina), March 10, 1993, pp. 1-2.
Edited by Dixon, John Morris. *Urban Spaces*. New York: Visual Reference Publications, Inc., 1999, pp. 170-171.
Forgey, Benjamin. "World Bank Capital Gains: HQ Investment Pays Off Grandly." *Washington Post*, February 8, 1997, Section B, pp. 1, 5.
Hall, Steven. "Security at the World Bank." *Security Management*, December 1998, pp. 77-81.
Ichniowski, Tom. "Worldly-Wise Bank Gets on Top of Trials." *Engineering News-Record*, December 4, 1995, pp. 28-30.
Pomeroy, William. "Calling the World Bank to Account." *People's Weekly World National Edition*, August 14, 1993, n.p.
Sands, David R. "President of World Bank Urges Funding to Aid Poor." *Washington, D.C. Times*, April 29, 1993, Section C, pp. 1, 3.

Sharoff, Robert. "At the World Bank, Architecture as Diplomacy." *New York Times*, March 9, 1997, n.p.
Silverstein, Kenneth. "Tenant Base Helps DC Deal with Recession." *Southeast Real Estate News*, September 1993, pp. 1, 18-21.
Starzynski, Bob. "Construction in D.C.: Some Big Walls Are on the Way Up." *Washington Business Journal*, October 17, 1996, n.p.

World Trade Center Amsterdam Renovation and Extension

"Biggest Dutch Redevelopment." *Vastgoemarkt*, April 14, 2000, n.p.
"Masterplan Zuidas." ["Masterplan Zuidas"] *Weekmedia* (The Netherlands), November 20, 1996, pp. 2-21.
"Uitbreidingsplan WTC Amsterdam." ["Plans for Extension of WTC Amsterdam."] *Vastgoedmarkt* (The Netherlands), n.d, p. 1.
"WTC Revamp." *Site*, June 1999, n.p.
Delargy, Melanie. *Building Magazine*, September 1, 2000, p. 12.
Kool, Willem. "WTC with Extra Tower." *De Telegraaf* (The Netherlands), April 14, 2000, n.p.
Lyall, Sutherland. "Buildings of Tomorrow." *Architect's Journal*, May 18, 2000.
Peeters, Frans. "New WTC as Breeding Ground for Young Business People." *Het Parool* (The Netherlands), April 14, 2000, n.p.

Selected Awards

1993

Dallas Urban Design Awards
Urban Design
The Federal Reserve Bank
Dallas, Texas

L'Ordre des architectes du Québec
Prix d'excellence en architecture
1250 Boulevard René Lévesque
Montréal, Canada

New York City A.I.A.
Distinguished Architecture Award
1250 Boulevard René Lévesque
Montréal, Canada

American Institute of Architects (National)
Brick in Architecture Award
Capitol Cities/ABC Headquarters
New York, New York

Houston, Texas A.I.A.
Distinguished Architecture Award
The Federal Reserve Bank of Dallas
Dallas, Texas

1994

General Services Administration
GSA Design Awards
Building Design Excellence
Mark O. Hatfield United States Courthouse
Portland, Oregon

American Institute of Architects (National)
Honor Award
DG Bank, Westendstrabe 1
Frankfurt am Main, Germany

New York State A.I.A.
Award of Merit
DG Bank, Westendstrabe 1
Frankfurt am Main, Germany

New York City A.I.A.
Distinguished Architecture Award
DG Bank, Westendstrabe 1,
Frankfurt am Main, Germany

1995

New York City A.I.A.
Project Design Honor Award
Buffalo Niagara International Airport
Buffalo, New York

New York City A.I.A.
Project Design Award
Shanghai World Financial Center
Shanghai, China

Presidential Design Awards
Federal Design Achievement Award
Independence Square
Washington, D.C.

1996

General Services Administration
GSA Design Awards
Honor Award in Architecture
United States Courthouse, Foley Square
New York, New York

General Services Administration
GSA Design Awards
Design Awards Citation in Architecture
United States Courthouse
Minneapolis, Minnesota

Progressive Architecture
Design Award Citation
Rodin Museum Samsung Headquarters Plaza
Seoul, Korea

New York City A.I.A.
Project Design Award
Rodin Museum Samsung Headquarters Plaza
Seoul, Korea

Washington Building Congress, Inc.
Craftsmanship Award
The World Bank
Washington, D.C.

Architektenkammer Hessen
Award for Exemplary Building in Hessen
DG Bank, Westendstrabe 1
Frankfurt am Main, Germany

1997

Portland, Oregon A.I.A.
Architecture Award
Mark O. Hatfield United States Courthouse
Portland, Oregon

New York City A.I.A.
Architecture Award
The World Bank Headquarters
Washington, D.C.

Westchester County, New York A.I.A.
Architecture Award
IBM Corporate Headquarters
Armonk, New York

New York City A.I.A.
Certificate of Recognition for a New Courthouse in Historic Context
Mark O. Hatfield United States Courthouse
Portland, Oregon

New York City A.I.A.
Certificate of Recognition for a New Courthouse in Historic Context
United States Courthouse
Minneapolis, Minnesota

New York City A.I.A.
Certificate of Recognition for a New Courthouse in Historic Context
United States Courthouse, Foley Square
New York, New York

1998

General Services Administration
GSA Design Awards
Honor Award
Mark O. Hatfield United States Courthouse
Portland, Oregon

American Institute of Architects (National)
Honor Award
The World Bank Headquarters
Washington, D.C.

Buffalo, New York A.I.A.
First Award for a New Building
Buffalo Niagara International Airport
Buffalo, New York

New York State A.I.A.
Award of Merit
Bloomingdale's
Aventura, Florida

The Chicago Athenaeum
American Architecture Award
IBM Corporate Headquarters
Armonk, New York

1999

New York State A.I.A.
Design Award of Excellence
Rodin Museum Samsung Headquarters Plaza
Seoul, Korea

British Council for Offices
National Urban Workplace Award
Thames Court
London, England

ID Magazine
Annual Design Review Awards
Environment Category
Rodin Museum Samsung Headquarters Plaza
Seoul, Korea

The Chicago Athenaeum
American Architecture Award
Rodin Museum Samsung Headquarters Plaza
Seoul, Korea

New York City A.I.A.
Architectural Awards Citation
Mark O. Hatfield United States Courthouse
Portland, Oregon

2000

A.I.A. Western International Design Awards Program
Honor Award
Mark O. Hatfield United States Courthouse
Portland, Oregon

Civic Trust Awards
Commendation
Thames Court
London, England

Nagoya City Government
Nagoya City Townscape Award
JR Central Towers
Nagoya, Japan

Railroad Architecture Institute Japan
Railroad Architecture Award
JR Central Towers
Nagoya, Japan

Chiba Architecture Award Committee
Chiba Architecture Award
JR Central Towers
Nagoya, Japan

2001

New York City A.I.A.
Architecture Award
Rodin Museum Samsung Headquarters Plaza
Seoul, Korea

New York City A.I.A.
Project Design Award
Endesa Headquarters
Madrid, Spain

New York City A.I.A.
Project Design Award Citation
Espirito Santo Plaza
Miami, Florida

New York City A.I.A.
Project Design Award Citation
Columbus Learning Center
Columbus, Indiana

New York Construction News
Best of 2001 Award
Project of the Year: Commercial Project Category
5 Times Square
New York, New York

New York Construction News
Best of 2001 Award
Project of the Year: Mixed-Use Project Category
Mohegan Sun Casino Phase II
Uncasville, Connecticut

New York Construction News
Best of 2001 Award
Award of Merit: Commercial Project Category
745 Seventh Avenue
New York, New York

New York Construction News
Best of 2001 Award
Award of Merit: Institutional Project Category
Baruch College New Academic Complex
New York, New York

Urban Land Institute Award for Excellence
Small Scale Office Category
Thames Court
London, England

Illustration Credits

Advanced Media Design, 348-353, 392-393, 403 right, 404-405, 492-493, 496-407

Peter Aaron / Esto 11, 182-191

Philip M. Brown, 252-253, 374-375 middle, 375 bottom, 381 top right, 381 bottom

John Butlin, 122, 126 right, 129, 280-281

Ray Chin, 500 left

Peter Cook, 142-143, 145-149

Hayes Davison, 394, 397-399

Michael Dersin, 8 top, 16 bottom, 33, 38-39, 42-43 top, 43 bottom left, 44-45, 318-319, 323, 408-413

Digital Box, 345-347, 369-371, 380, 475, 480, 481 top, 482-483, 440-441

Jae-Sung E, 81

Edge Media, 160 right, 161-164-165

H. G. Esch, 15 top, 65, 123-126 left, 127-128, 170-174, 176-179

Dennis Gilbert, 8 bottom right

Dicky Herras, 196 top, 196 bottom left, 197

Timoth Hursley, 10 bottom, 12, 13 top, 37, 41, 43 bottom right, 54-61, 67-73, 92-99, 198, 201-202, 205 top, 207-209, 234-236, 238-239, 320-322, 324-331

Nicolas Katz, 504 left

Jeff Kaufman, 499-500 right, 501-503, 504 right, 505 left

Kim-Yong Kwan, 13 bottom, 203, 205 bottom, 206

Wayne N. T. Fujii, 6

Barbara Karant, 8 top

Ava Lugtu, 194-195, 196 bottom right

Eamonn O' Mahony, 150, 154-155, 212, 217, 297-298, 301, 386, 418-419, 433-435, 442, 447-448

John Marshall / Wordsearch 277, 282-283

Cheto Monge, 423

Michael Moran, 16 top, 219, 224-233

Courtesy, Mori Building Company, 302

Tim Nolan, 132-137, 266-271, 274-275, 332-333, 336-338top, 339

Jock Pottle / Esto, 15 bottom, 76-77, 101, 119, 162-163, 237 left, 241, 243, 246-248, 251, 254 left, 293-295, 346, 354, 372, 379, 384-385 left, 390, 422, 427-428, 439, 454, 457-459, 463-465, 476-479 left, 481 bottom, 487 left, 494, 498

Jeremy Rendell, 506 right, 505 left

Christian Richters, 109, 112-117

Skyscraper Digital, 382

Courtesy, Space Magazine (Singapore), 238 bottom

David Sundberg / Esto, 307-313

Courtesy, Taisei Corporation, 48-51

Tom Turturro, 358-359

Vergara Photography, 180 bottom

Seung-Hoon Yum, 83-89

All other images were provided by Kohn Pedersen Fox in New York and London.

Editor's Acknowledgement

An endeavor of this scope and complexity required the effort of a great many people.

The body of work cataloged in this volume reflects the uncommon collective talent of the Principals, Directors, Senior Associate Principals, Associate Principals, and the entire professional staff of Kohn Pedersen Fox in New York and London. In particular, this book is a testament to the shared vision of A. Eugene Kohn, William Pedersen, Robert Cioppa, William Louie, and Lee Polisano. I am grateful for the opportunity to play an integral role in creating this volume.

I would be remiss if I did not single out the generosity of David Morton, Steve Case and the staff of Rizzoli International Publications; the eloquence and concision of contributing essayists Joseph Giovannini, Carol Krinsky and Kenneth Powell; and the unique vision of designer Massimo Vignelli and Vignelli Associates.

I would also like to extend thanks to David Leventhal and Peter Murray for their editorial input, and Piera Brunetta at Vignelli Associates for her role as design coordinator.

This book required the careful attention of all who were involved in its production. Marjorie Rodney-Goodin was crucial in coordinating the selection of material relevant to the work of the London office. The efforts of Duncan Bainbridge, Pierre Lemaire, Ted Neilan and Roxana Asad in providing all the visual, graphic and textual information is greatly appreciated.

In the New York office, I would like to cite the contributions of Gale Chaney, Siobhan Lowe, Tony Morgan, Fanny Lee and Ilona Rider, who assisted in collecting all the visual information; Spencer Rand, Jeremy Gardner, Jeromy Powers, Jessica Broas, Jennifer Rios, Michael Tunkey, Trudy Brens, Hogan Chun, Pedro Font, Mark Debrauske, James Suh, Warren Kim, Hughy Dharmayoga, and Peter Niles, who assisted in cleaning up hundreds of drawings; Julia Murphy, Gabriel Wick and Laura Blintzer, for compiling drafts of the appendices; Danielle Gastall-Philbrook, Robert Whitlock, Eric Höweler, Jason Zerafa, Trent Tesch, Michael Aniero, Helen Leshinsky, and Paquita Bass for their editorial assistance.

I am especially indebted to Rachel Wohler, Thomas Tsang and Eugene Lee. As editorial assistant, it was Ms. Wohler's near-untenable task to compile, edit and type the drafts for the body of the book. Mr. Tsang was responsible for ensuring a consistent graphic identity for the line drawings within the portfolio. Mr. Lee contributed invaluable production and printing advice. Without their diligence, patience and sheer force of will, this book would not have been possible.

Ian Luna

JAC

First published in the United States of America in 2002 by
Rizzoli International Publications, Inc.
300 Park Avenue South
New York, NY 10010

Library of Congress Cataloging-in-Publication Data
Kohn Pedersen Fox: architecture and urbanism, 1993-2002 /
Edited by Ian Luna and Kenneth Powell; introduction by
Joseph Giovannini; essays by Carol Krinsky and Kenneth Powell.
Includes bibliographical references.

ISBN 0-8478-2506-X(HC)   0-8478-2508-6(PB)
Library of Congress Catalog Control Number: 92–33347
1. Kohn Pedersen Fox (Firm). 2. Architecture, Modern-United States. 3.
Architectural practice, International. I. Luna, Ian. II. Giovannini, Joseph.

2002 2003 2004 2005 2006 / 10 9 8 7 6 5 4 3 2 1

Printed in China

Designed by Massimo Vignelli
Design Coordinator: Piera Brunetta